GALASHIELS

THROUGH TIME

Sheila Scott

AMBERLEY

The top front cover photograph shows the 61397 morning train (Class B1 4-6-0 *St Margaret's*) to Edinburgh in 1957 leaving Gala Station. The bottom image shows the Royal Train, pulled by the steam locomotive *Union of South Africa* entering the town on 9 September 2015. With Her Majesty the Queen, Prince Phillip and Scotland's First Minister Nicola Sturgeon on board, it was heading to Tweedbank for the official opening of the new Borders Railway.

First published 2010
Reprinted 2011
This edition published 2016

Amberley Publishing
The Hill, Stroud
Gloucestershire, GL5 4EP

www.amberley-books.com

ISBN 978 1 4456 5033 3 PRINT
ISBN 978 1 4456 5034 0 EBOOK

British Library Cataloguing in Publication Data.
A catalogue record for this book is available from the British Library.

Typeset in 9.5pt on 12pt Celeste.
Typesetting by Amberley Publishing.
Printed in the UK.

Introduction

Having been a professional photographer in the town for around thirty years, I have become aware that I am playing a small part in a historical recording process, started many years ago by previous photographers. They probably never gave a thought to the interest that would be shown in their work so many years on. I hope this book will give future photographers something to work from when they produce the next version in 100 years time!

I have been fortunate to have records and memories from both my mother and father's families who both had strong connections with the town. My great grandfather Andrew Walker moved to the town in the mid to late 1800s to work as a Slater. His son, my grandfather James Walker (born Church Street in 1885) ran a post office and general store in Huddersfield Street for thirty-three years, and my mother, Margaret worked for Goodsirs (cabinet makers and furnishers) and R. P. Adam (dry-salter's).

This book has been compiled with the help of memories left by them. The following poem was found written in my grandfather's memoirs in the 1950s and I feel the words are as appropriate and meaningful today as they were then.

The auld toun's disappearing, the hooses bit by bit.
The auld folks either deeing or else they're havin tae flit.
But the Cross is still standing, it'll stand a lang, lang time,
Tae mind the lads of Gala and the days o' auld lang syne.

I doubt there has been such a change in appearance in any other Border town as there has been in Galashiels since 2000. Galashiels is rich in history – in its heyday the centre of the Scottish textile industry. It was known for woollens by 1733 but earliest indication of the woollen trade in the town is contained in a manuscript (Mr Scott of Gala) dated 1581 when 'waulkmills' are mentioned as pertinents belonging to the barony.

Large, grand mansion houses, built by mill owners' new found wealth, are still to be seen in the town, however many have now been converted to flats or a hotel in the case of Kingsknowes. The town's mills and chimneys long gone with the demise of the industry, having been replaced with large shopping complexes which now offer the townsfolk work in retail rather than mills.

Although the textile industry is all but lost we still have the famous College of Textiles, although now known as Heriot Watt University, it boasts a splendid campus facility in Netherdale. This attracts students

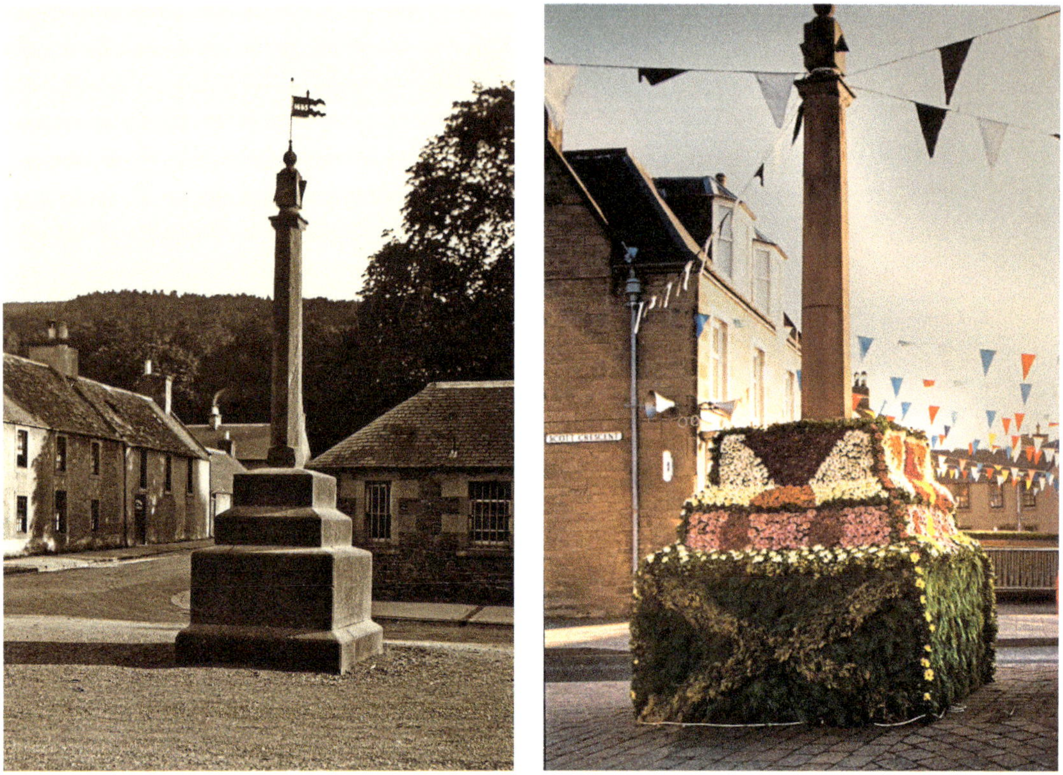

Photographs show Old Town Cross and also decorated for Braw Lads' Day 2000.

from all parts of the world to the town to learn design and business management.

In 1622 over 400 people lived in Galashiels. In 2014 the National Registers of Scotland gave a figure of 12,670, albeit much changed in appearance, but one which is now multicultural, friendly, and above all full of history.

Fishmongers

The arrival of the railway to Galashiels in 1849 brought many benefits, not least the easy transportation of coal to power the tweed mills' looms, replacing water power. It also allowed fishwives from Newhaven to sell fresh fish in The Borders. This traditional garbed fishwife with her creel and basket was photographed by Kirkwood of No. 21 Bridge Street around 1860. The recent image shows Dave Crichton with Julia Noble in Noble's Fishmongers in Bank Street. Fishmongers have been in these premises for approximately 100 years.

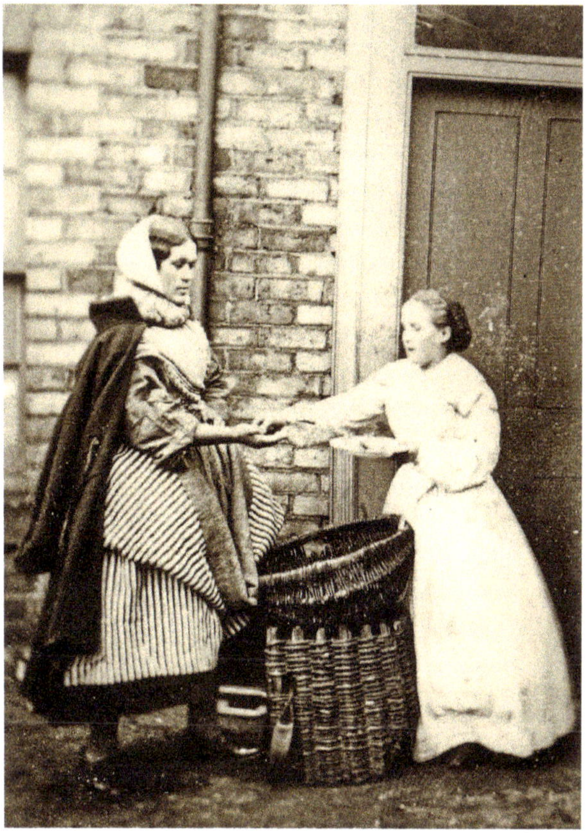

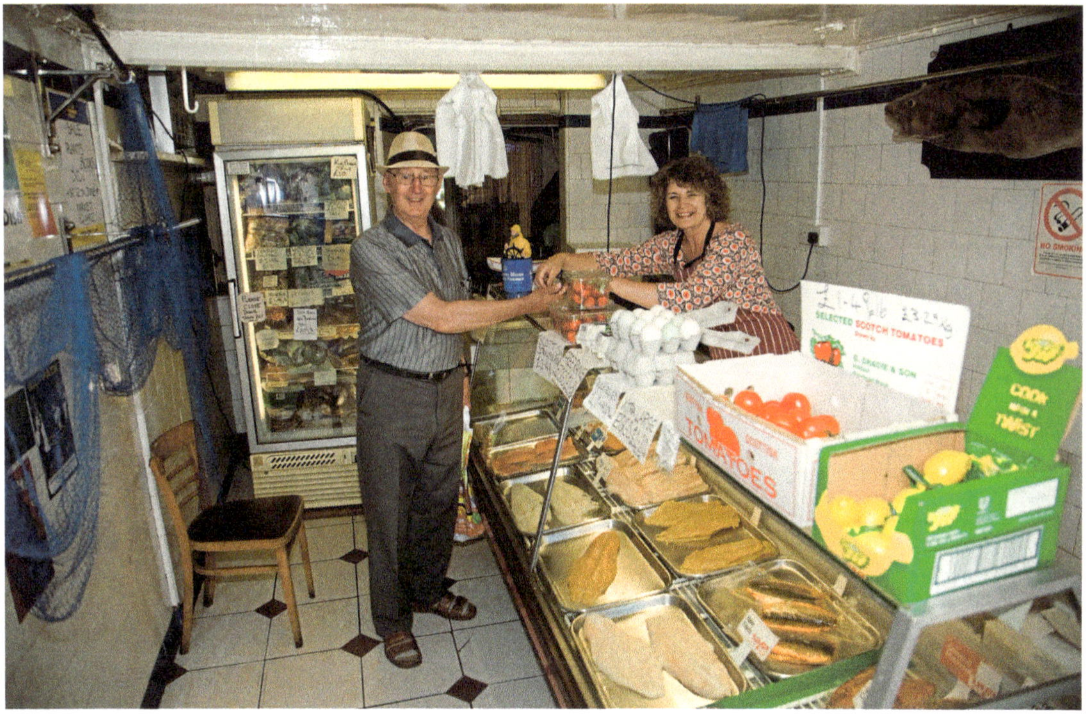

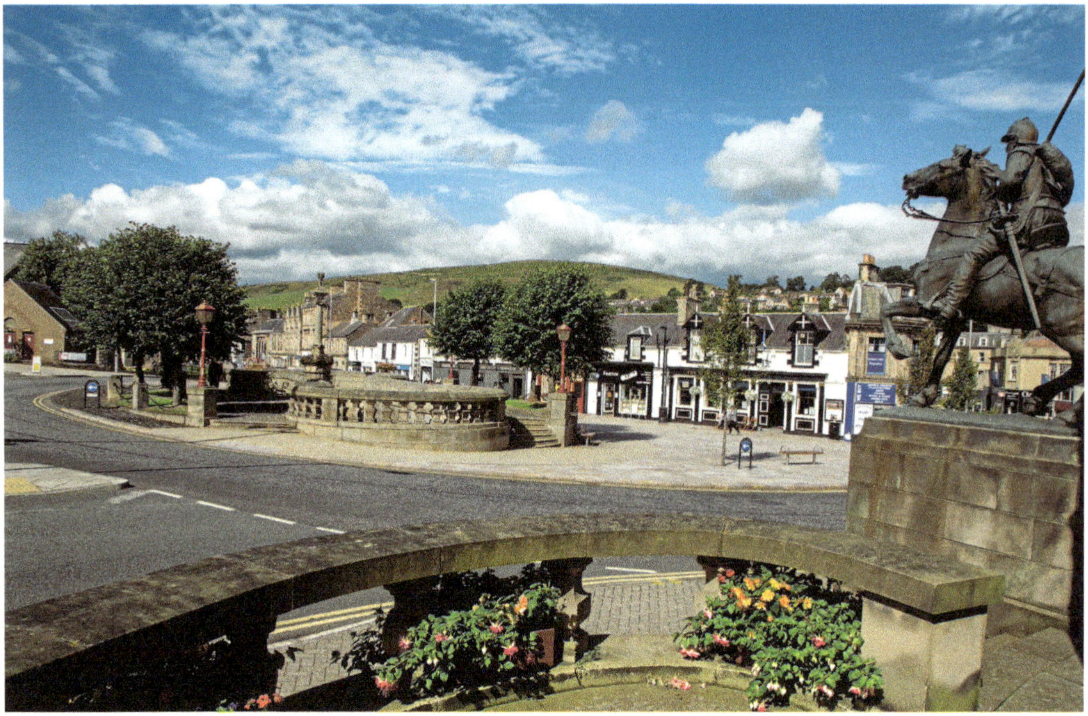

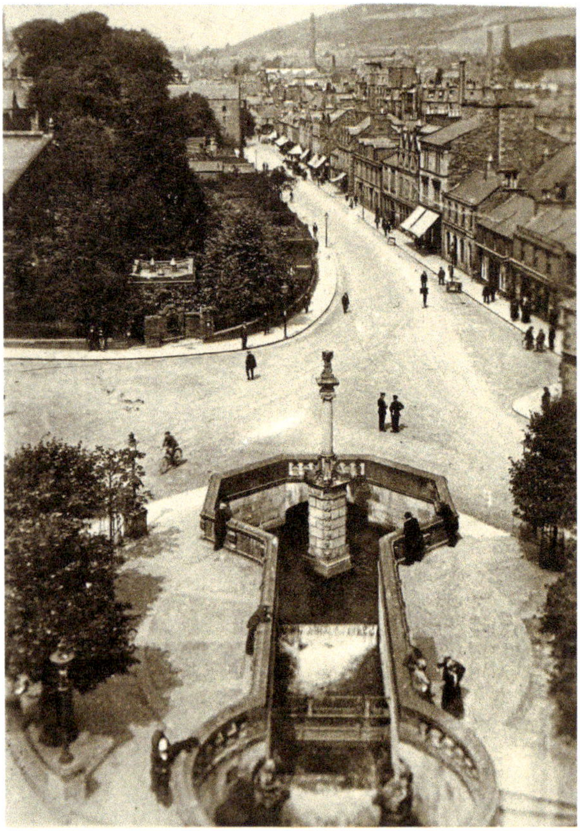

War Memorial and the Fountain

Although the layout of the buildings remains similar a huge amount of work has been done to give Galashiels a lovely pedestrian area around the Fountain, opposite the War Memorial.

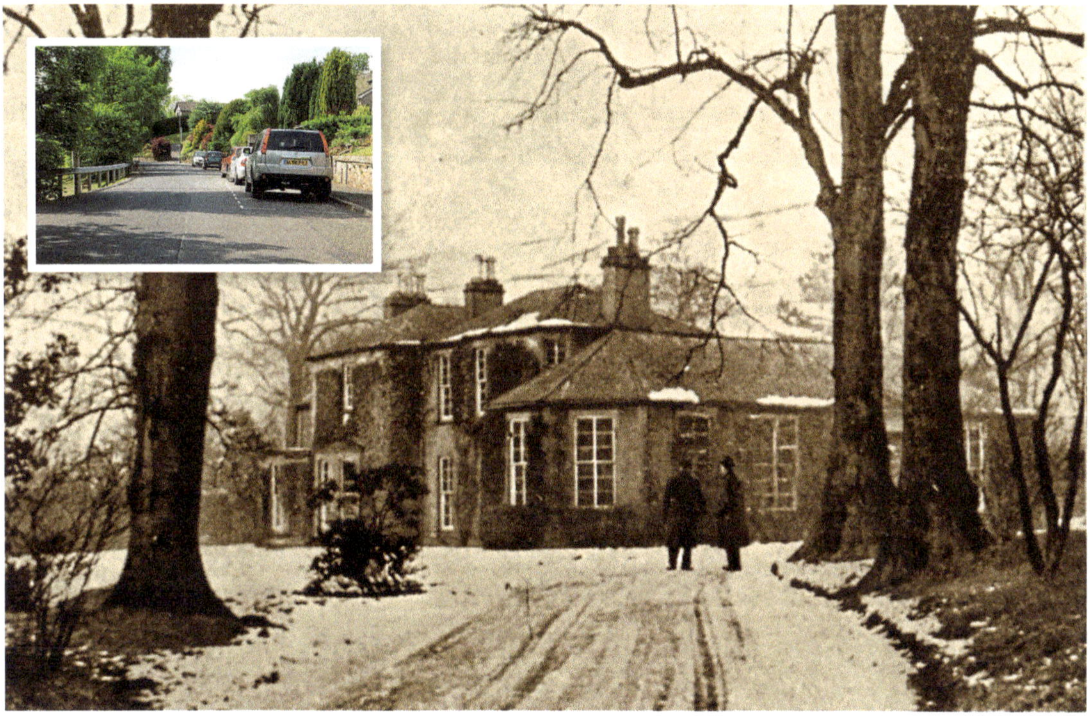

Ladhope House

Ladhope House, long gone, is now a large private housing estate entered from High Buckholmside. The image from 1907 shows the Lodge House and drive at the end of the High Road. Unlike this tranquil scene, the road is now used as a traffic 'short cut' from the A7 to Melrose Road.

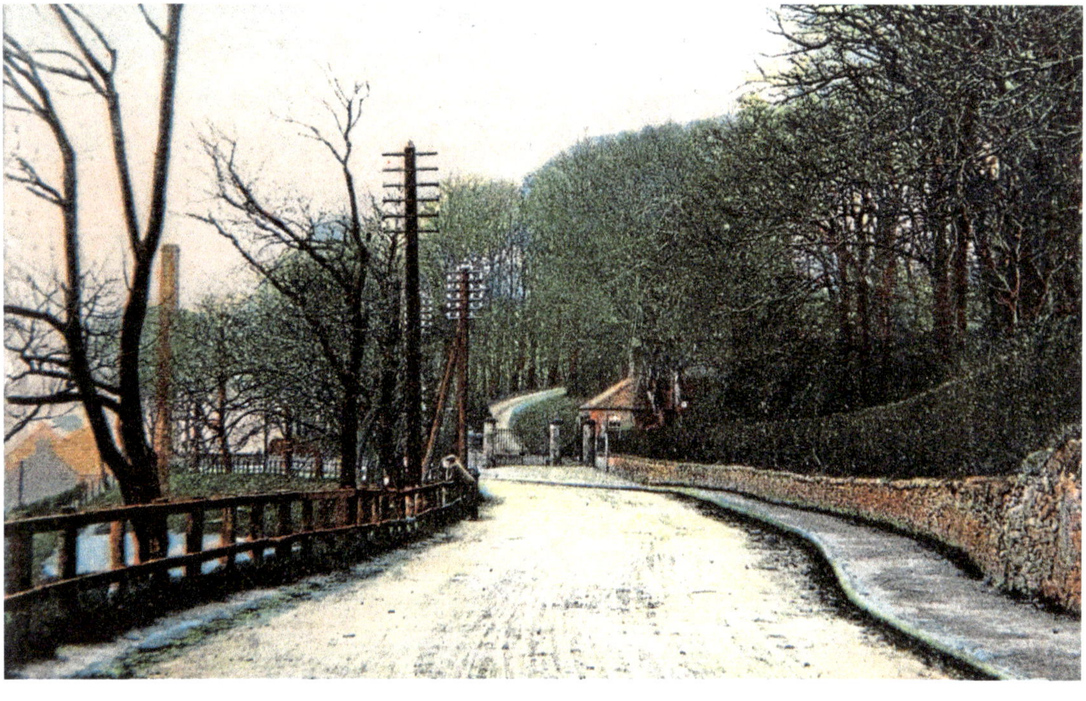

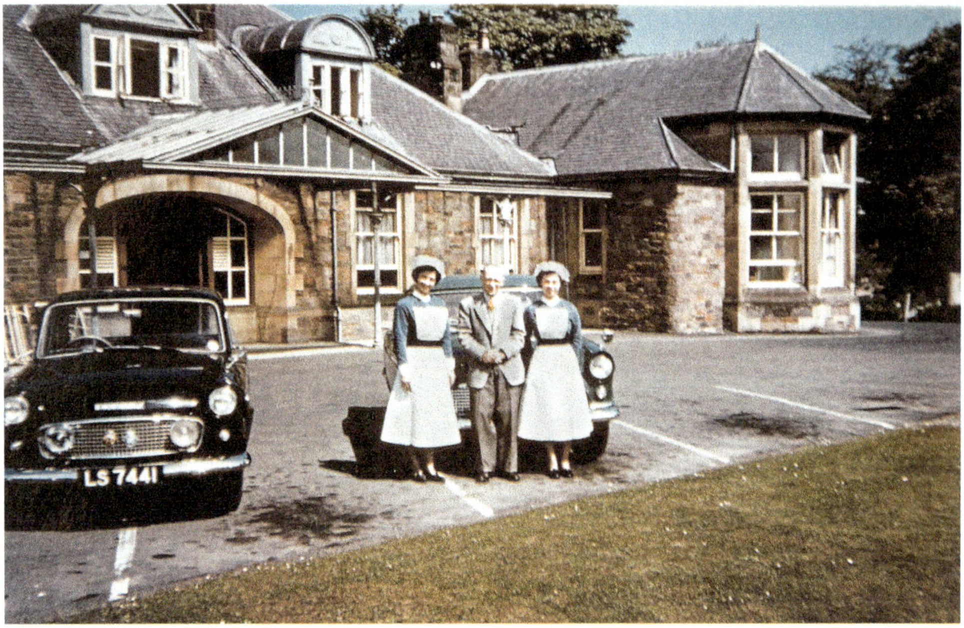

The Cottage Hospital

Having been the local hospital since 1893, 'The Cottage' stopped being used as a maternity and general unit in recent years and became a psychiatric unit. Sister Neta Weatherly is pictured here in 1959 with Dr Anthony and Sister Midwife Mary Dickson. Sister Weatherly became Matron, and was in charge of approximately fifteen maternity and twenty-two general beds. The hospital grew their own vegetables, had their own kitchens and laundry, performed operations every Tuesday and removed tonsils and adenoids every Friday. The cottage also had its own X-ray and casualty department. The outside now is relatively unchanged.

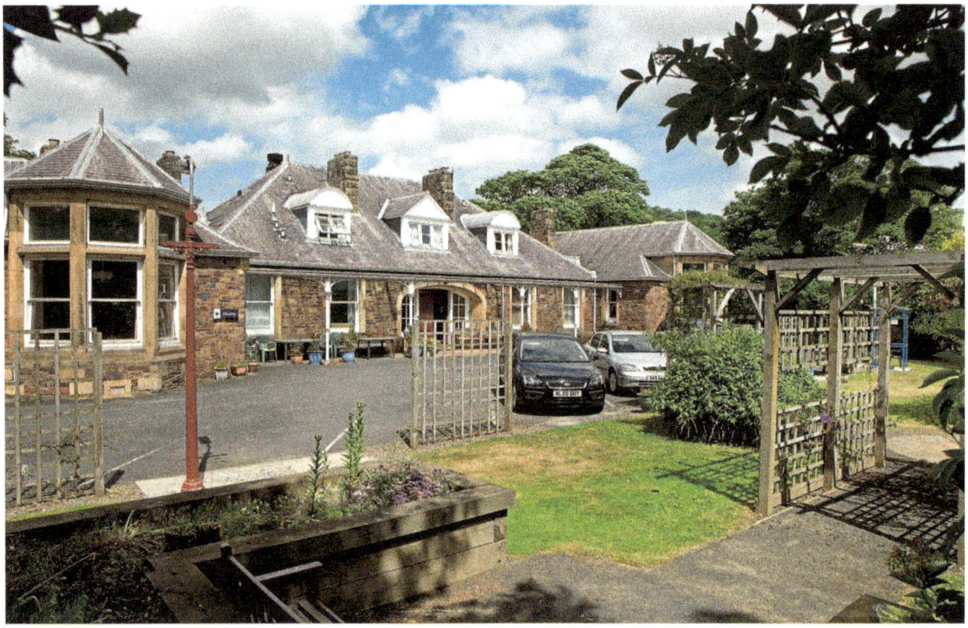

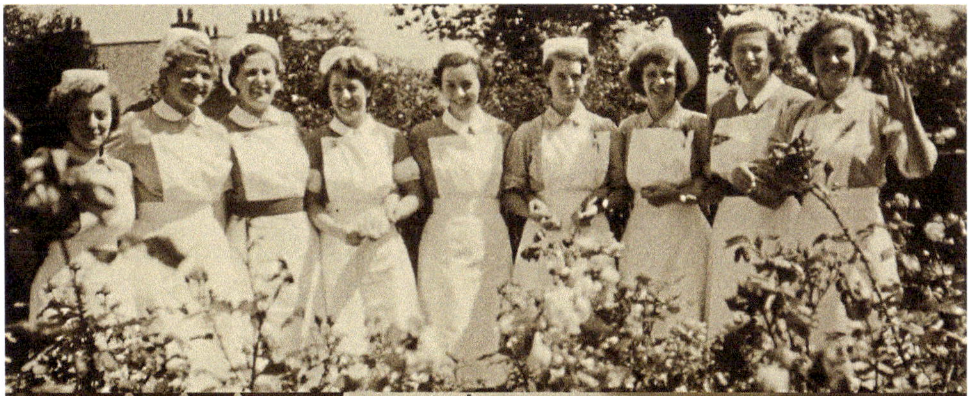

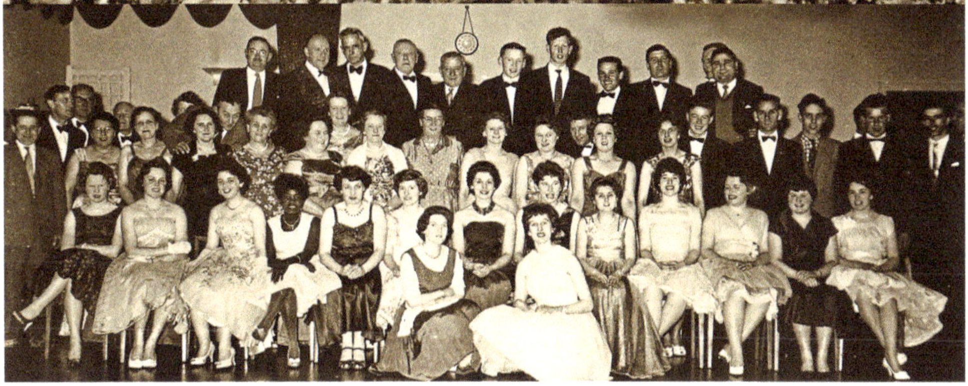

Maternity Unit

Many local people have fond memories of the maternity unit within The Cottage Hospital. Pictured is Sister Effie Devlin who retired in 1984 alongside Sister Joanne Ballantyne. Their 'service' for mothers was a seven-day stay after the birth, with the husband being allowed, for just one night, to take his wife out while the midwives did the babysitting. A great treat along with the milk stout allowed during the stay! Changed days indeed. The other image shows a hospital night out with nurses and doctors, and a group of young nurses in the gardens in 1956.

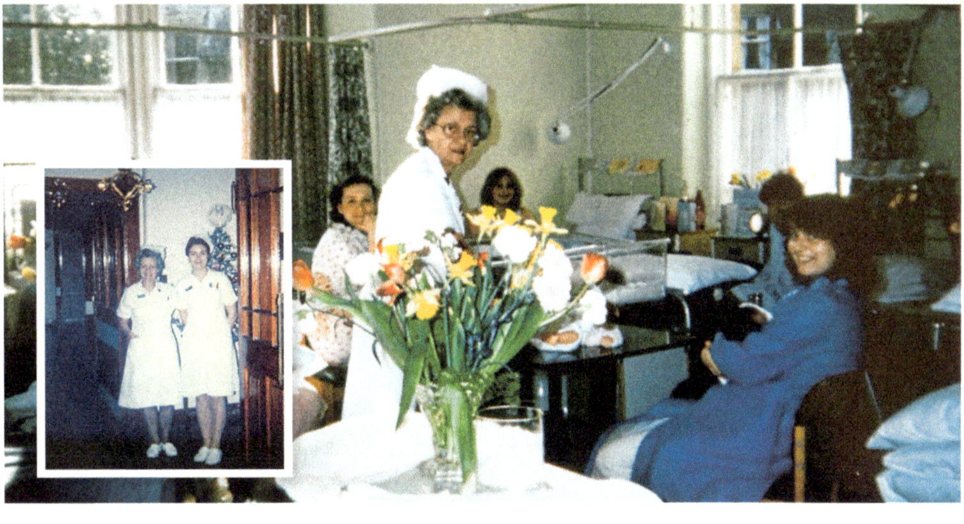

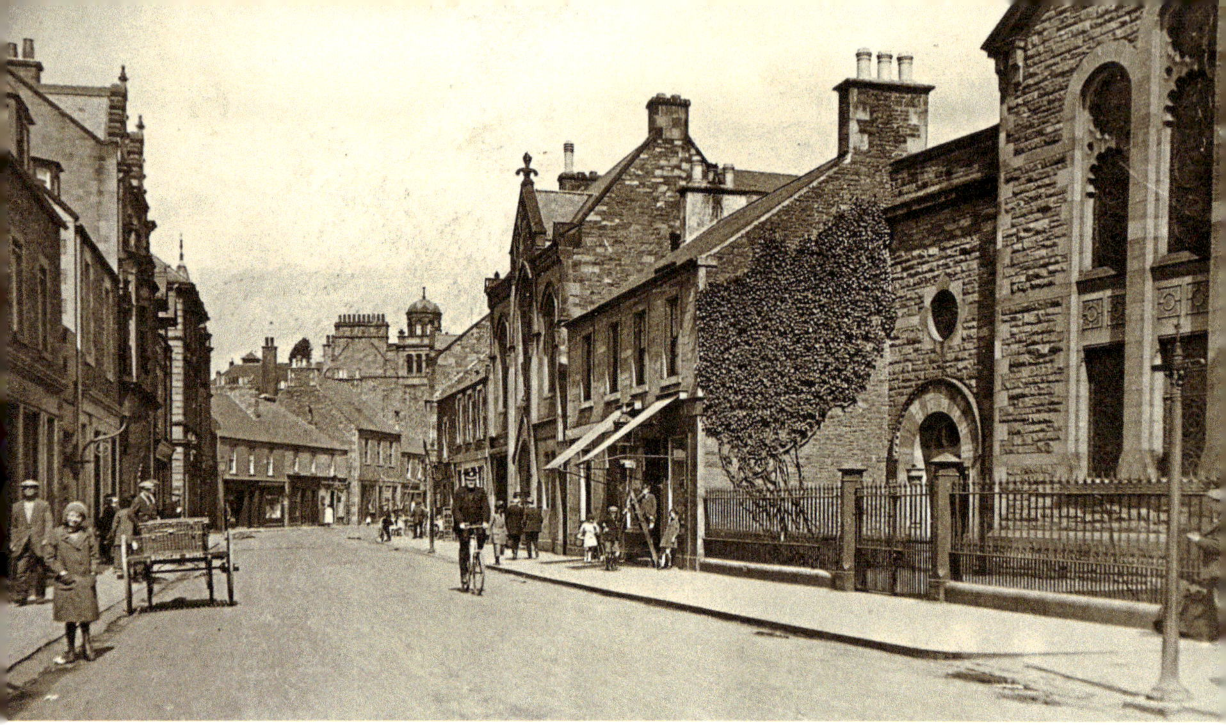

The High Street

The road layout is similar apart from the pedestrian crossing outside Trinity Church. It is now a requirement for the two lane, one-way traffic, something not necessary in the thirties.

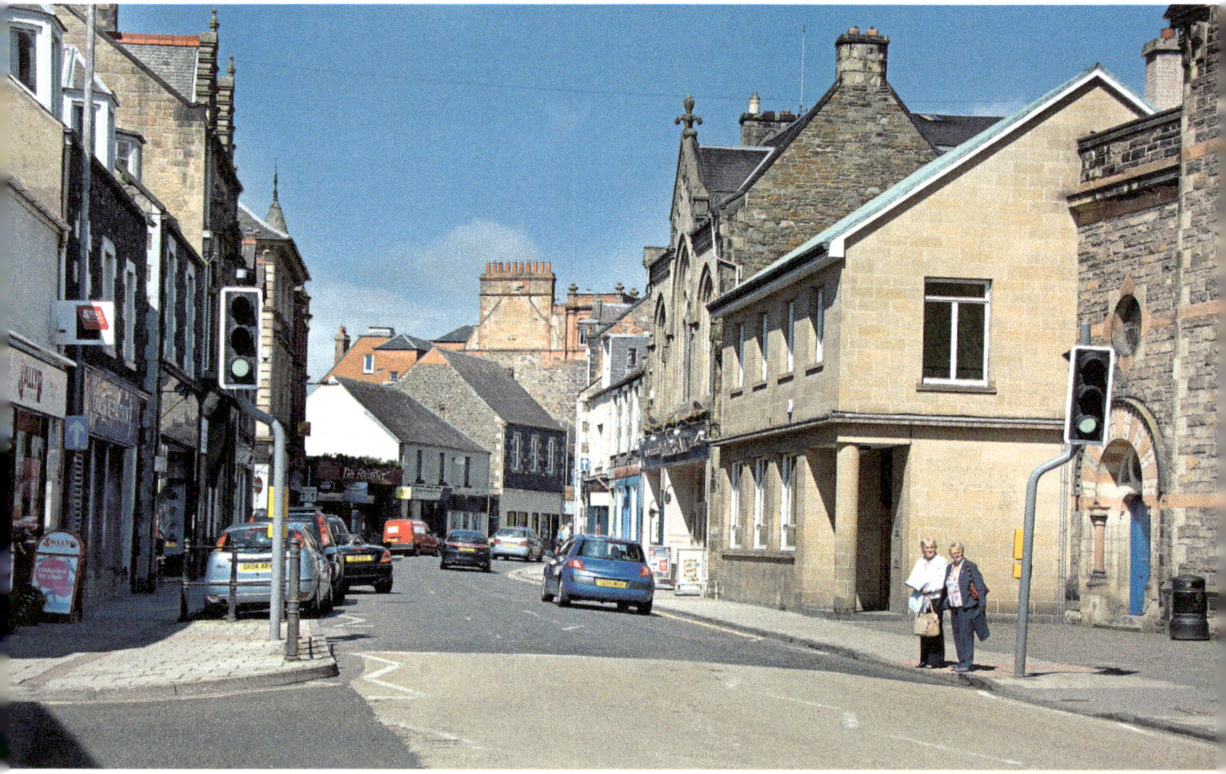

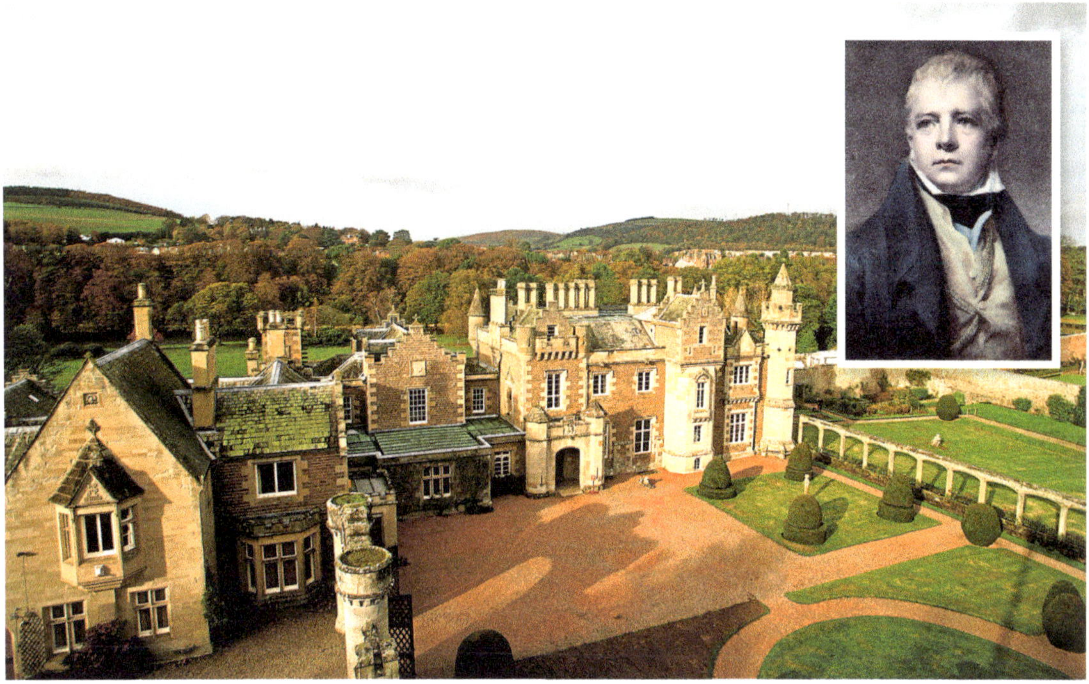

Abbotsford House

Home of Sir Walter Scott, who was born 1771. In 1812 he had moved there from Ashiesteel, having purchased the property known as Cartley Hole (seen in the old image) on which he built Abbotsford. He was the first to wear a pair of trousers made of Scottish shepherd check plaid. It is a custom for these checks to be made for, and worn by all Braw Lads on the Gala Day.

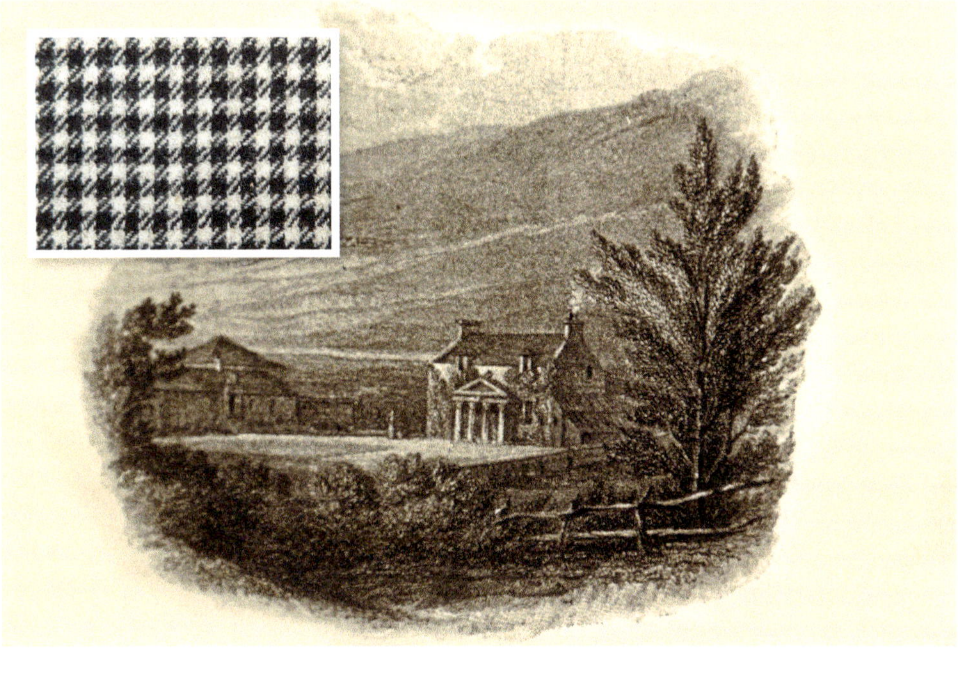

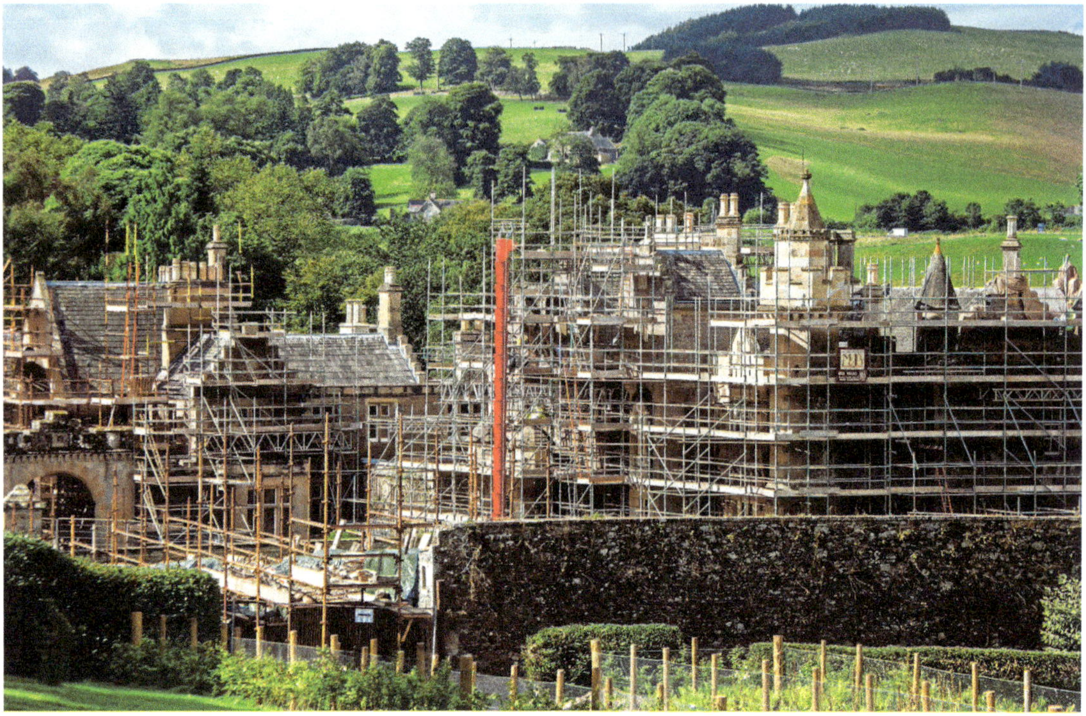

Abbotsford House

Abbotsford received a multi-million pound renovation and restoration during 2011–2013. Closed to the public during this time, it was officially opened by Her Majesty the Queen in 2013.

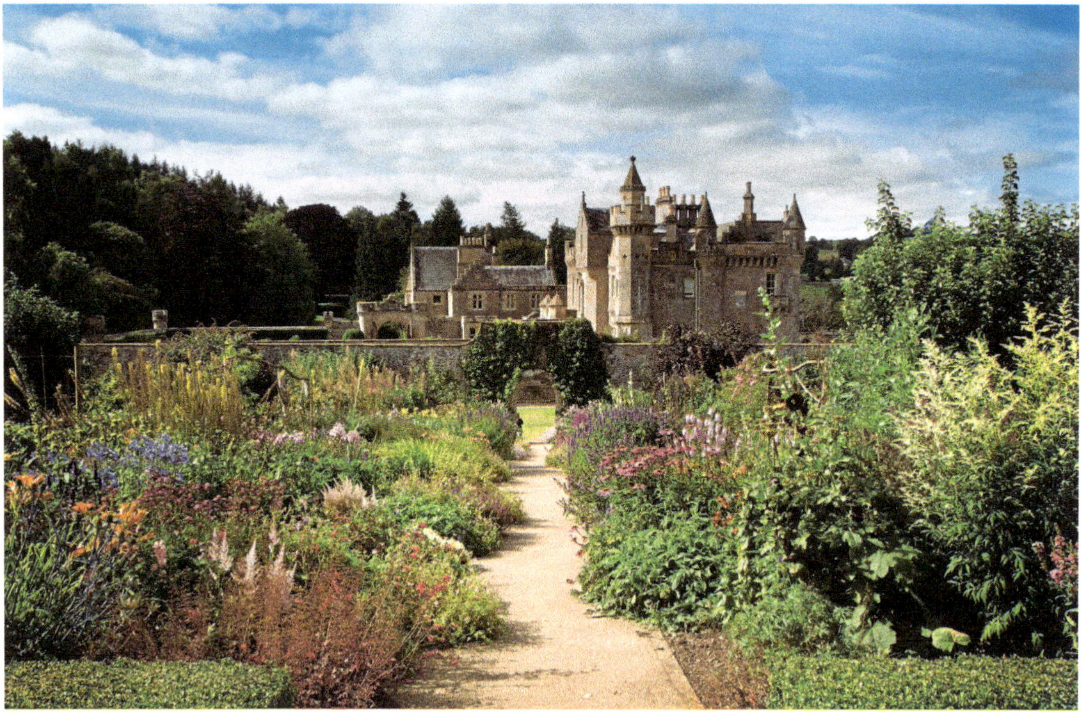

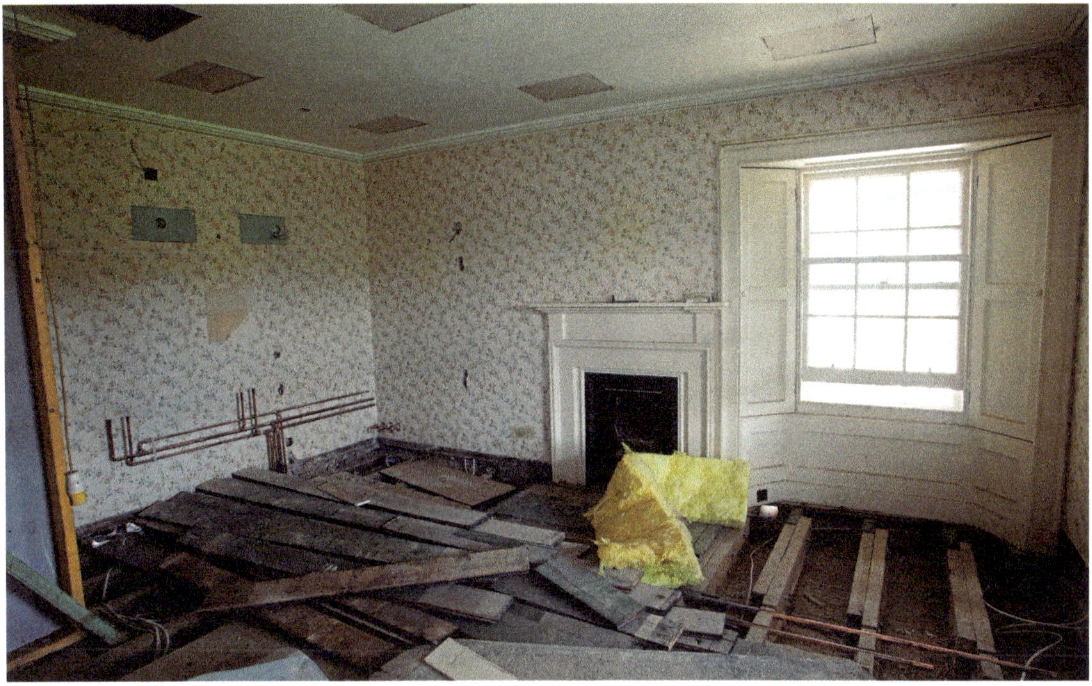

Hope Scott Wing

This wing of Abbotsford was originally created as an extension of Sir Walter Scott's original home. In 2013 it too was completed and reopened, giving the public the opportunity to rent this luxury, 5-star accommodation wing with seven individually styled bedrooms. The images show a previous bedroom being transformed into a disabled bathroom for guests.

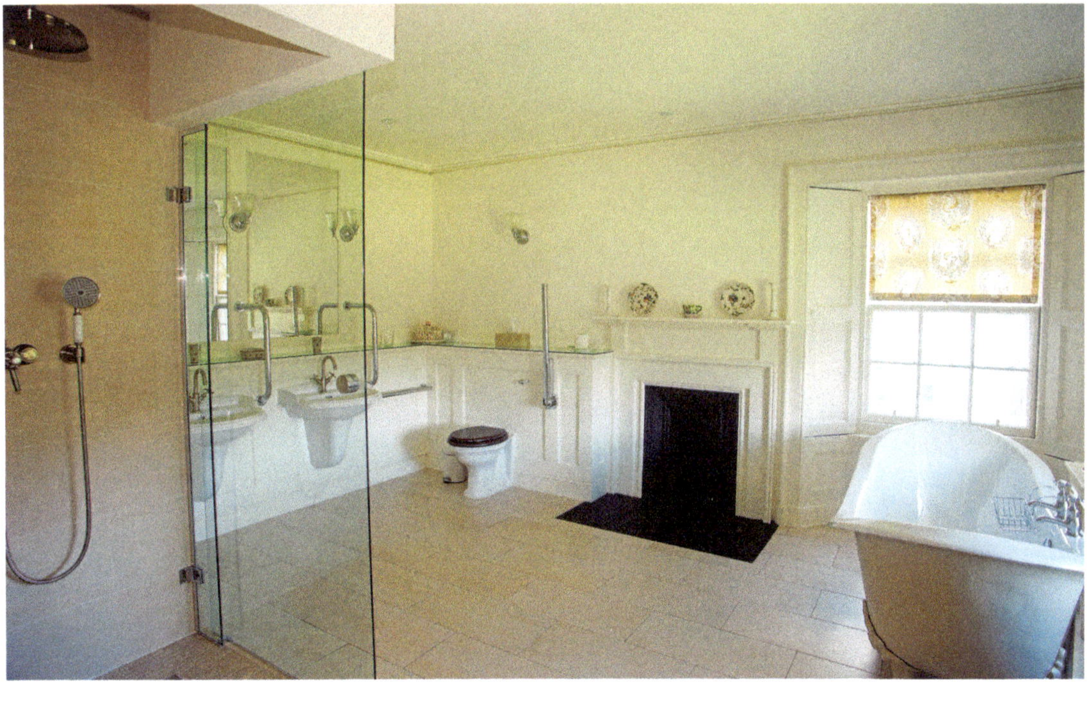

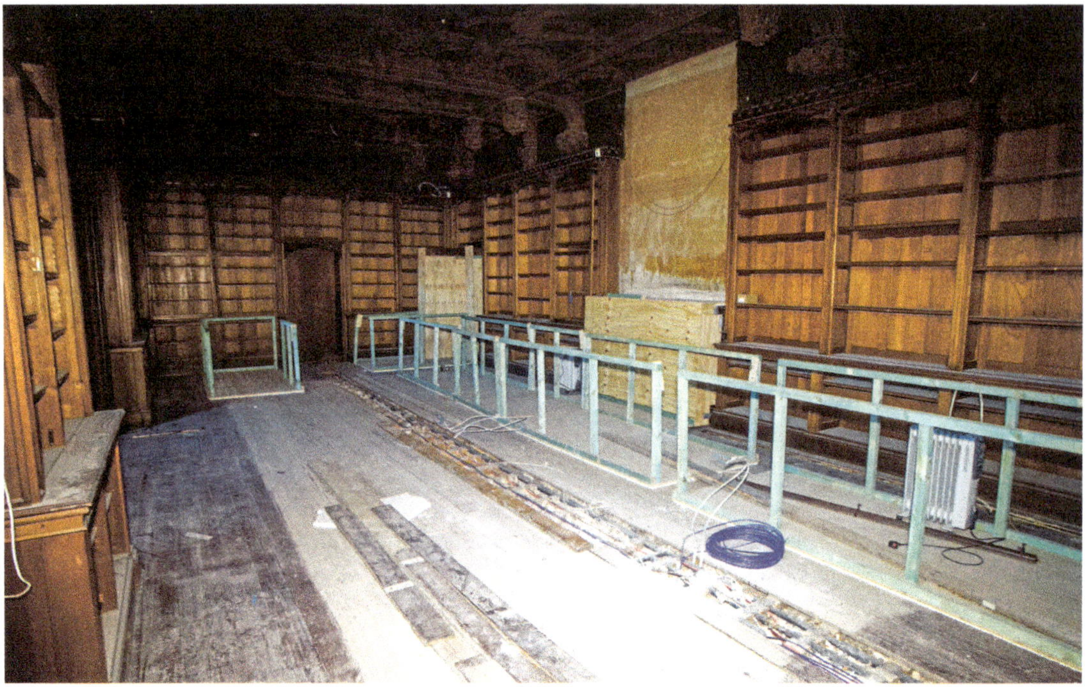

Sir Walters Scott's Collection

Scott's library and study contents had to be removed prior to renovation work taking place in Abbotsford. The historic collection was carefully removed to the Faculty of Advocates in Edinburgh. The two photographs show the library prior to and after the renovation.

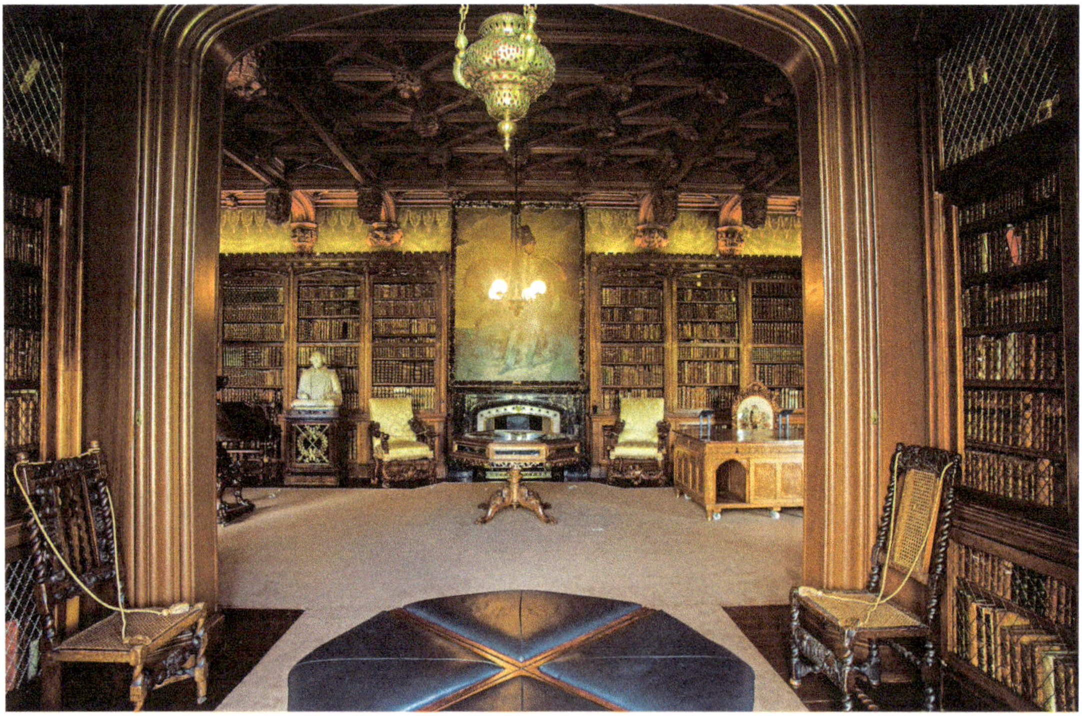

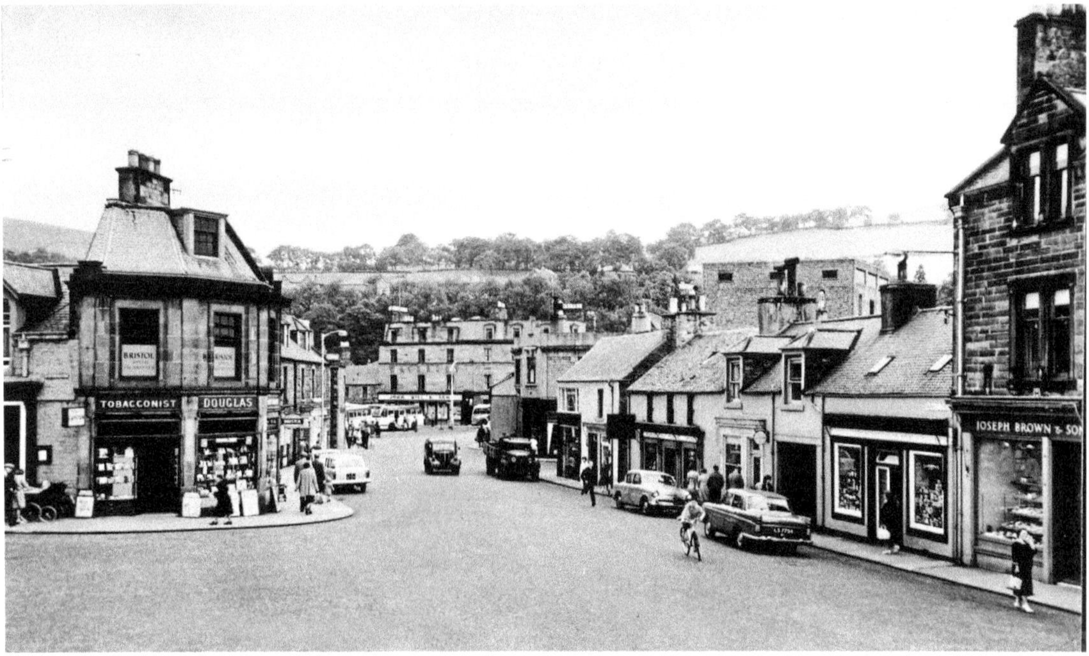

The Old Bus Stance

The old bus stance in Market Square at the bottom of Channel Street can be made out in this image taken in the late '50s. The older image shows a Brooke & Company vehicle and workers, from Albert Place. The company is recorded in 1923, by then Brooke & Amos, as starting a service between Galashiels and St Boswells for a fare of *6d.* They were taken over by SMT in 1926. Following this SMT started the first direct bus service to Edinburgh from Galashiels in 1927.

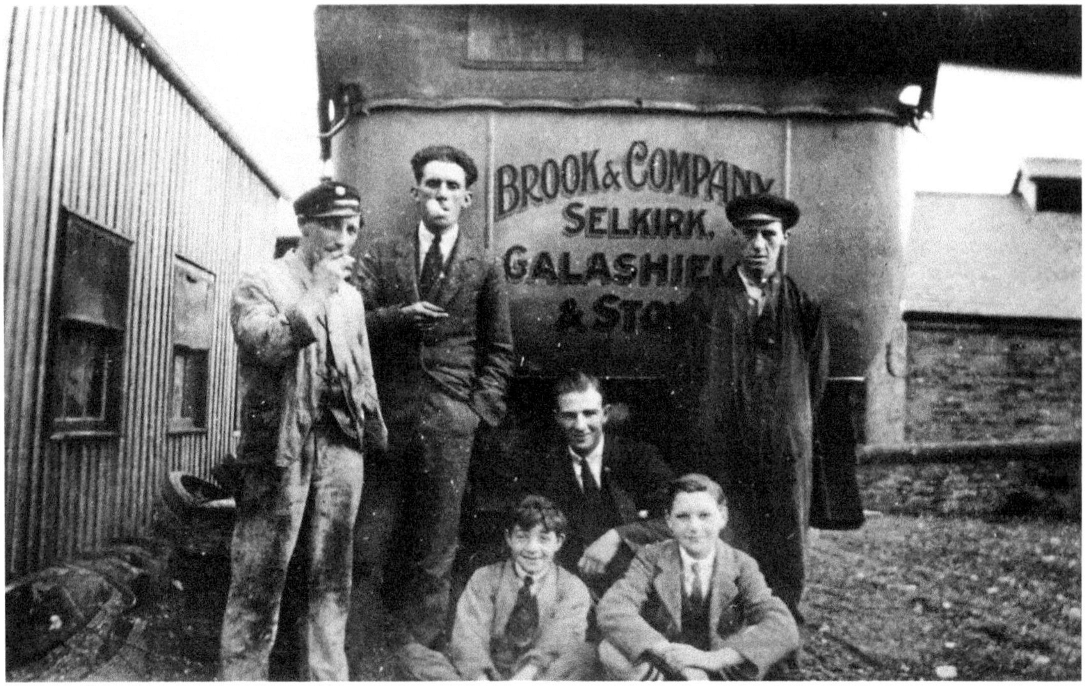

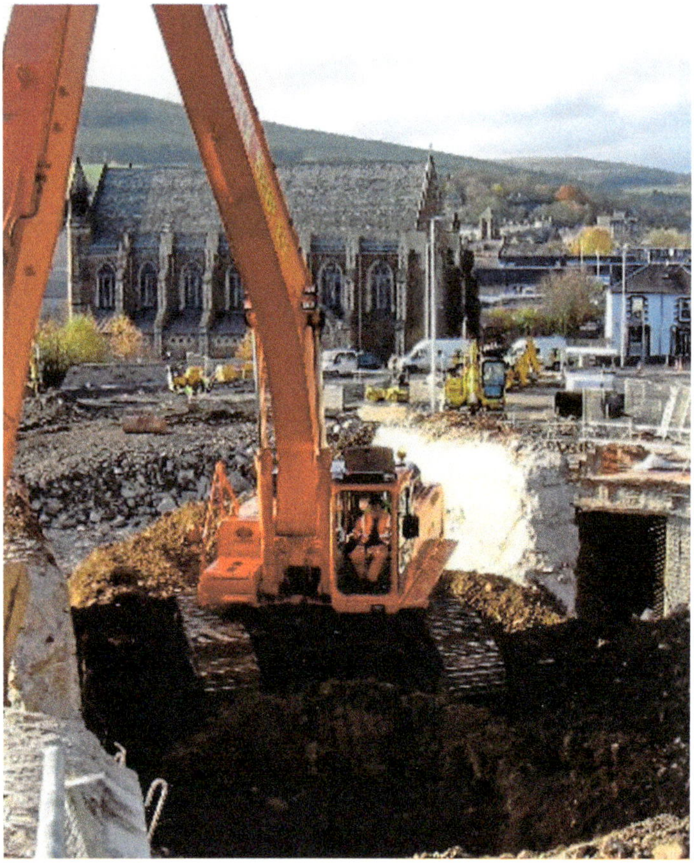

The Borders Railway

The closure of the railway back in 1969 proved a very controversial subject, but politicians and supporters finally succeeded in their efforts and had it reinstated in 2015. The demolition of the Station Brae took place in 2006. The new photo shows the line once again running through Galashiels in September 2015.

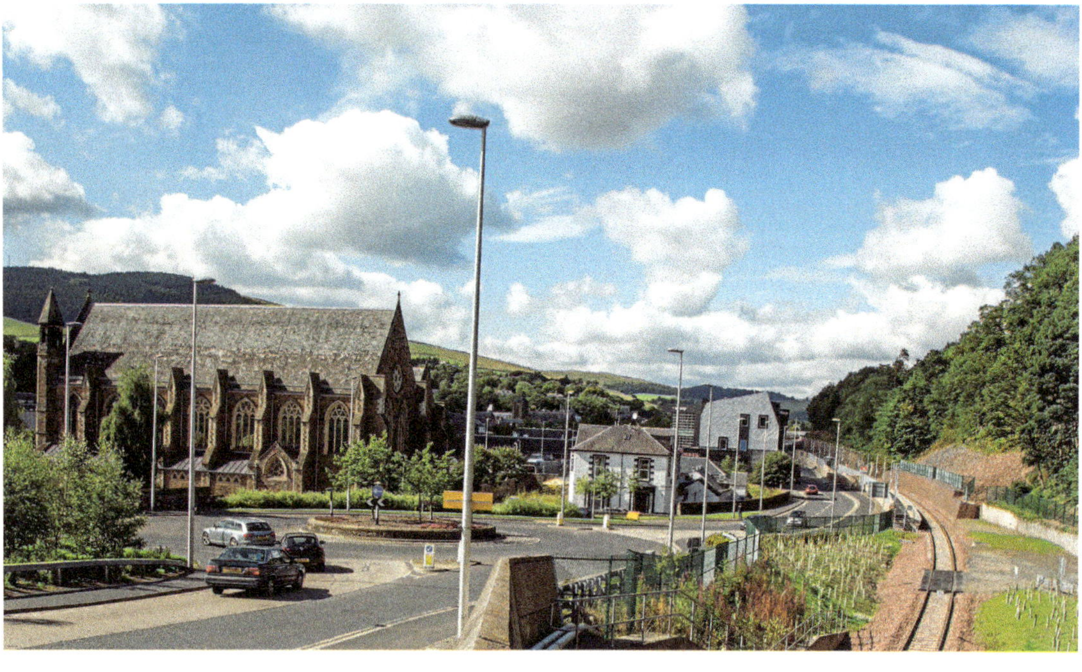

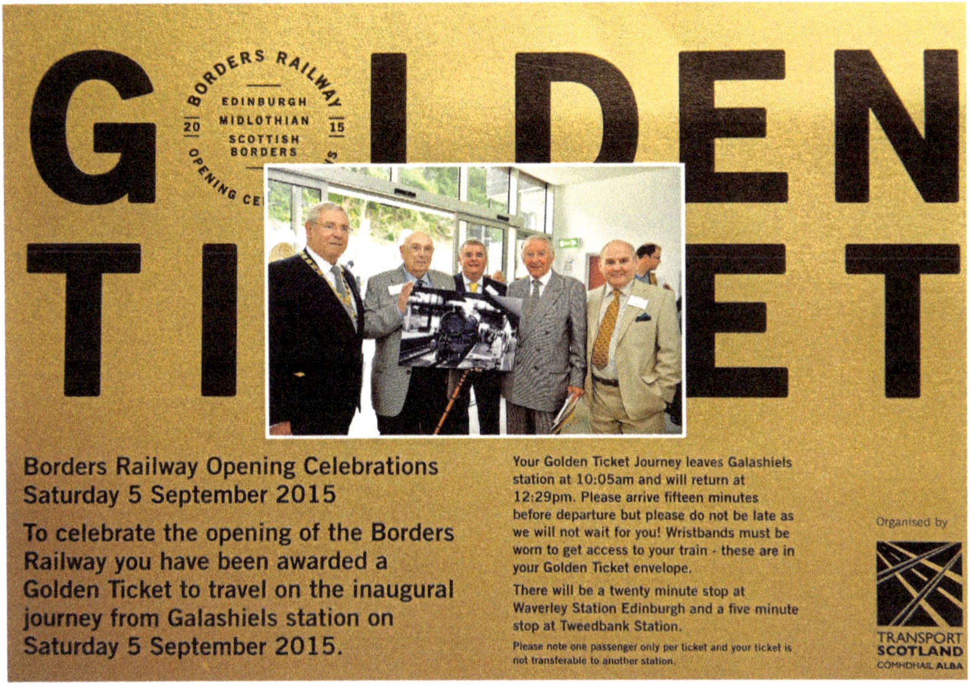

Golden Tickets

To celebrate the return of the train to the Borders, a number of people were nominated to receive a 'Golden Ticket'. This invited them to travel on the 5 September 2015, on a special day prior to the railway opening to the public. Jim Walker, FRPS, who was born in Gala in 1925, presented a copy of a photograph he took back in 1957. Seen in inset image with Councillor Garvie, Council Leader David Parker, Sir David Steel and Councillor Herd.

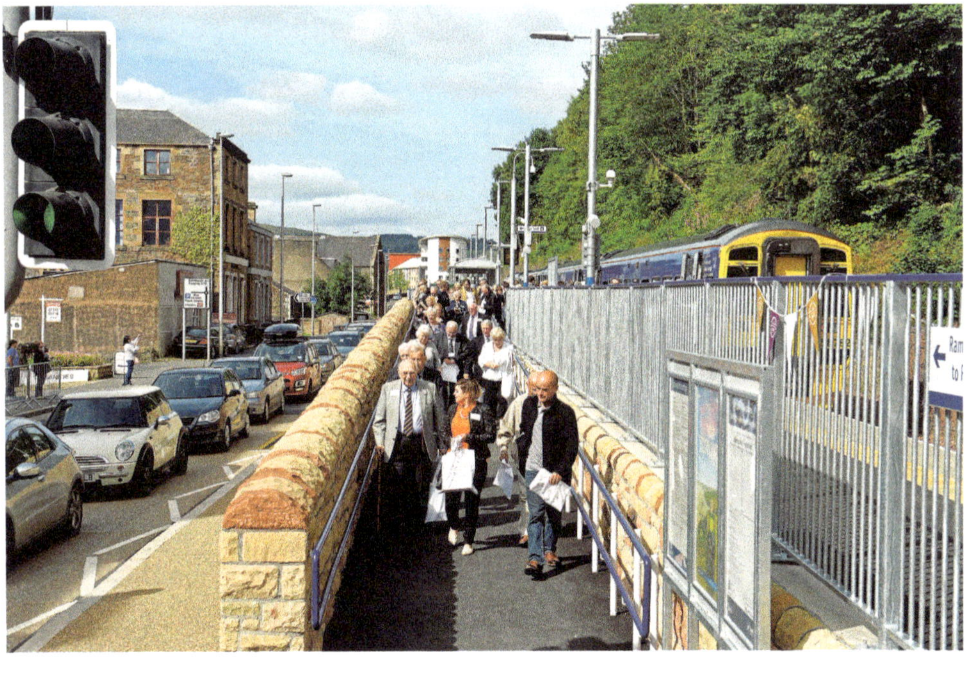

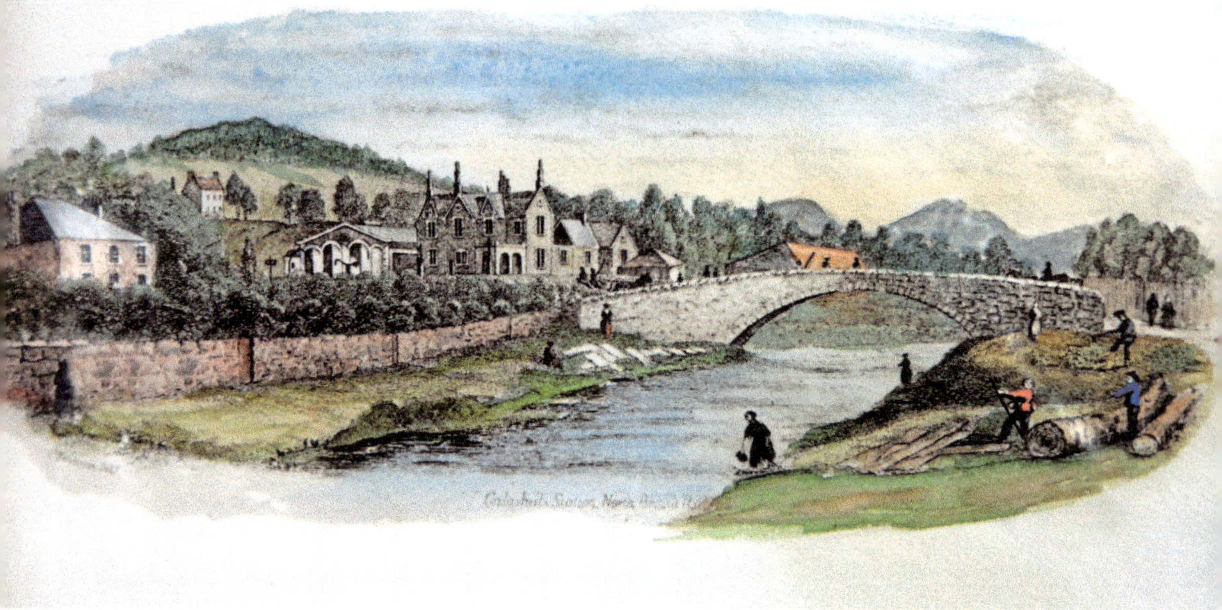

Galashiels Station

This scene titled *Galashiels Station, North British Rail,* shows women washing clothes by the river with the railway station buildings to the left. In 1917 the cost of the fare to Edinburgh was put up from 1*d* to 1½*d* a mile (old currency) 'as the train had got faster'. The train seen in the photograph has, unusually, two engines which suggests it was carrying a heavy load.

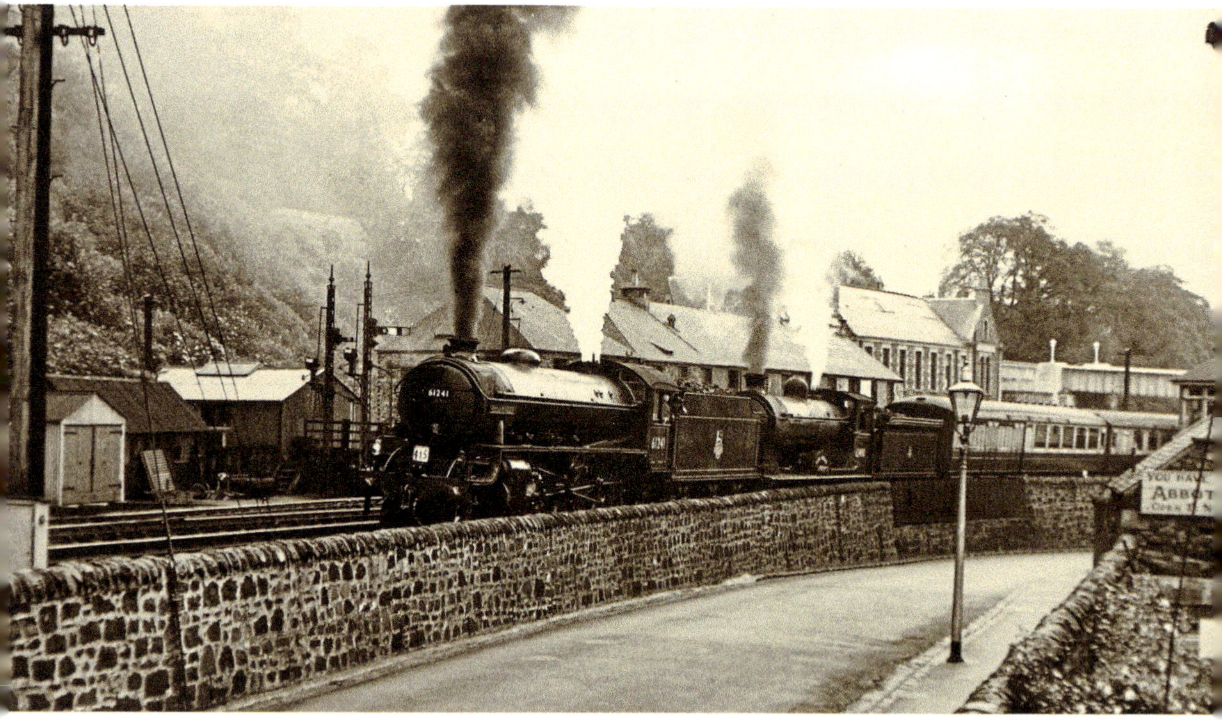

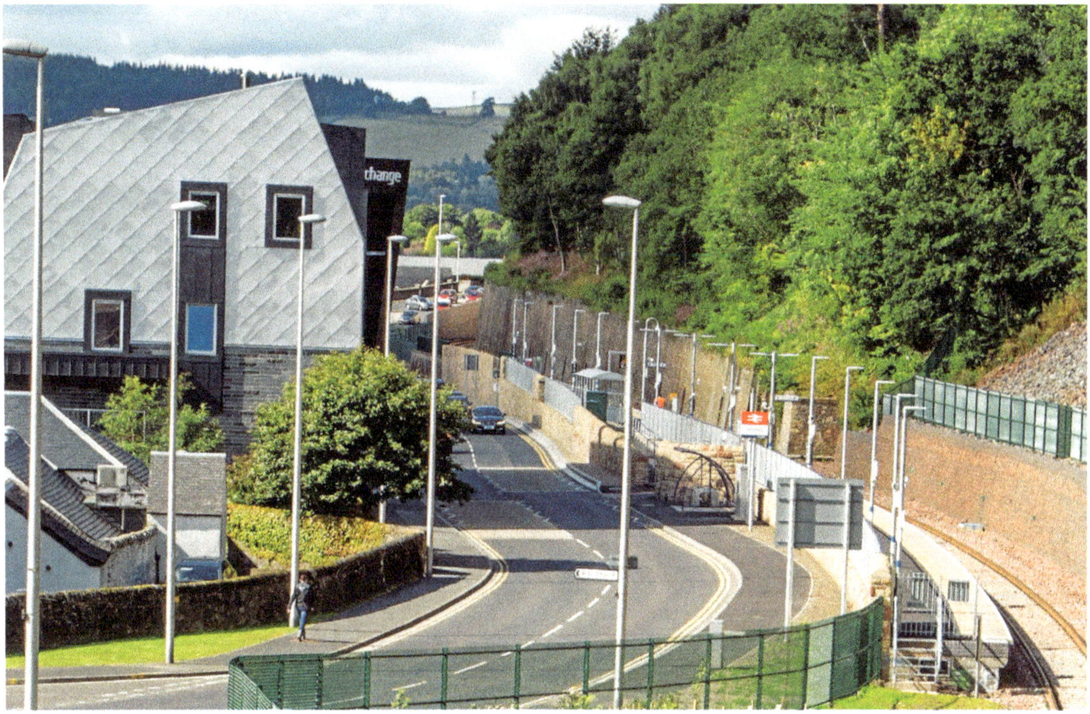

New Transport Interchange

In 2015 Ladhope Vale with two-way traffic and a railway line alongside. The new interchange building is used by both the railway and new bus station, accessed from Stirling Street and Ladhope Vale.

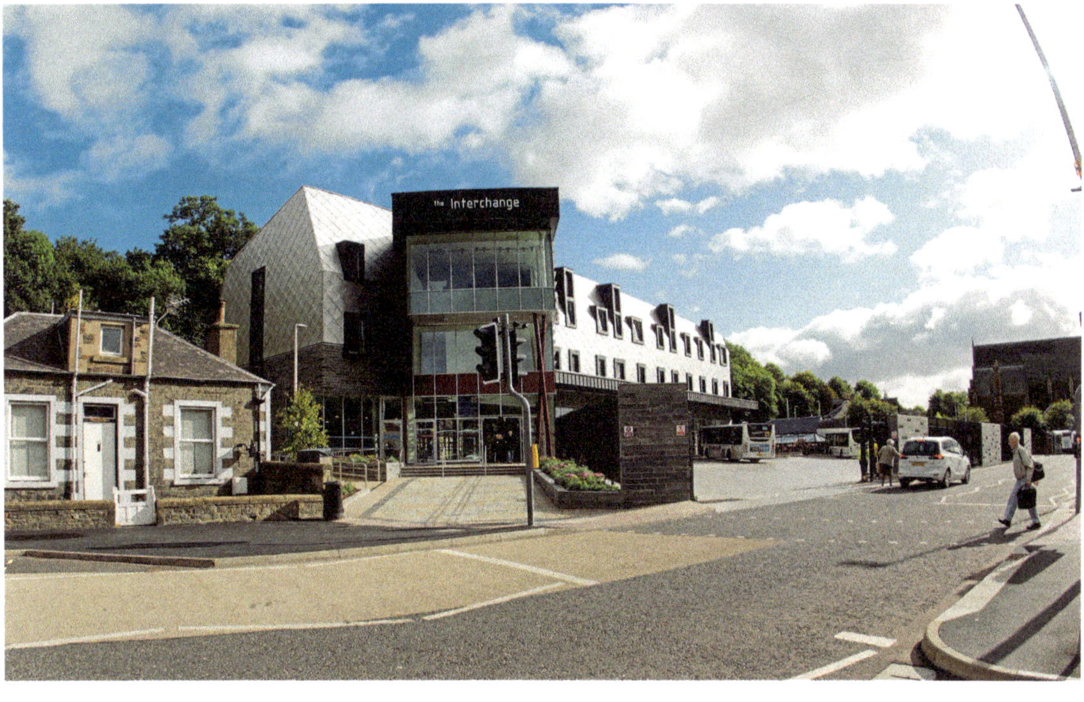

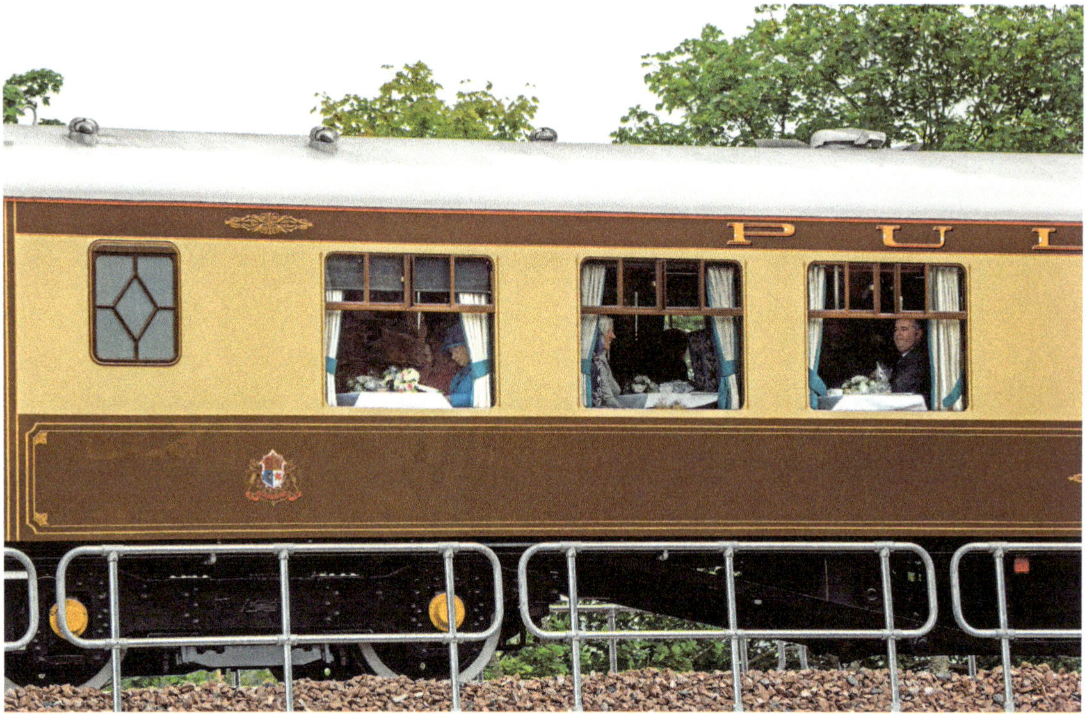

Her Majesty The Queen

Her Majesty The Queen travels through Galashiels to Tweedbank to officially open the new Borders Railway on 9 September 2015. This was also on the day she became the longest-serving monarch in UK history. The top image sees The Queen in one window and David Parker, Leader of Scottish Borders Council in the other. The bottom image shows the train travelling alongside Curry Road.

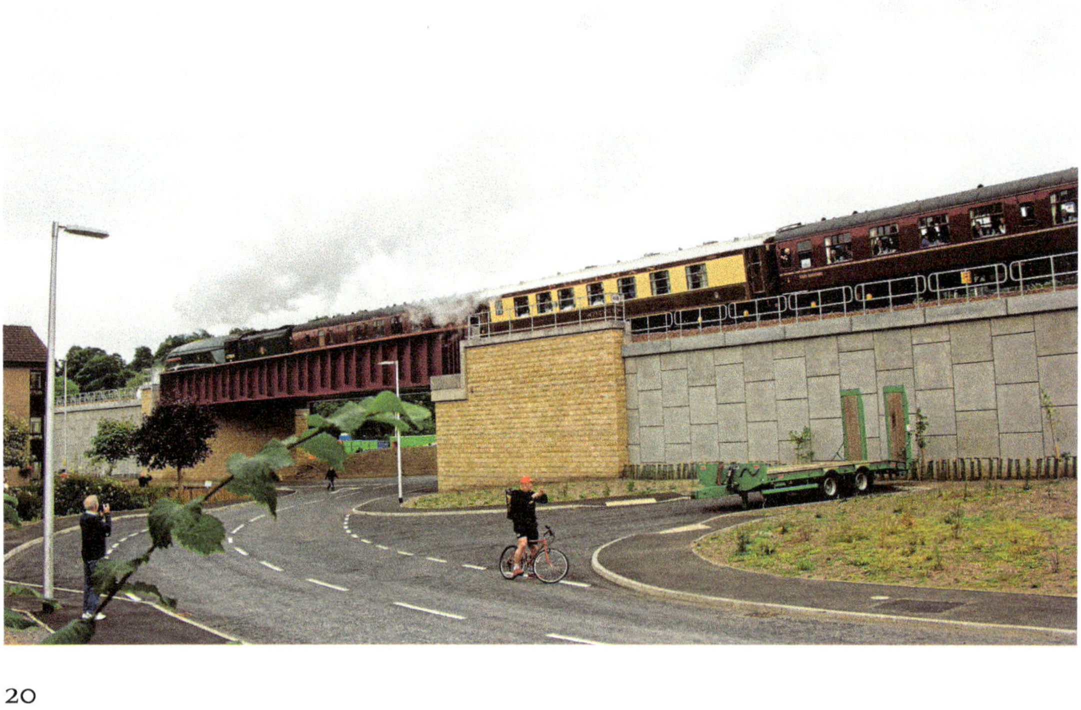

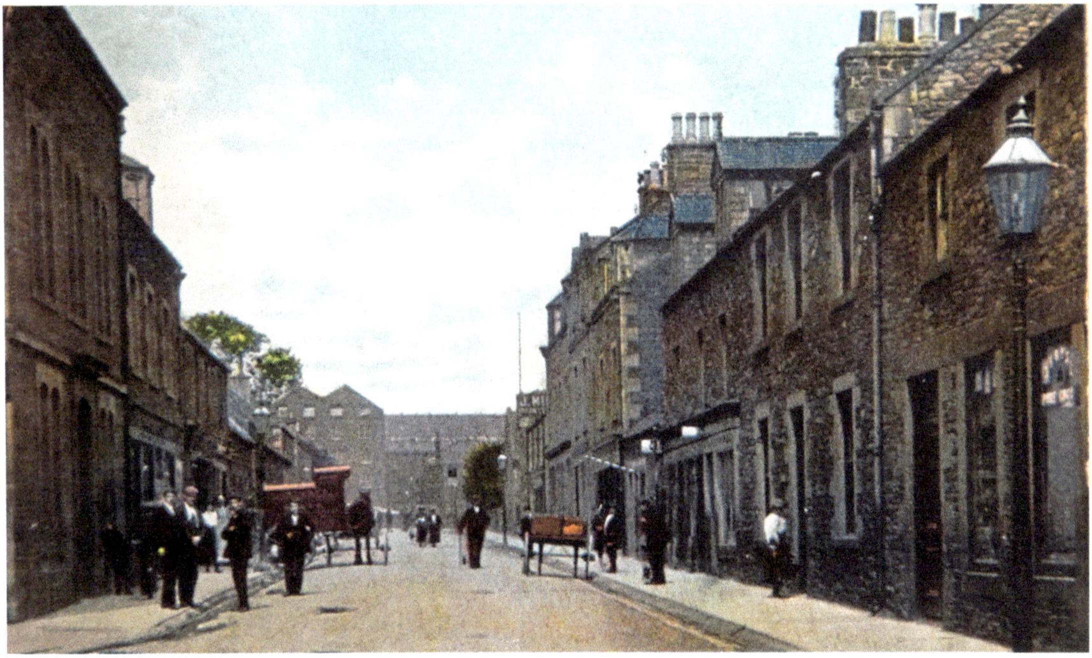

Island Street

Alex Dalgetty & Sons can be seen in the old image, where the baker's horse and cart stand on the left. The original bakery was in Galapark and moved to Island Street in the early 1900s. This is still a family business. Craig Murray, great-great-grandson of Alexander Dalgetty, is seen in the new image in the bakery. The ovens still in use are over 100 years old.

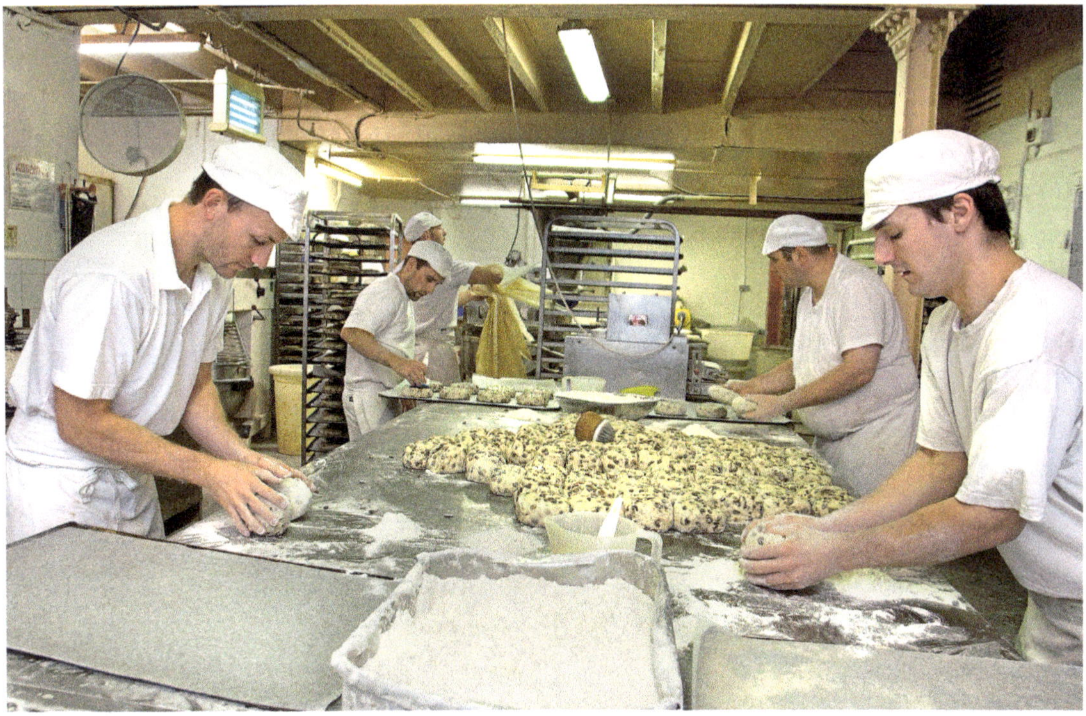

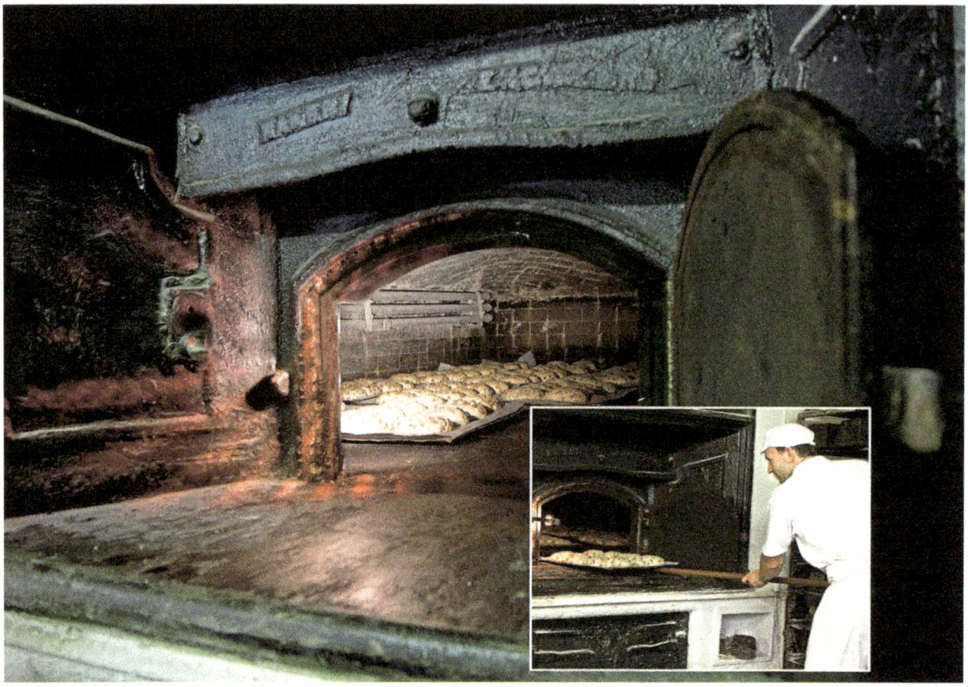

The Selkirk Bannock

Next door we see what was Michael Moore's constituency office. He became the first backbencher in living memory to go straight to Cabinet minister in 2010 when he was appointed Secretary of State for Scotland. One of his first duties was to host a reception at Dover House in London for 100 dignitaries, for which he ordered six large Selkirk Bannocks from Dalgetty's to serve to the guests. Craig Murray seen here on the left making Selkirk Bannocks at 4.30 a.m. using his great, great grandfather's recipe.

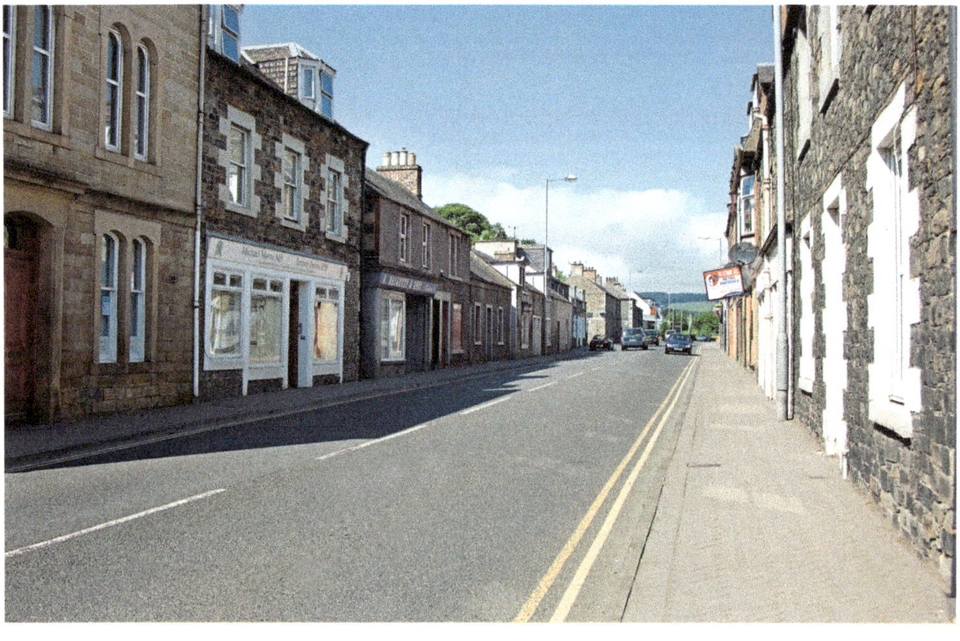

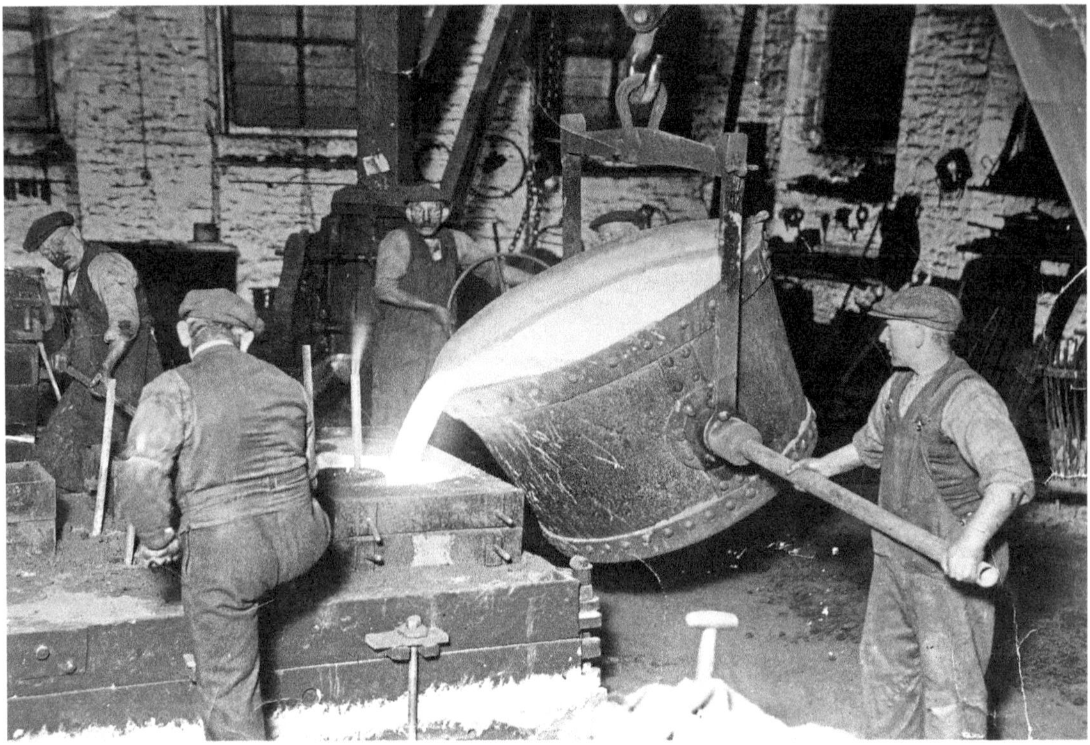

Aimers McLean Ironfounders
The top image shows brothers Andrew, Johnny and Walter Baillie at work with Aimers McLean Ironfounders. The all-male workforce lined up below for the photographer (pre-First World War).

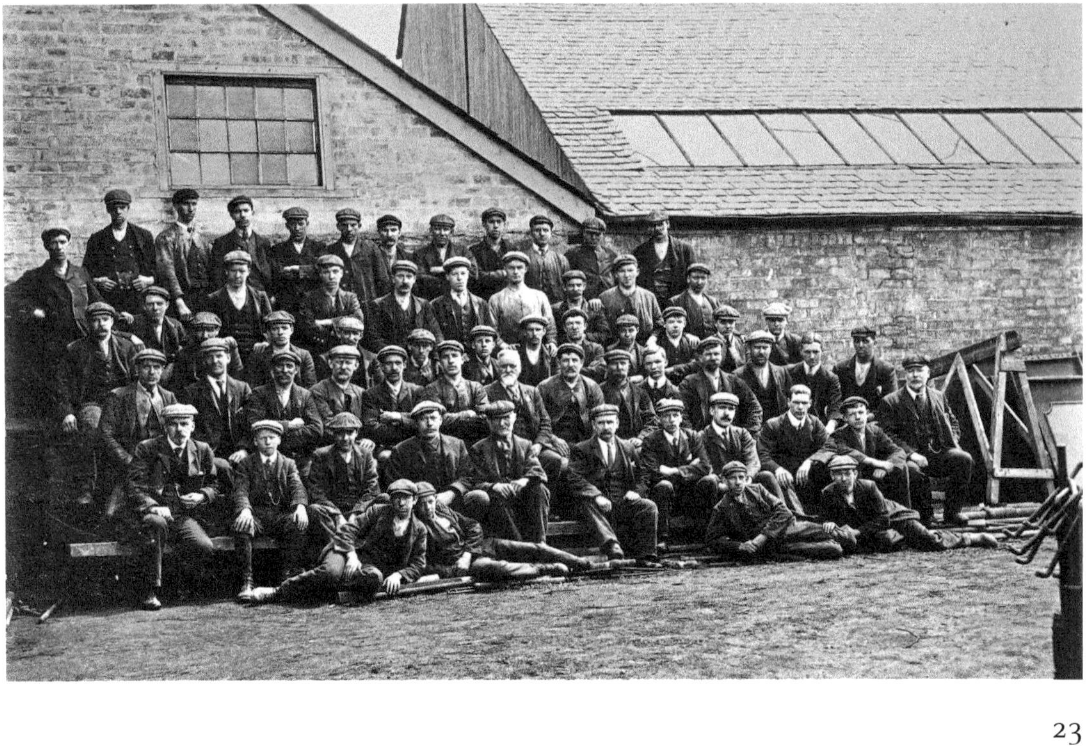

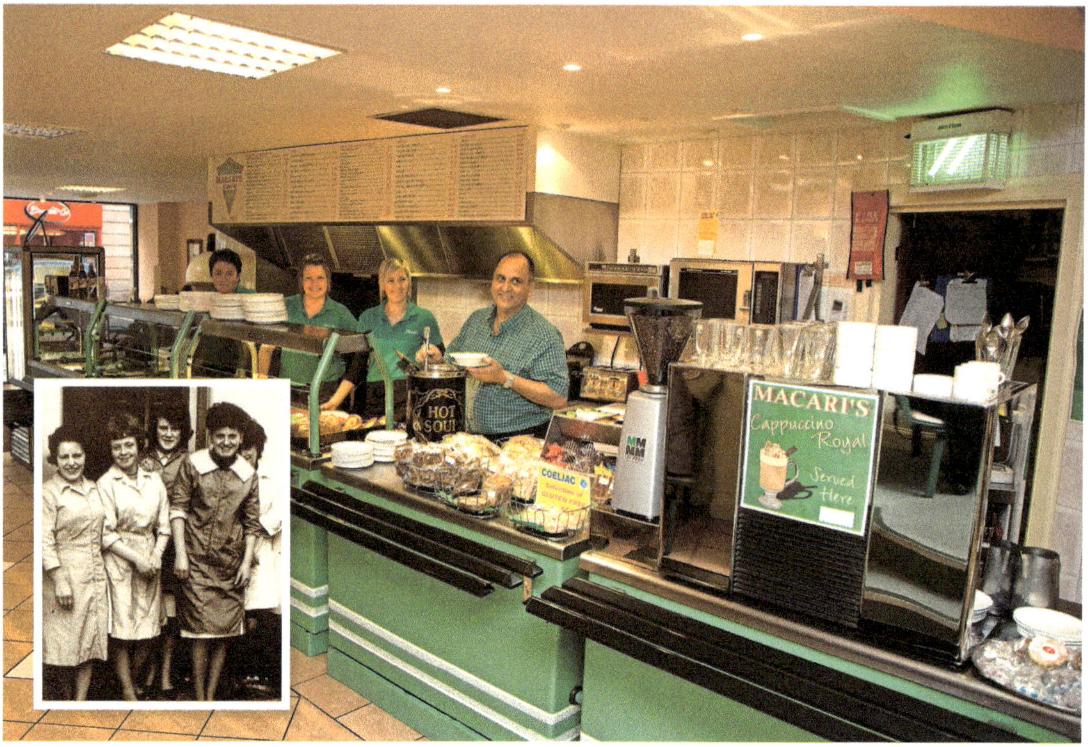

Macari's

Giovanni was the first of the Macari family to come to Galashiels, opening The Gala Soda-Fountain in 1924. He was followed by his son Tony and in turn, his son Phillip who now runs the Macari family business in the town seen here in the same premises today. The inset image shows sister Sylvia alongside café girls in 1965: Nikki Fitzgerald, Maria Macari and Christine Reid.

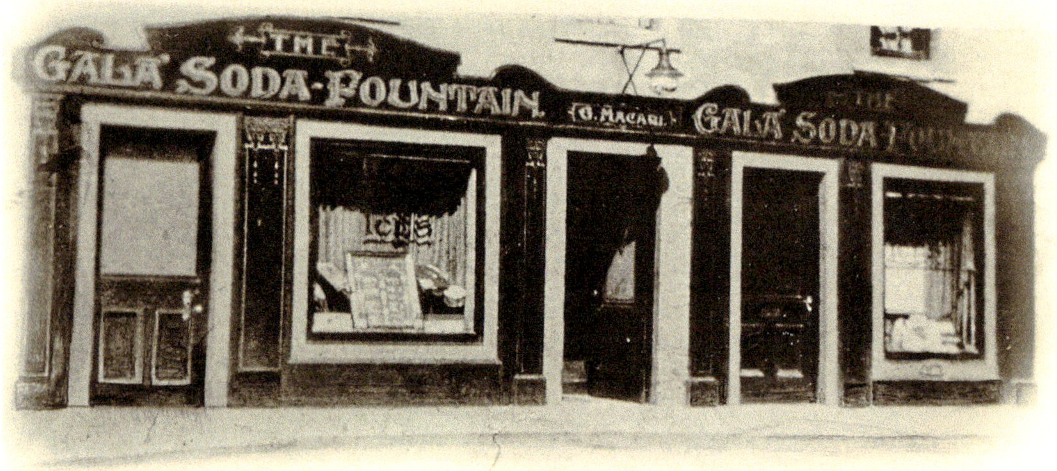

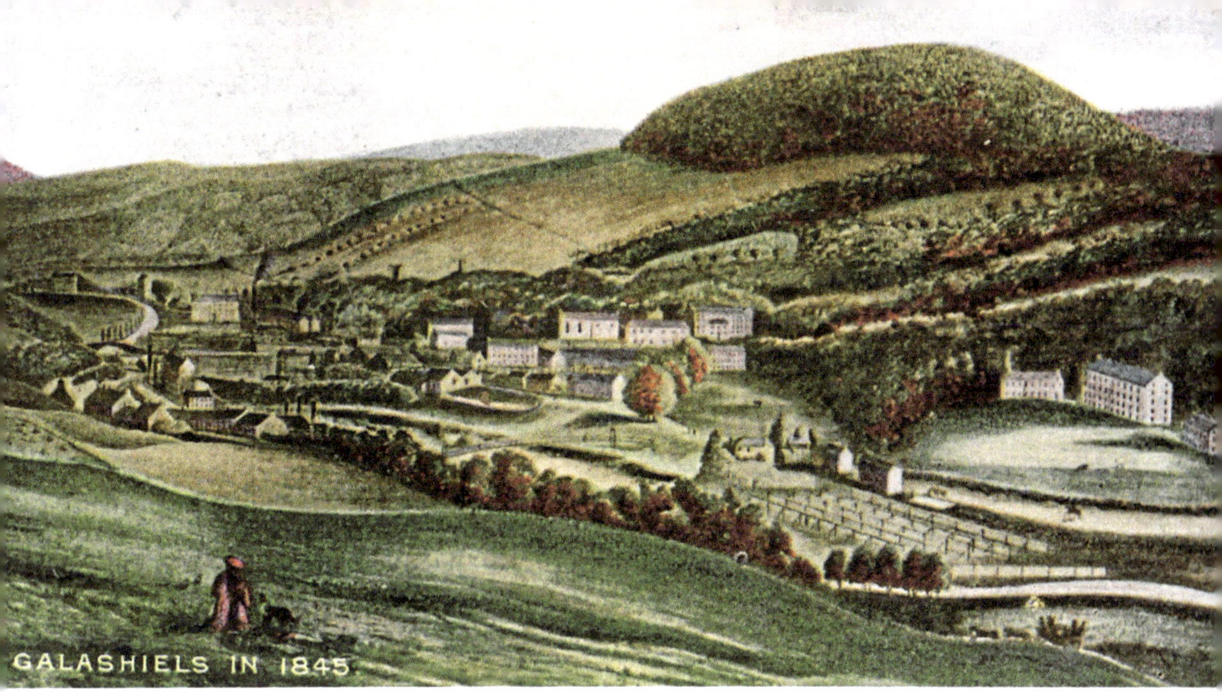

Gala Hill

Looking toward Gala Hill, this early engraving above is quite a contrast from the Galashiels we know today – Gala Hill being the only familiar sight. The foreground shows wooden 'tenters' where the cloth would be hung on hooks overnight (tenterhooks).

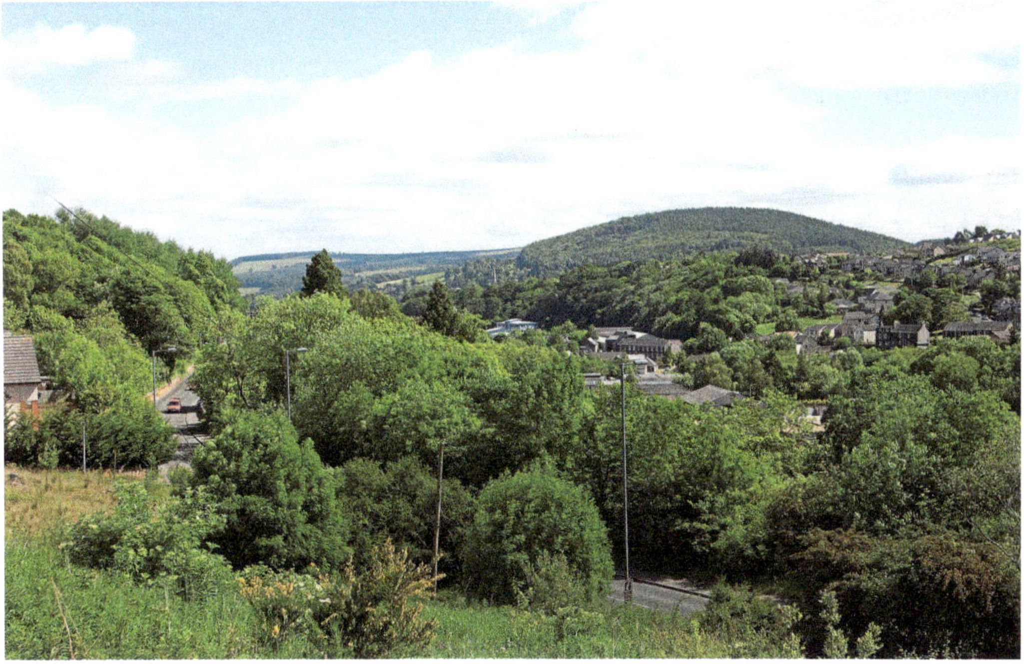

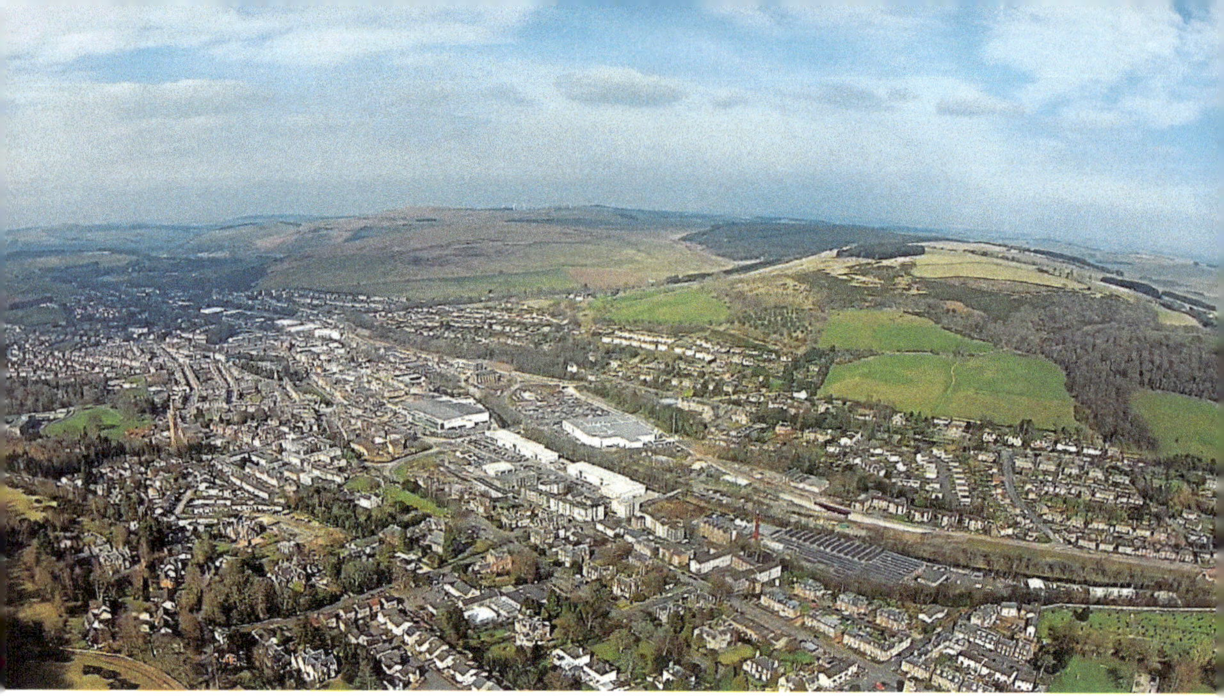

Oatlands Terrace

Photographed with a drone, this shows how much more densely populated Galashiels is, in particular areas such as Ellwyn Terrace, Ladhope Golf Course, and Halliburton (top of picture), Parsonage Road towards Oatlands Terrace (bottom left of picture). The town centre in the middle, is dominated by the large superstores instead of the old mill chimneys seen in the old photograph.

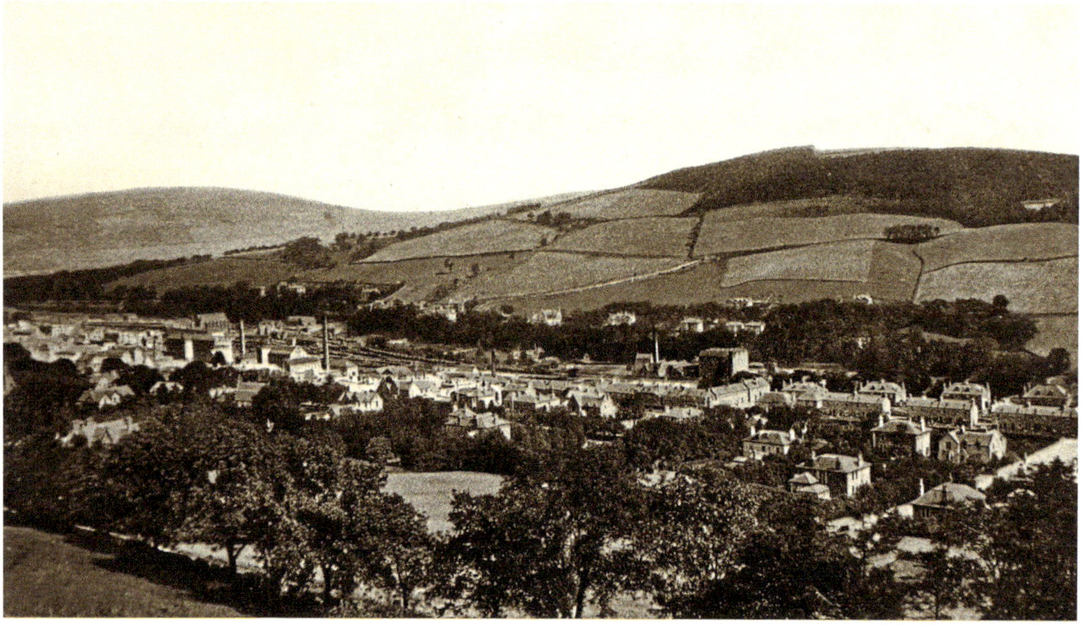

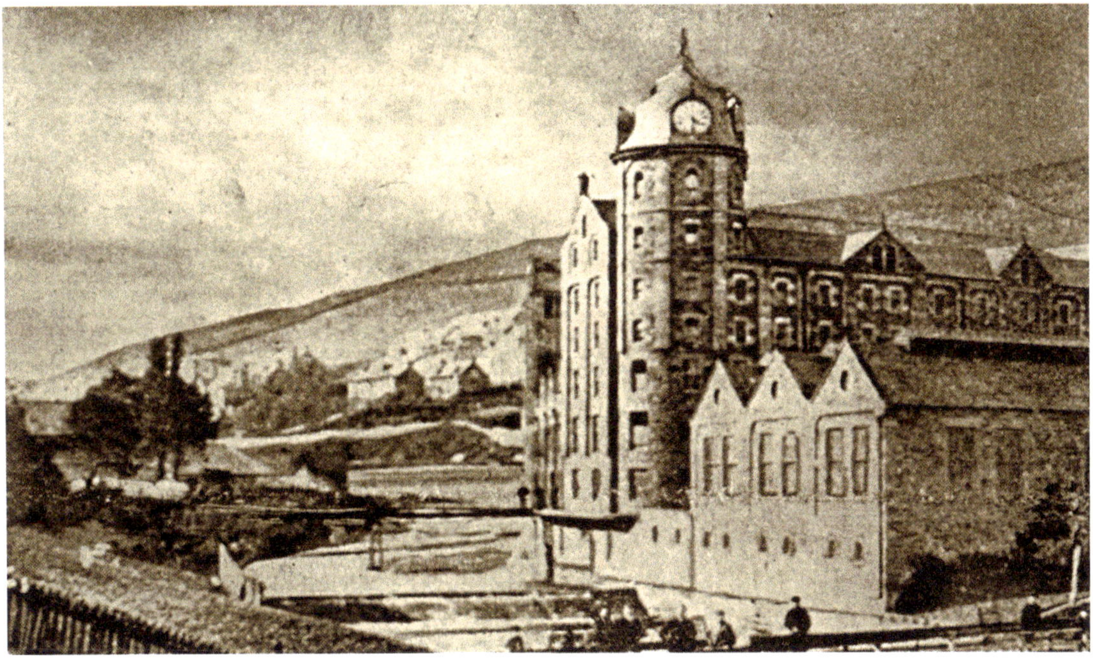

Sanderson & Murray

Founded in 1844 as a fellmongers and wool merchants in Wilderhaugh, Galashiels. The business suffered three fires during its time, rising from the ashes on each occasion – 1873, 1882 and 1923. The old image here shows the Clock Tower which was never rebuilt after one fire. There is no longer any sign of the skinworks which at its peak, would employ around 300 people. All that is left are the offices, now occupied by Cameron Architects.

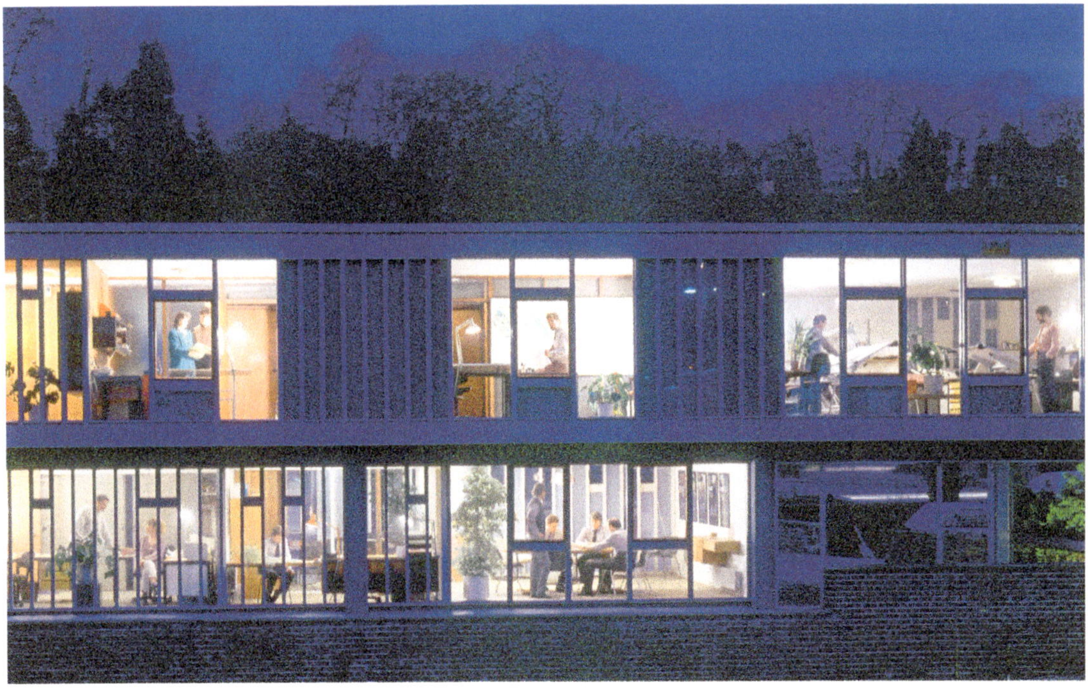

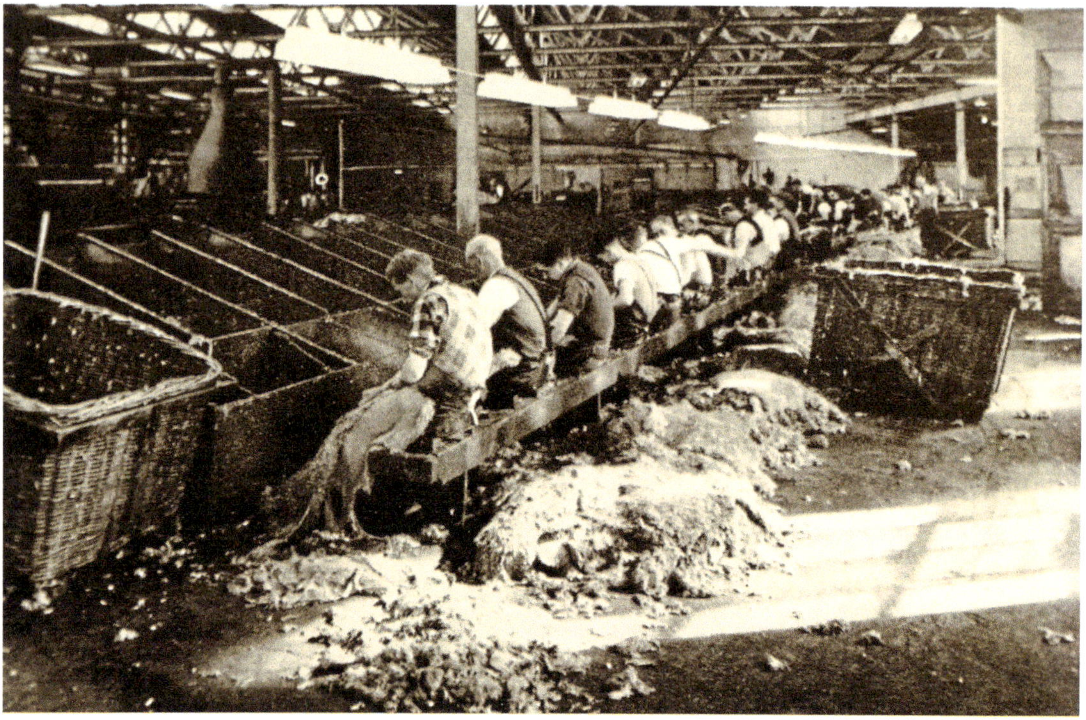

At Work

Workers are pictured 'pulling and grading' the sheepskins. Inset Dr Edwin Winton, who arrived around 1947 as Chief Chemist and was a director of the company until its closure in 1981.

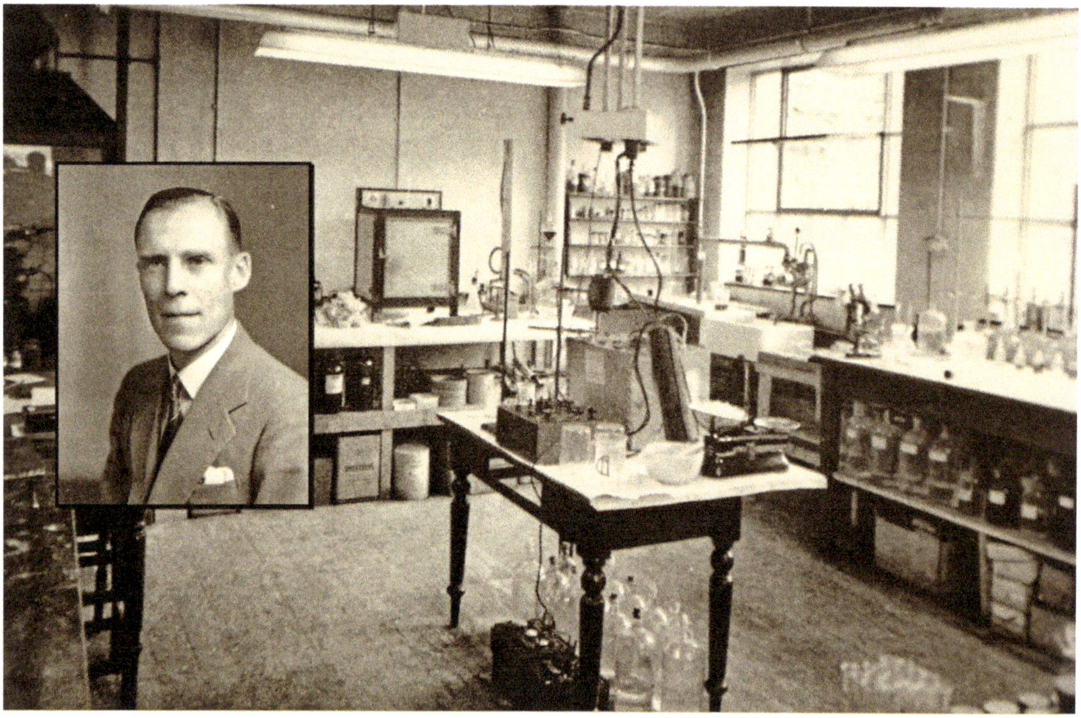

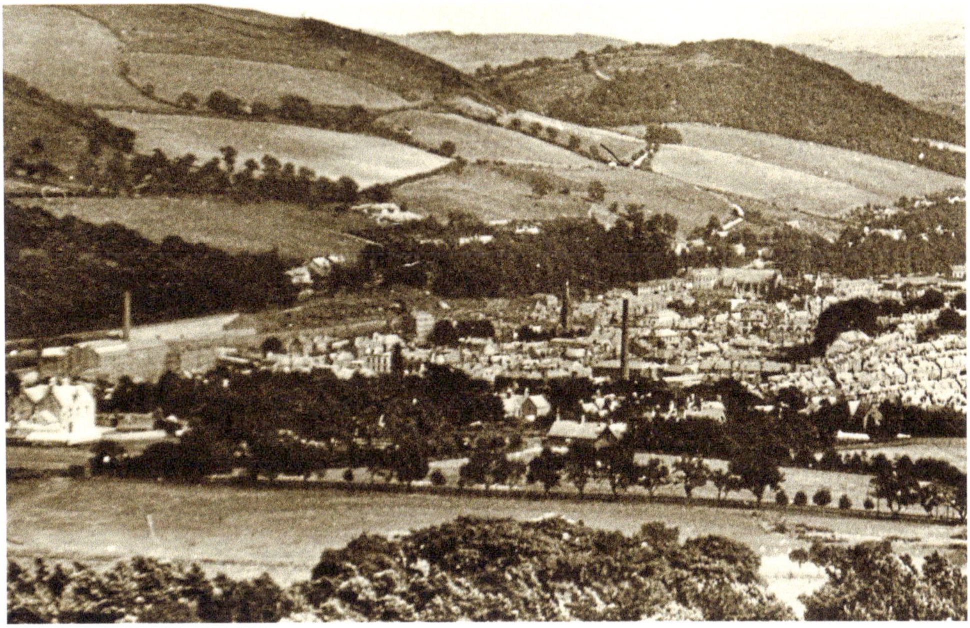

Galashiels in History

Views have been difficult to copy exactly due to extensive growth in trees, but photographing from the hills on the outskirts in 2010 leaves me feeling we are privileged to have such a beautiful setting in which to live. Former Provost Rutherford makes reference in his book in 1930, *Galashiels in History,* to 'the great primeval forest', 'appearing in recorded history in the days of the Romans, and being described by Roman writers as vast and dense.' This density we again have of trees is the compensation for the vision of the white roofed, bland buildings which have appeared in the last ten years.

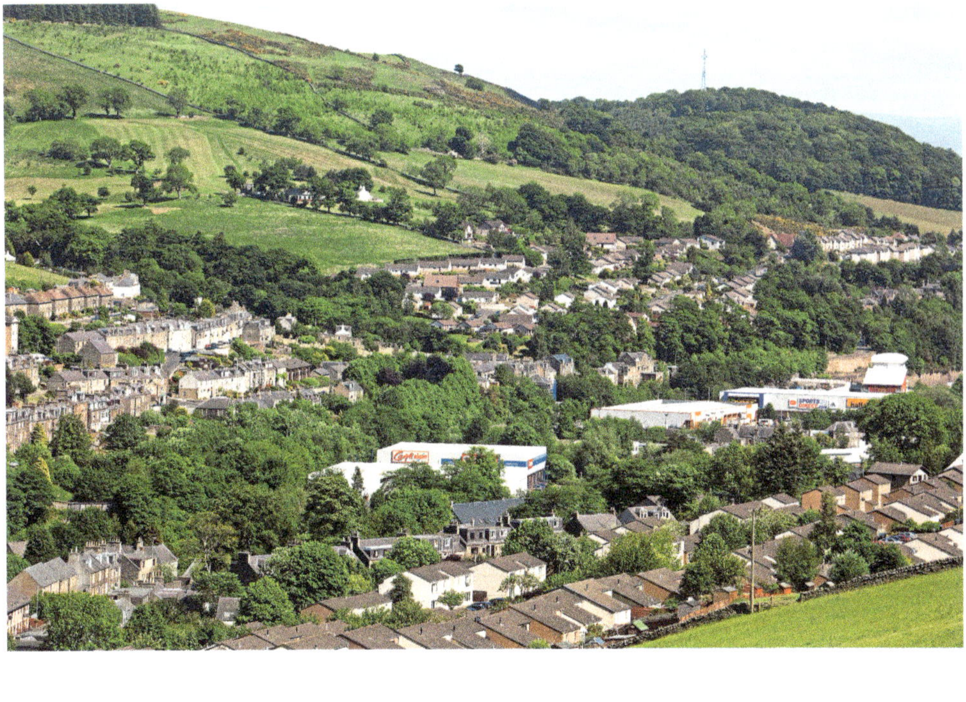

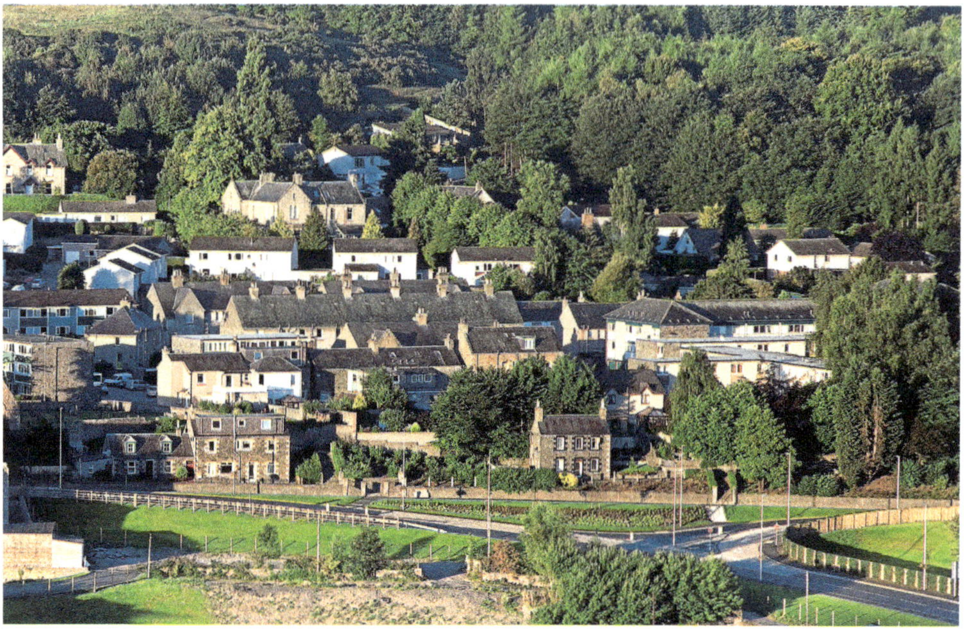

The Bow Butts

Below – View from The Bow Butts in 2010. Image looks over to Albert Place down to Huddersfield Street and up on the hillside to Ellwyn Terrace and Ladhope areas. The Bow Butt steps got their name from the first quarter of the seventeenth century when villagers over twelve and under sixty 'found opportunity for practice with bow and arrow on Sabbath afternoons at the conclusion of church service'. The Bow Butts was also the site of Logan's stables in the late 1800's, where corporation carts and pigs were kept. The other image is taken from the opposite side of the town looking over to Albert Place.

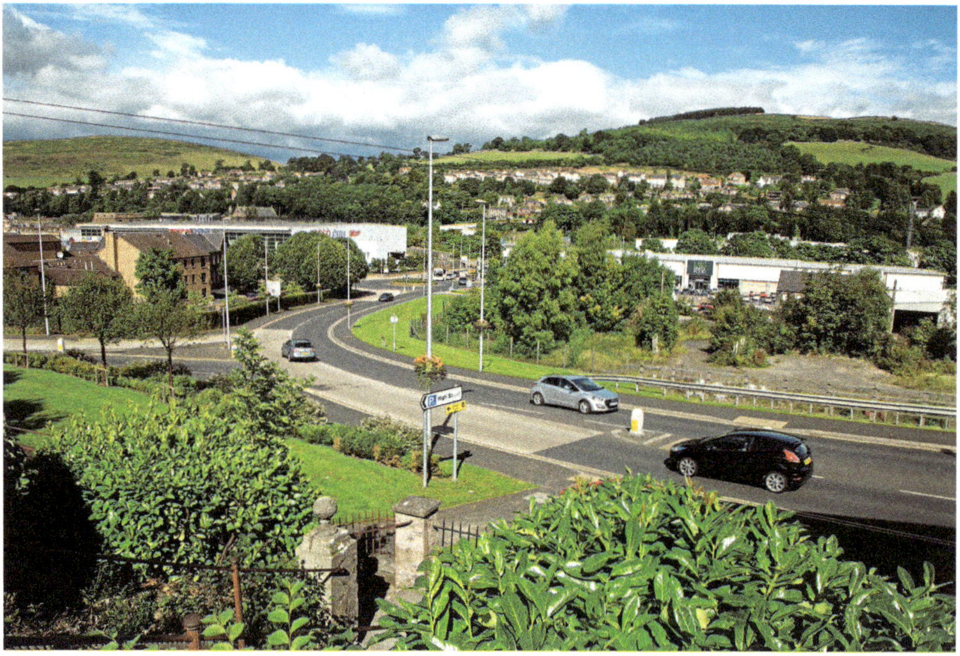

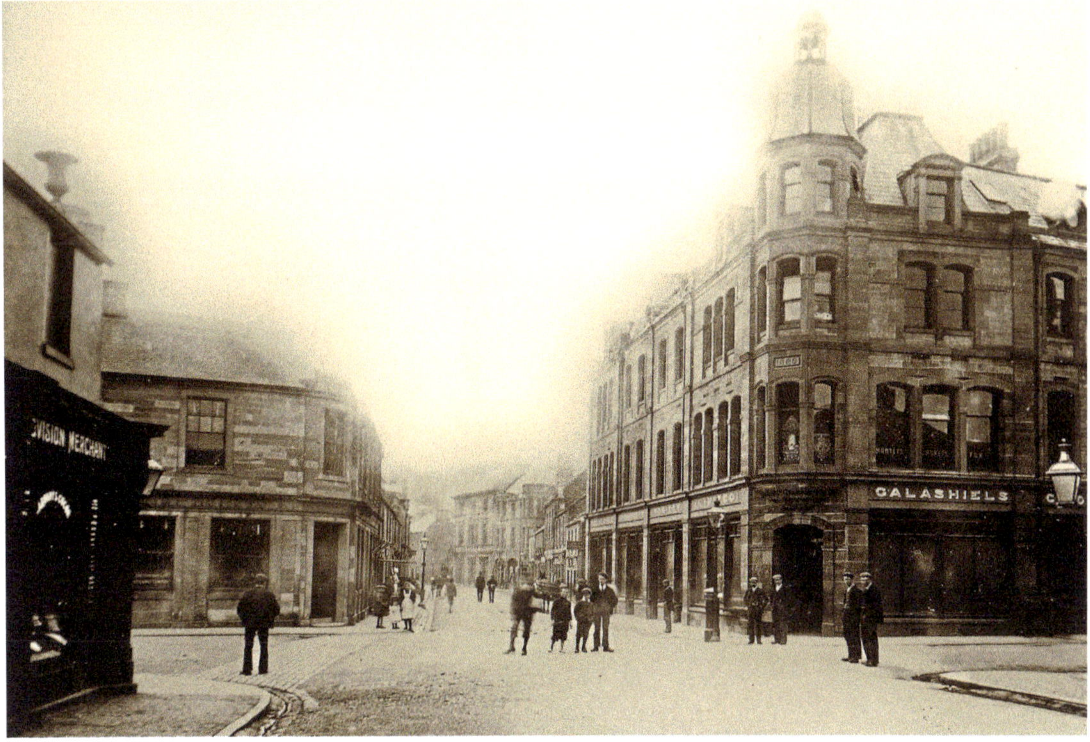

Island Street Junction

The junction of Island Street and High Street is a part of the town centre that still has a similar layout as it did in the 1890s. What was the old Royal Bank can be seen on the left hand side – latterly The Golden Lion – is now a pub. Now we have a one-way system up High Street to the junction with Island Street. The premises on the left in the new image is occupied by The Bridge Inn and to the right Murray & Burrell.

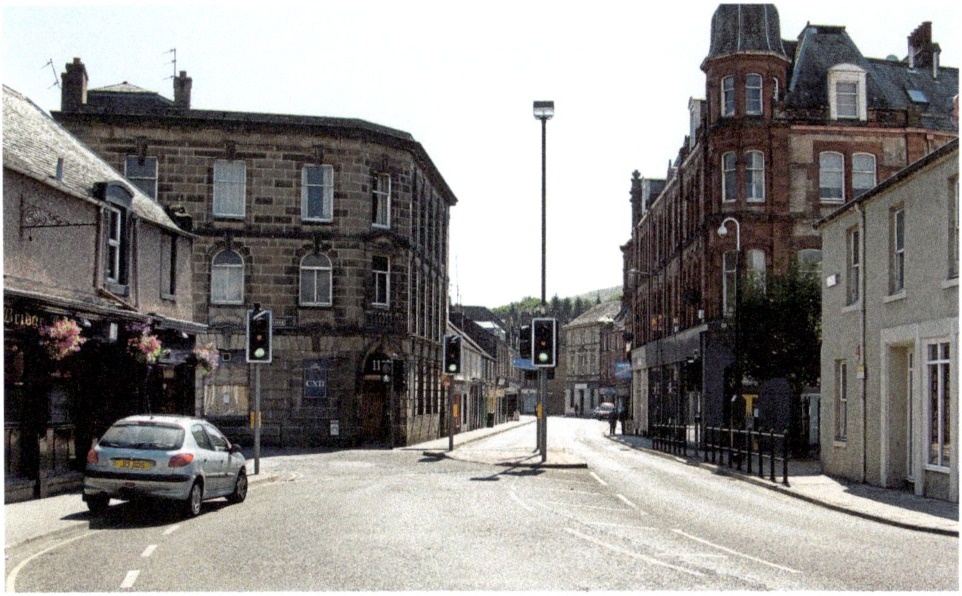

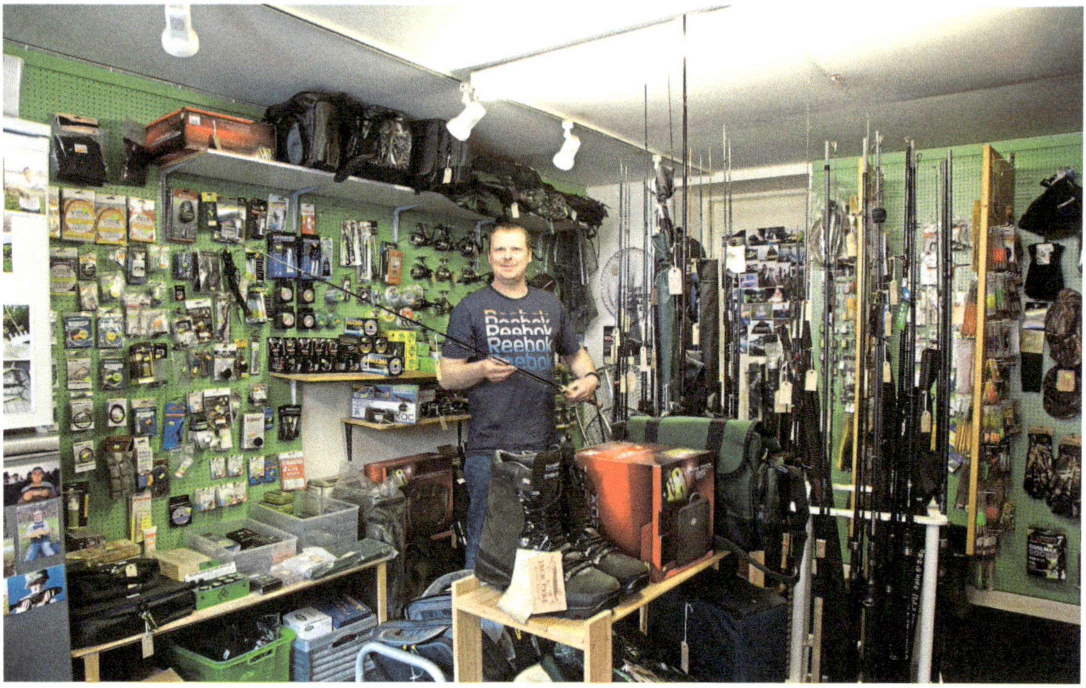

The High Street

Further down High Street the old photograph shows John Thomson who operated a saddler's business at No. 97 *c.* 1930s. There are no saddlers working in the town now, and having taken many forms over the years, this shop is now run by Mike Allan of the Border Angling Centre. Back in 1946 the Almanac and Directory published by John McQueen and Son recorded two saddlers and four fishing tackle makers in Galashiels.

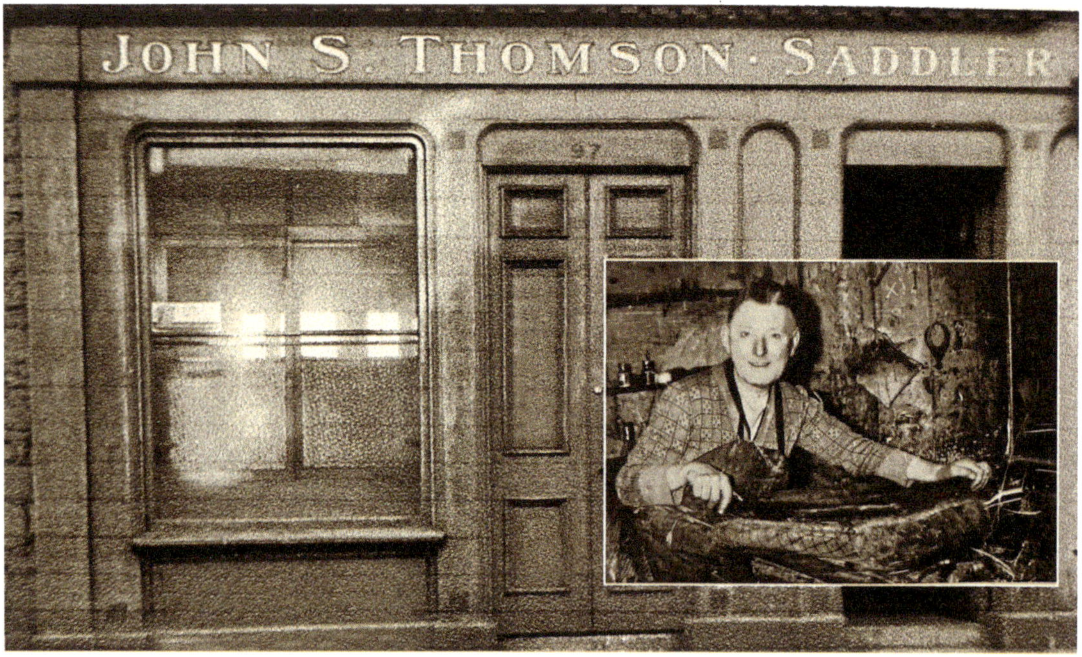

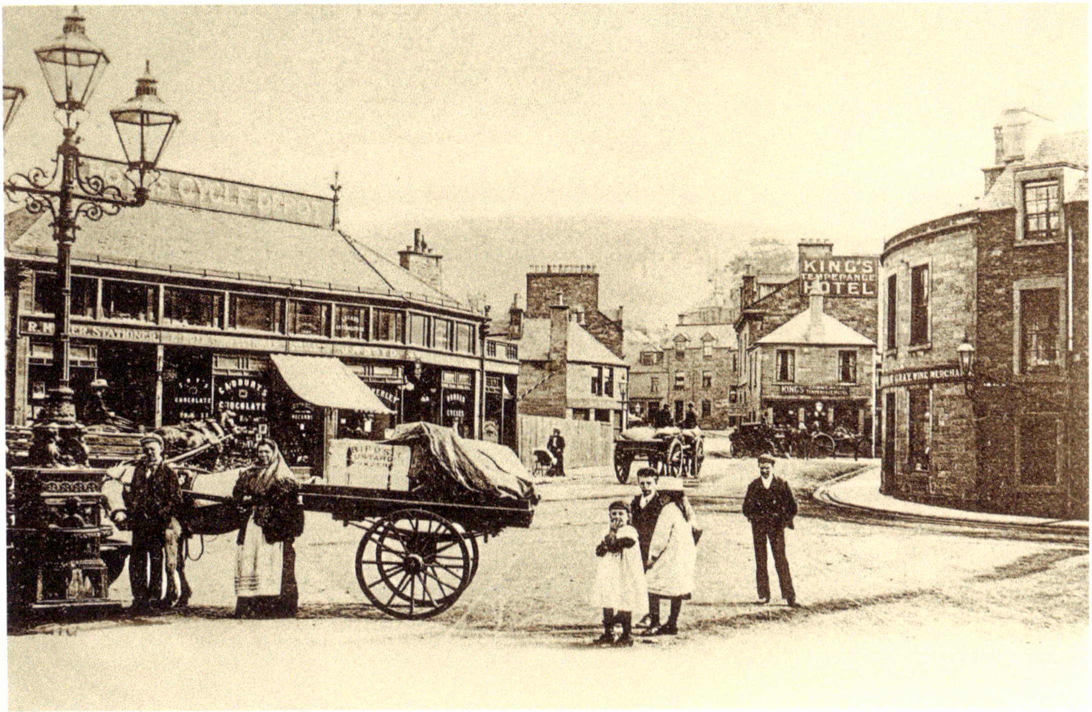

The Market Square

The two images strangely look as busy as one another, despite being so many years apart! The new image sadly shows the town as it is in 2015 with too many empty shops.

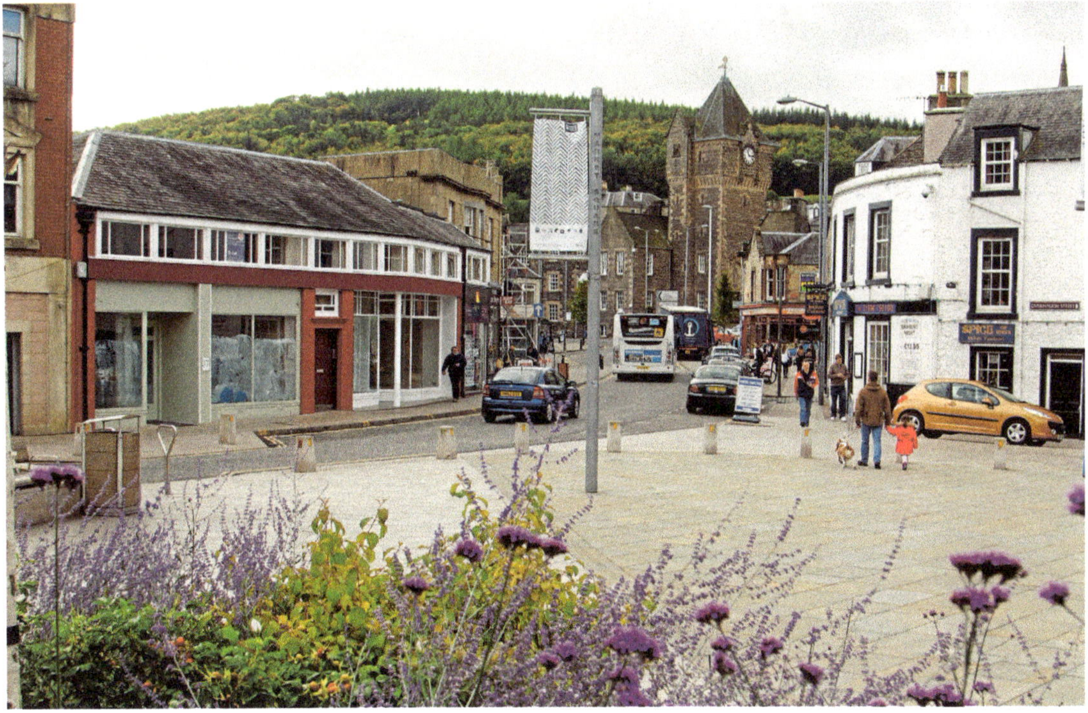

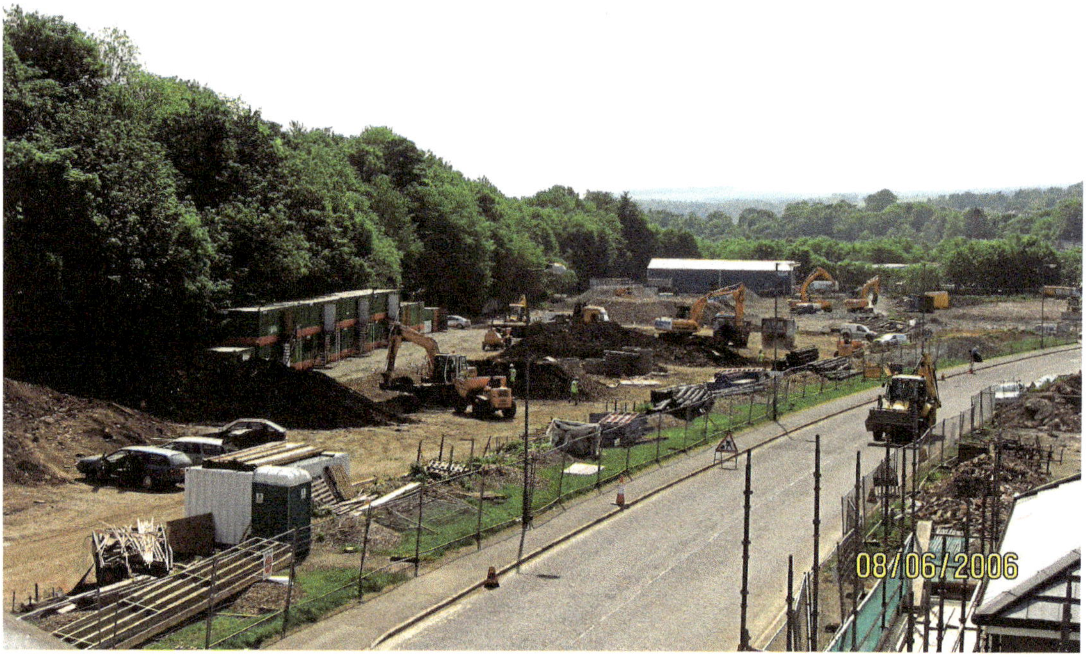

Curry Road

The superstore and the health centre sit alongside the new railway line heading down towards the Glenfield area on its way to Tweedbank. Gala Hill in the distance (top right in new image).

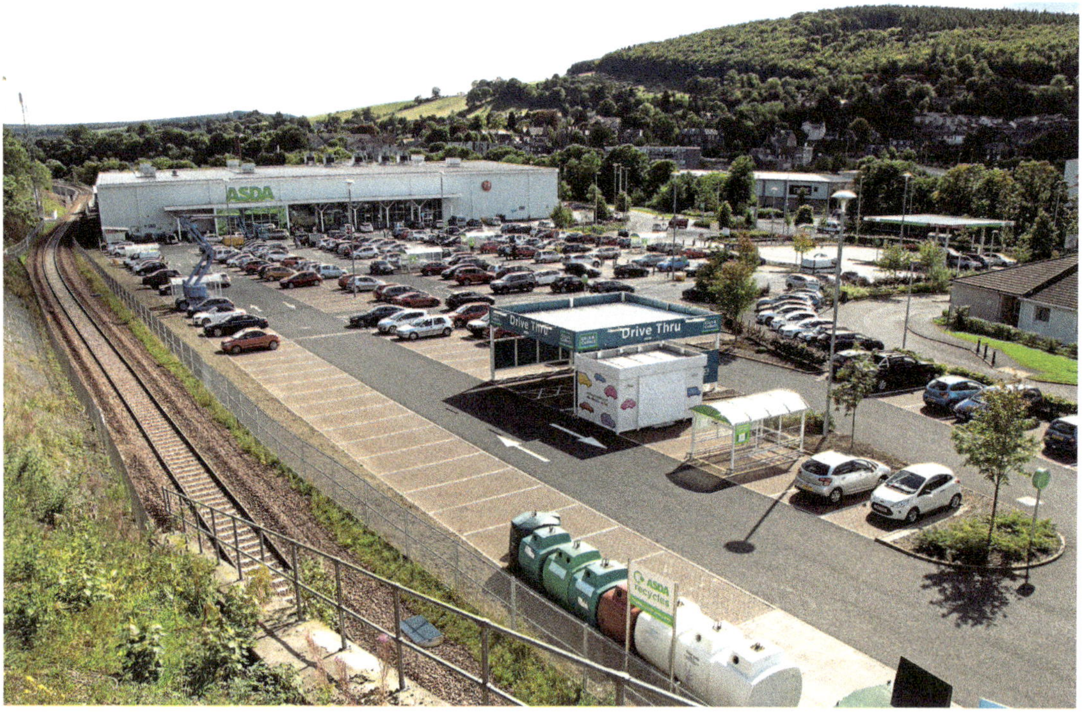

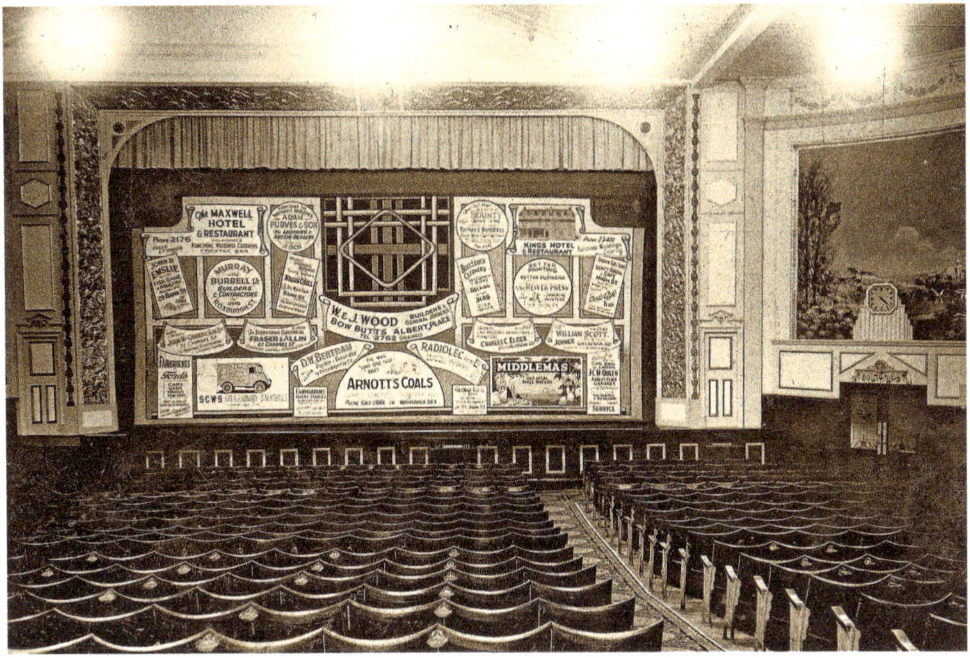

The Pavilion

'The Piv' (The Pavilion) in Channel Street, home to cinema and other productions, was demolished in 1970. This image was taken after the new proscenium was added along with the extension of seating etc. to the right-hand side (1930s). Below the interior of The Playhouse, which was situated further down at the bottom end of Channel Street and opened in 1920. This building is a cinema and bingo complex but now uses the name 'The Pavilion'.

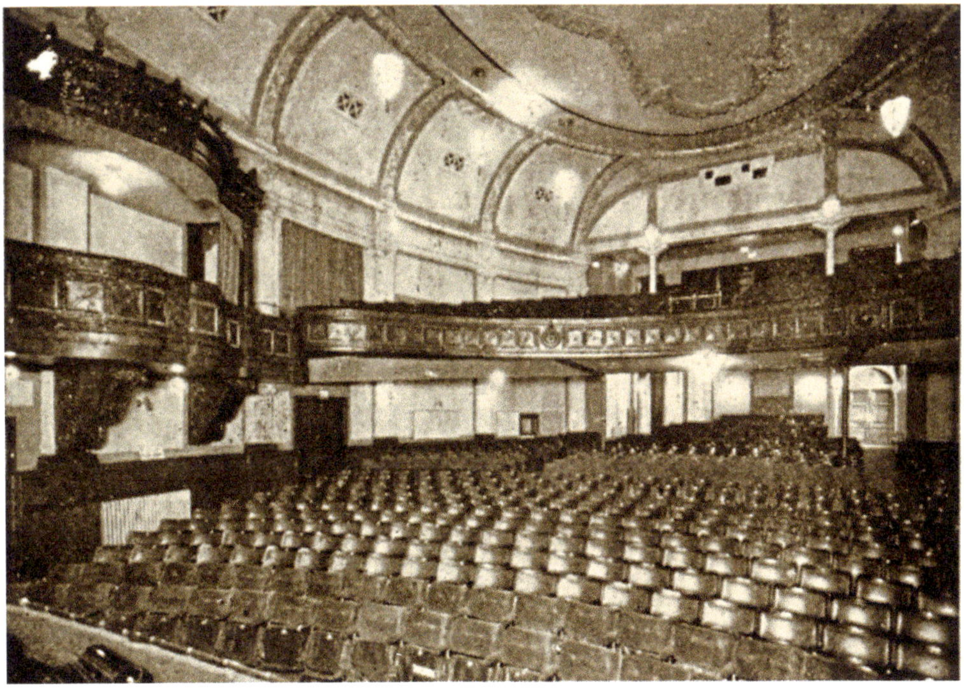

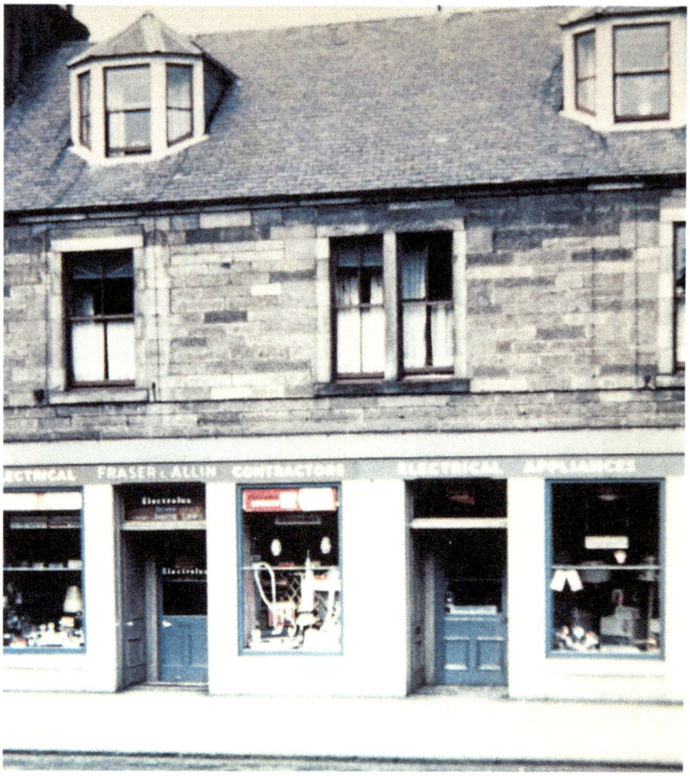

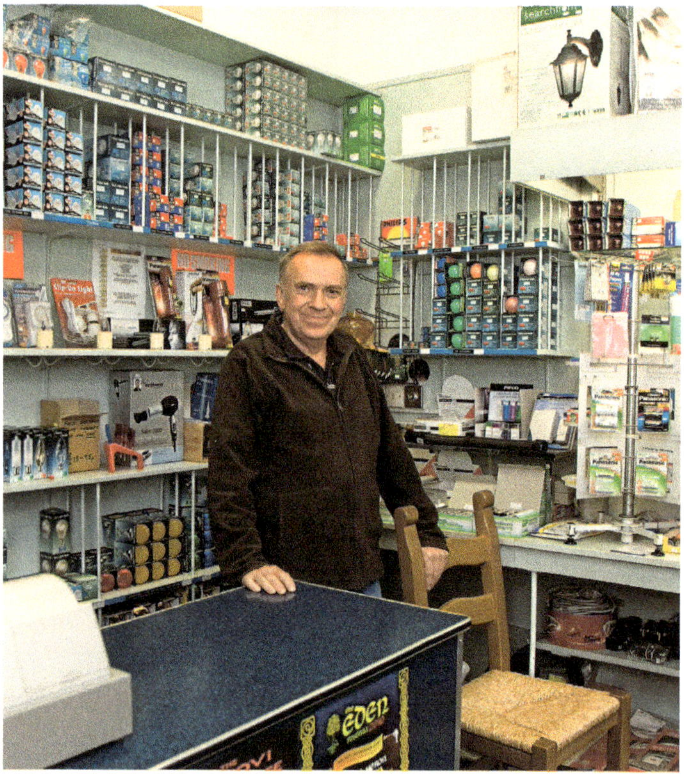

Fraser & Allin

The fire curtain seen on the previous page in 'The Piv' is a sad reminder that only a few of the businesses remain. One however is Fraser & Allin, whose premises are seen in the picture at No. 67 Channel Street (previously No. 25 Island Street). Jim Fraser and John Allin met in the trenches during the First World War and said if they survived they would start in business. Owner today, Jim Lees (pictured) runs the business from Bank Street. He joined his father as an apprentice in 1960, later taking over from him in 1972.

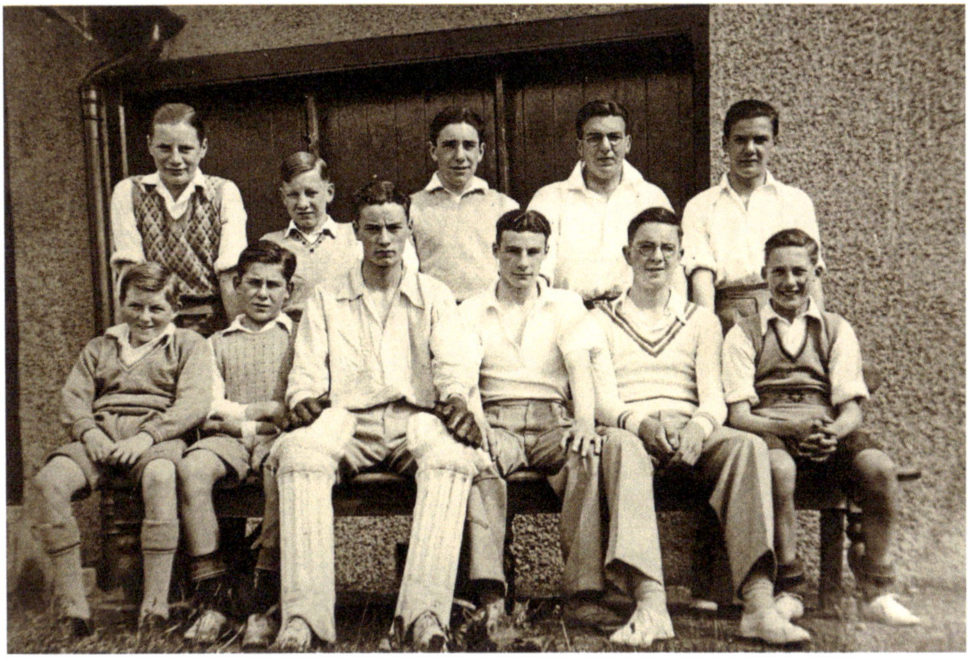

Gala Cricket Club

Gala Cricket Club was founded in 1853, having moved in 1900 to the foot of Meigle Hill. A very successful and popular club, and winners of the Borders League again in 2010, they currently train up to fifty youths on a Saturday. The photograph above shows the Gala Academy Team in 1938, with the new image (below) of some of the 2010 players. The new shirts, presently worn by the team, have 'Rowan' on them as a mark of respect for Rowan Bowland, a talented youngster who had tragically collapsed and died at the club.

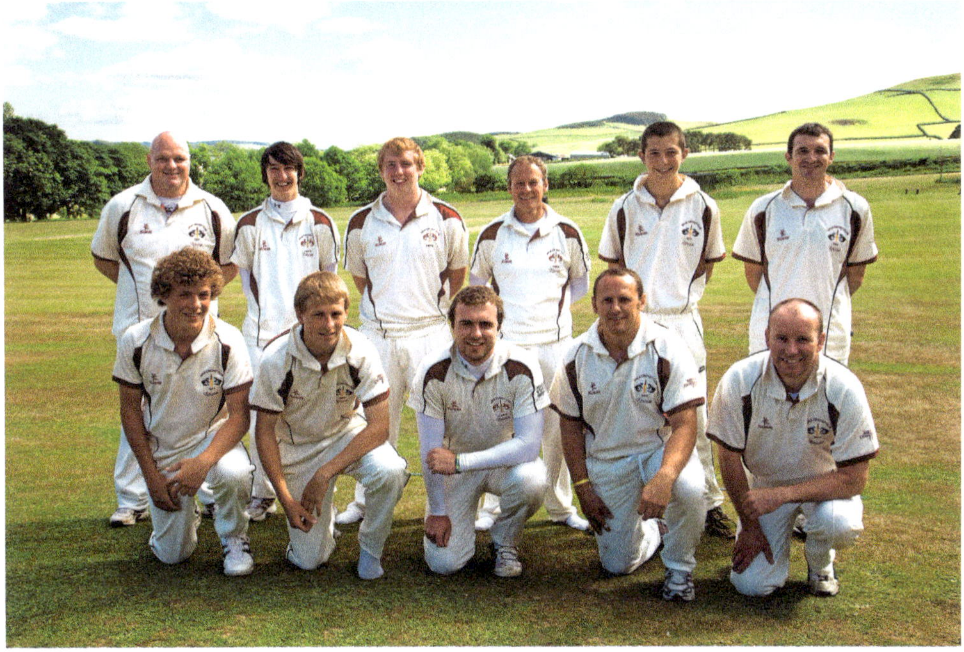

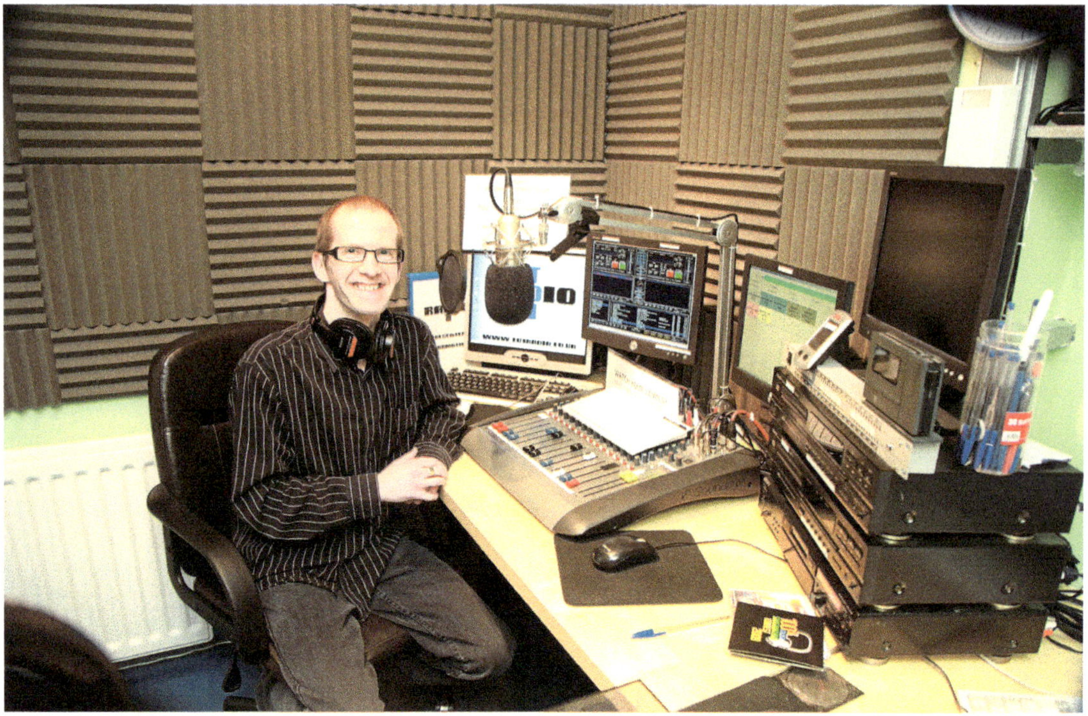

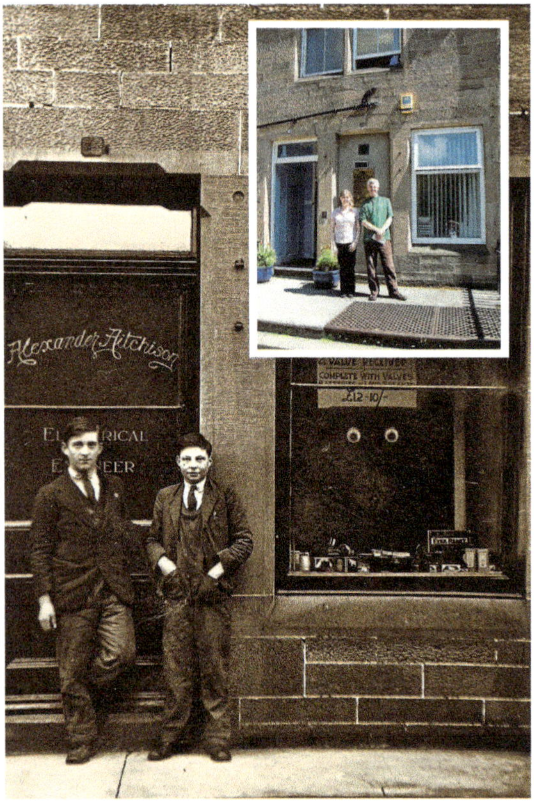

Changes

The image on the right is of Bert Clark and George Goodfellow who were apprentice electricians with Alexander Aitchison in Albert Place in the early thirties. Inset, the two dental practitioners Frances Munro and James Thom, who occupy the premises today. There is an advert in the window for a Melophone receiver and speakers – £12.10*s*.-*d*. Today's technology allowed David Henderson, in the photograph above, to turn his bedroom, in his Victoria Street house, into a radio station, broadcasting 'TD1 Radio' to listeners over the internet.

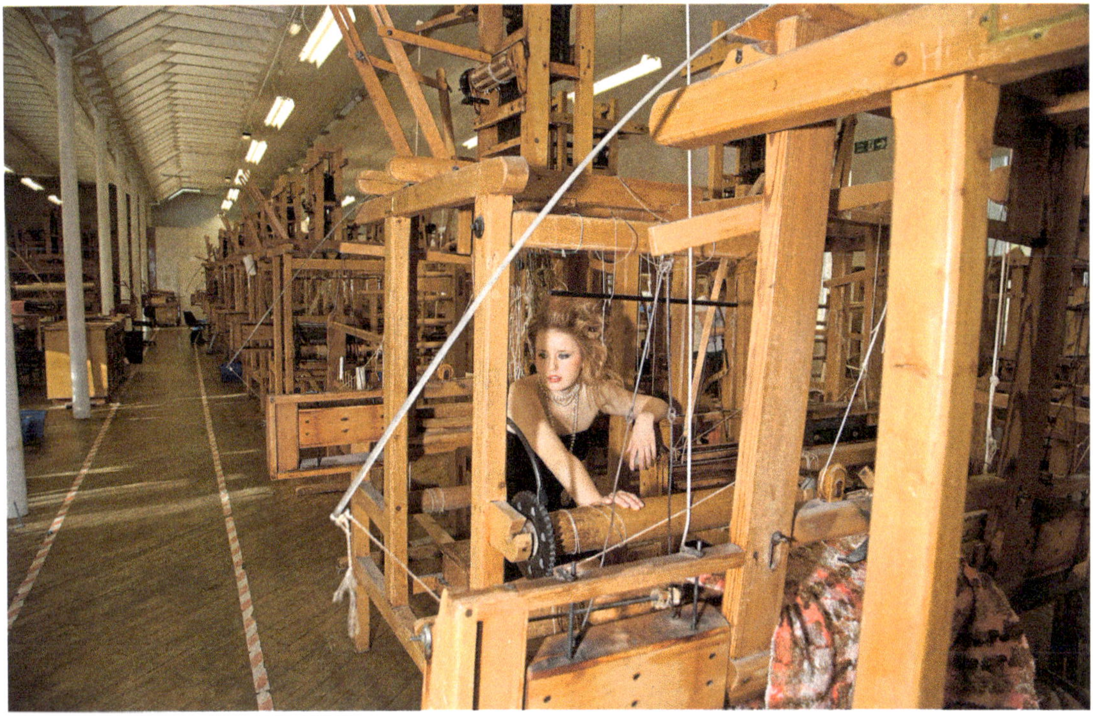

Looms

Although the woollen and textiles industries have seen a drastic decline, looms can still be seen in the town. The image of the young student (above) was for a fundraising calendar and was taken within Heriot Watt University at the end of 2009. The image on the left shows the last remaining mill chimney in the town at Schofield, Dyers and Cloth Finishers in Huddersfield Street.

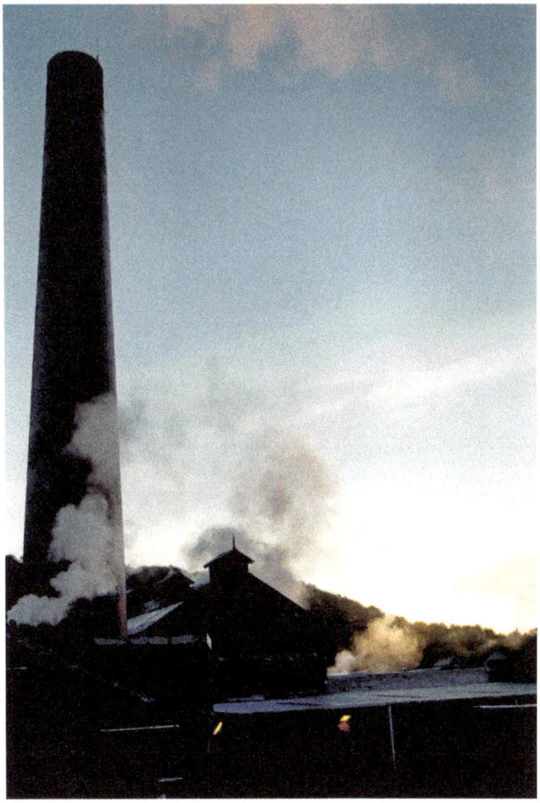

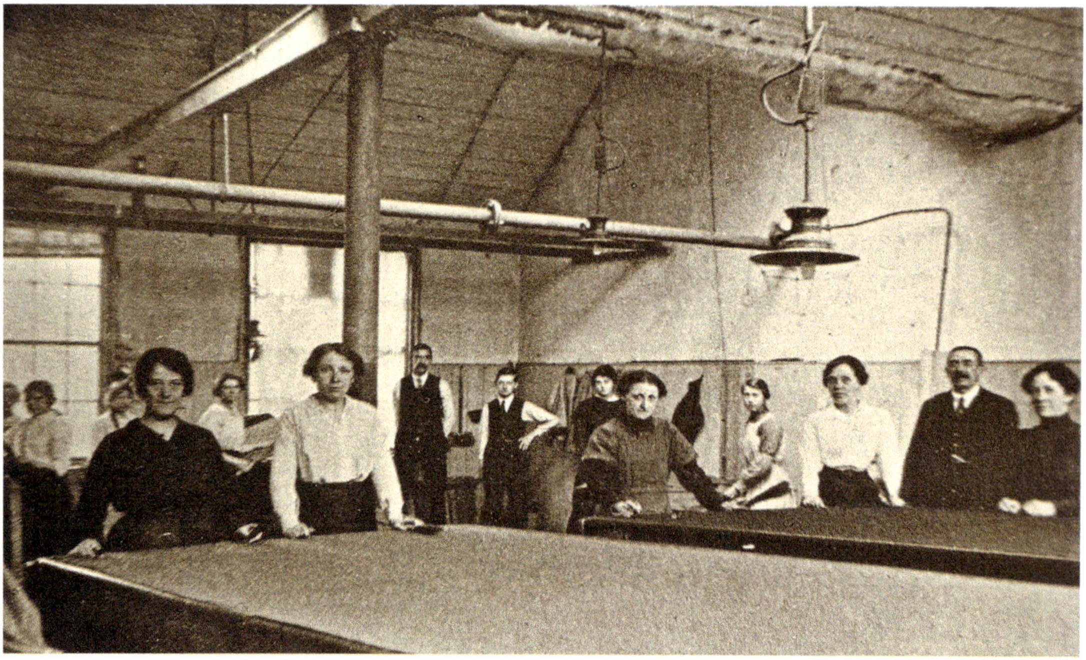

Workers

My grandmother, second from the left, a darner in Botany Mill in the early 1900s. Also a group of ladies from Ovens Mill's darning department pose for a group photograph in the early 1920s. One tradition among the millworkers in years gone by was to get a coat or jacket belonging to a 'bride-to-be' and decorate it with small household items and hang it outside the mill where she worked. Later she would wear it home.

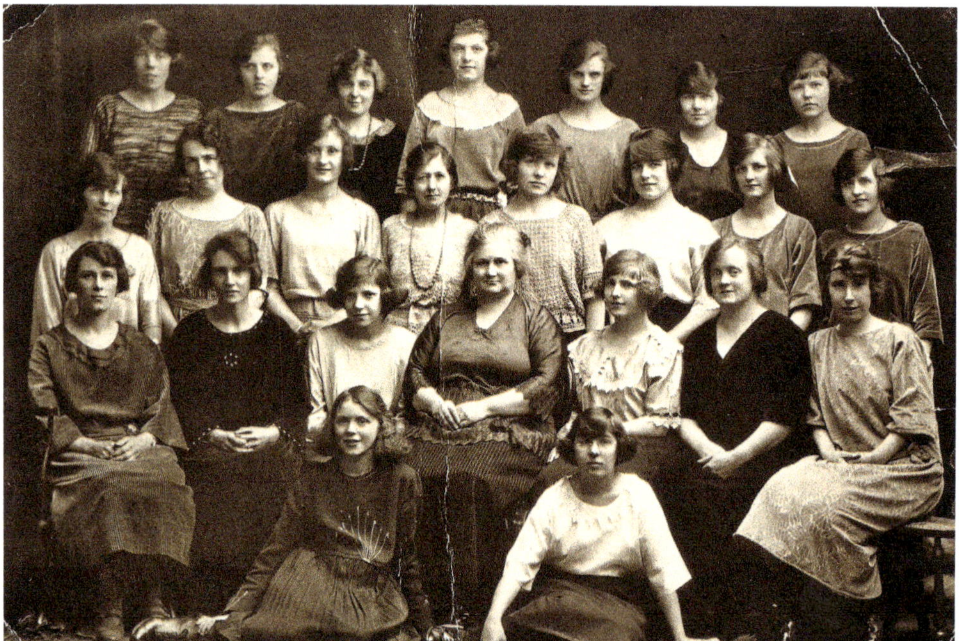

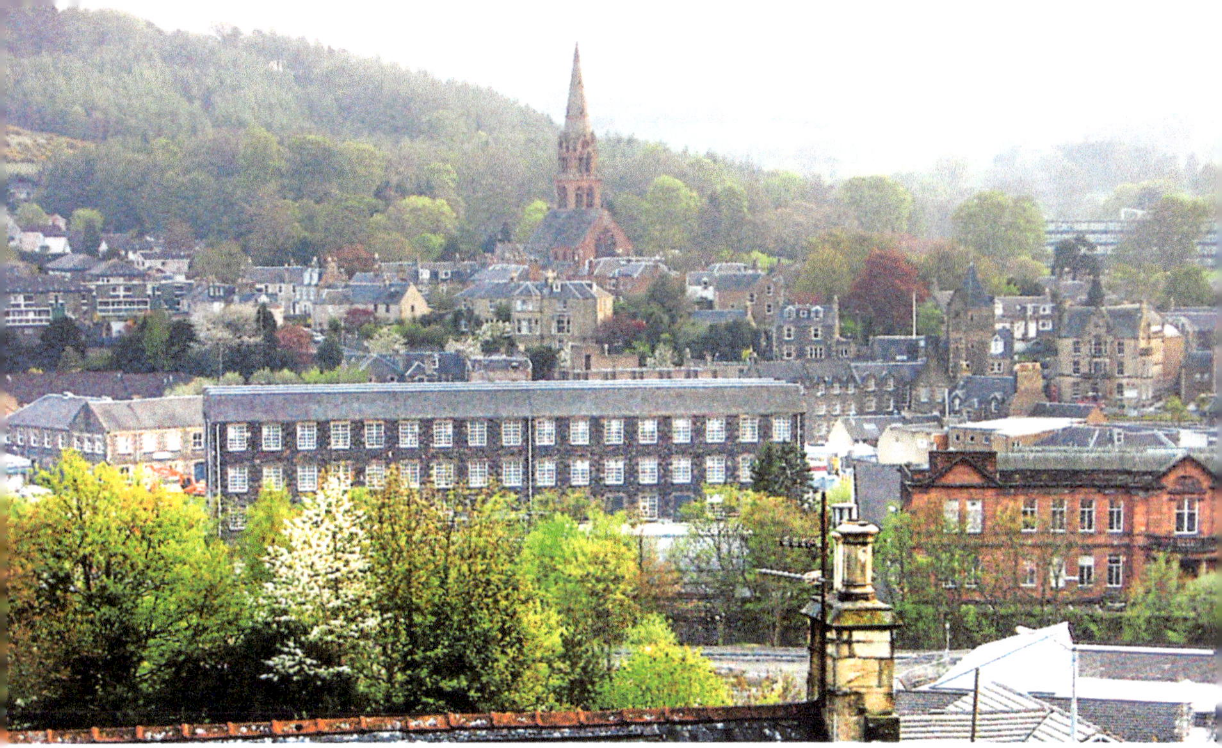

Valley Mill

Valley Mill, and at the moment of demolition in 2004 to make way for the new shopping centre in the town.

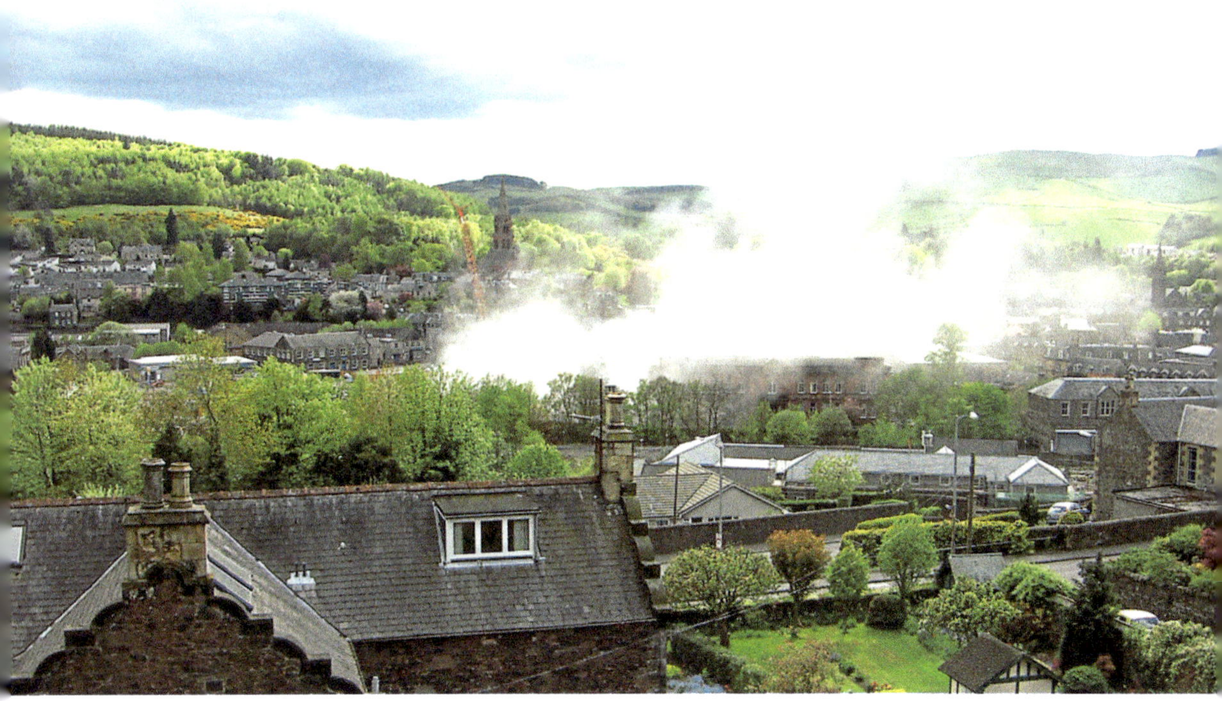

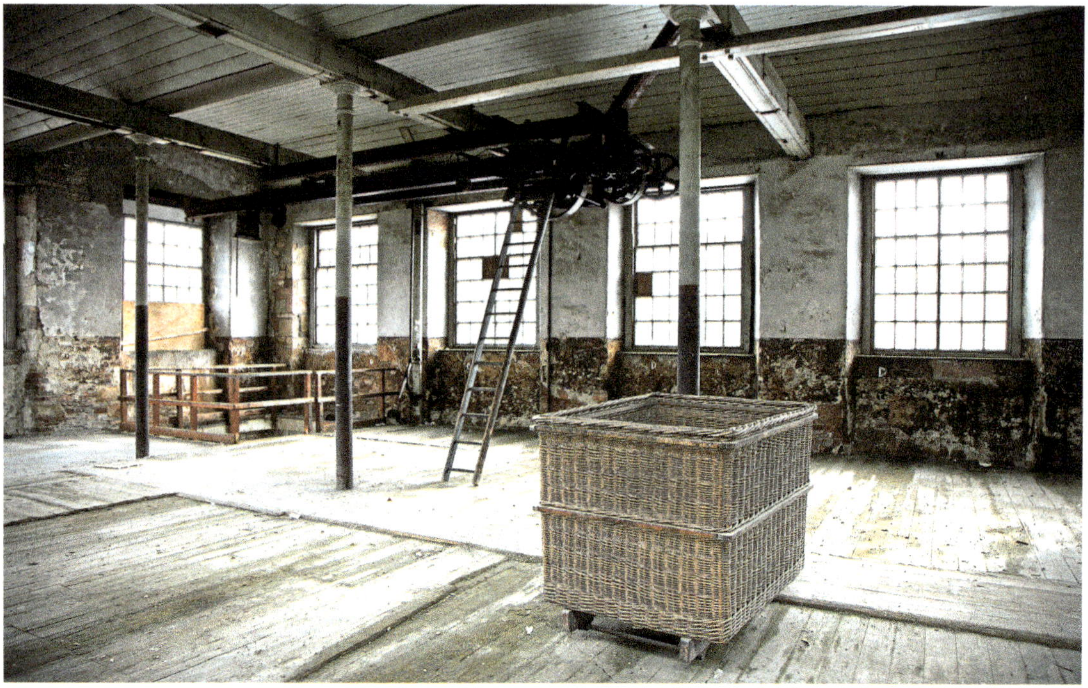

Mill Drawings

An old, empty flat within the mill uncovered some interesting drawings and signatures on the walls.

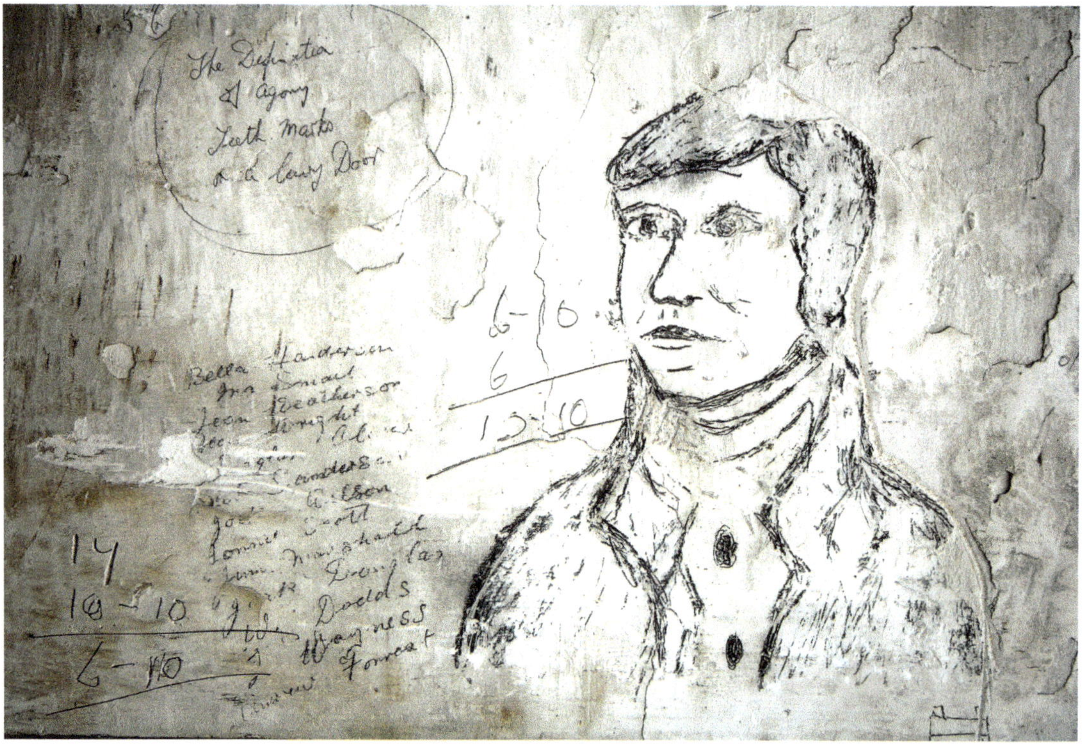

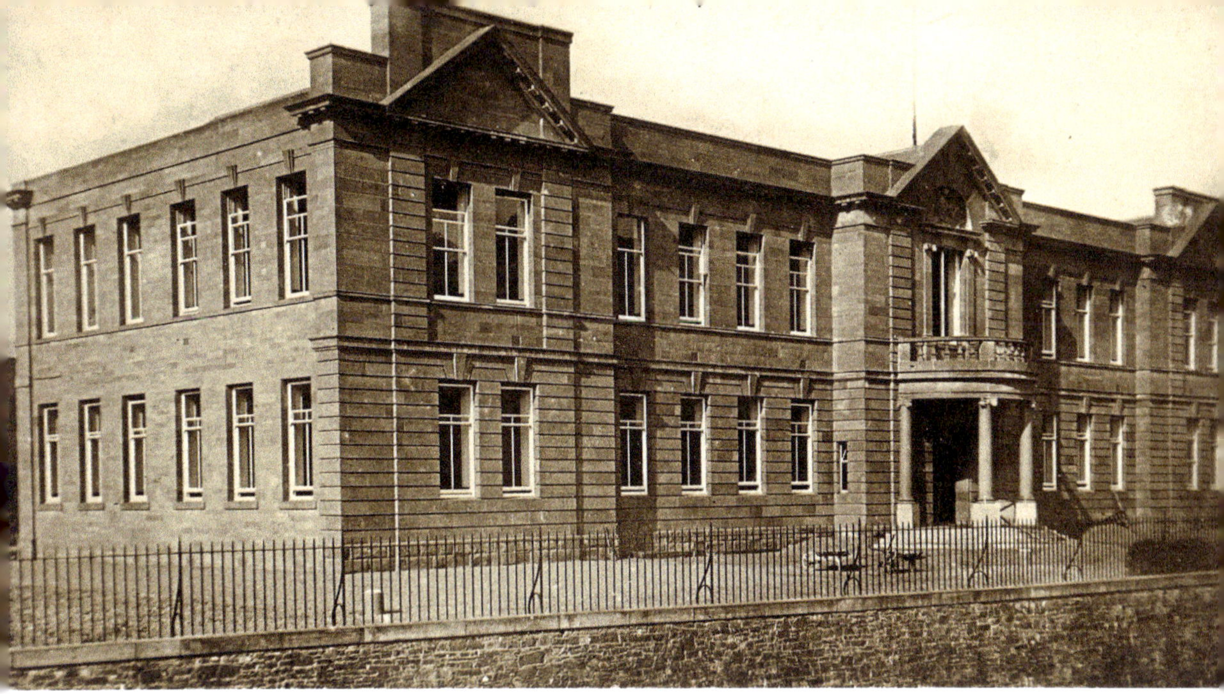

South of Scotland Technical College

Built in 1909 for a cost of £24,000 this was the South of Scotland Technical College. The building was removed, stone by stone in 2006 to make way for a Tesco superstore. It was agreed the stone would be used for a future project in the area. The aerial shot shows the present college and university facilities available in the town, sited in Netherdale, close to the Gala Rugby and Fairydean Football pitches.

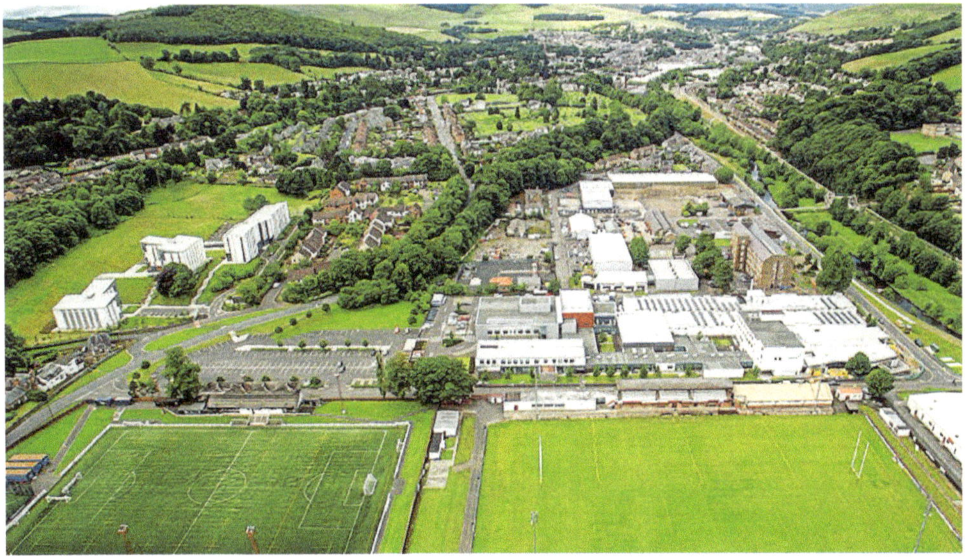

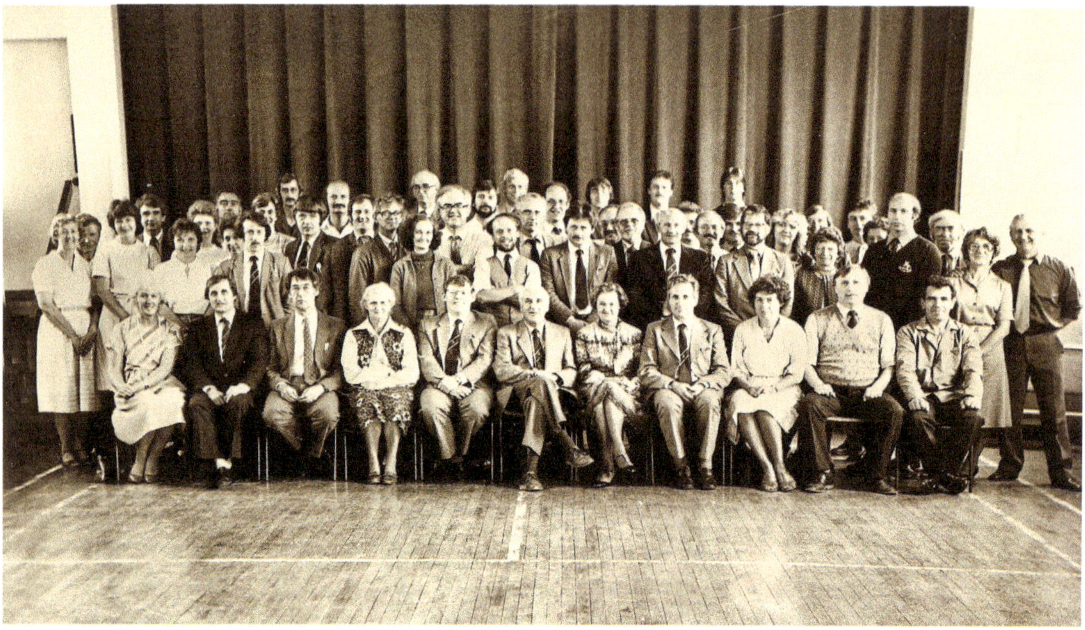

Borders College

In 2009, Borders College moved from Melrose Road to within the Heriot Watt University Campus at Netherdale. This is a great facility in the town. The old image shows staff and lecturers in the early 1980s. The image below shows a recent image of Borders College staff at the campus building.

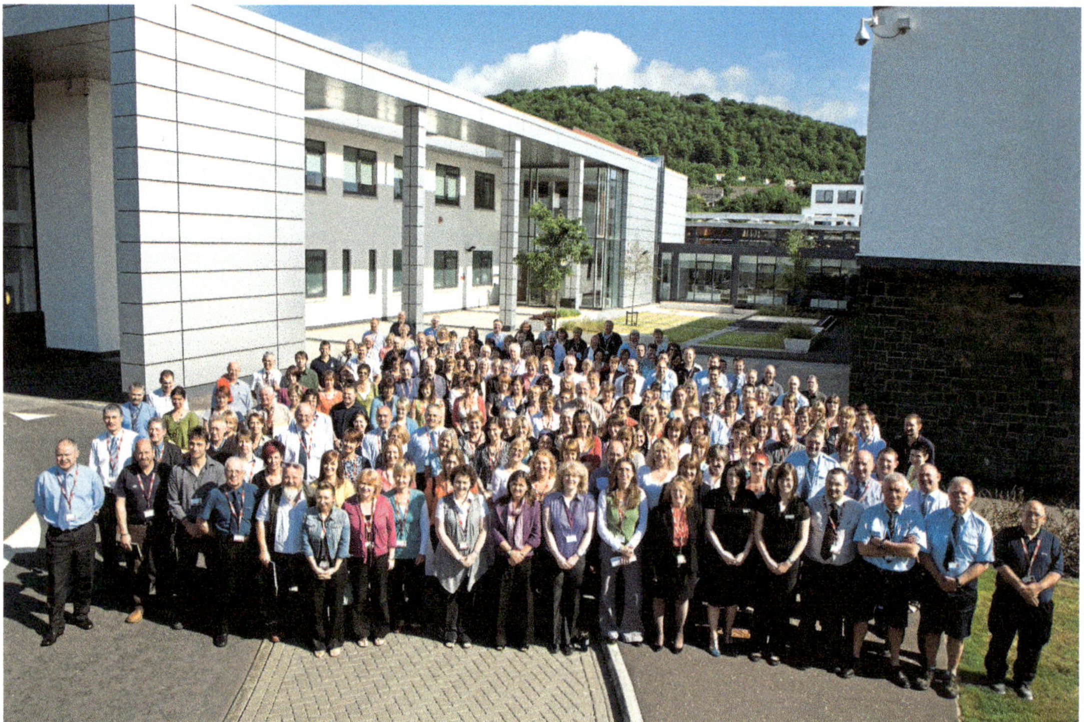

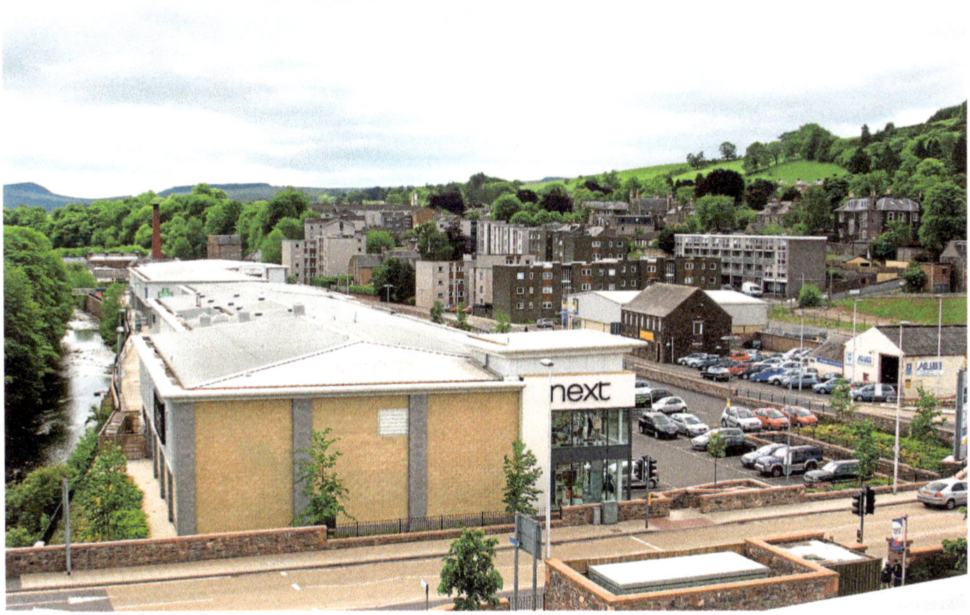

George Craig

Locharron of Scotland's mill building in Huddersfield Street, being demolished in 2006, having moved their head office and weaving production to Selkirk. The new road crosses the George Craig Bridge. George Craig (1783–1843) was a lawyer and agent of The Edinburgh & Leith Banking Co., the first bank to be established in the town. Situated in Elm Row, it failed in 1842. While out hunting with Sir Walter Scott one day Mr Craig was accidentally hurt. This was part of Sir Walter Scott's account of the incident:

> Queen Mab lifted up her heels against Mr Craig, whose leg she greeted with a thump like a pistol shot. Mr Craig would not permit his boot to be drawn off, protesting he would faint. Some thought he was reluctant to exhibit his legs in their primitive and unclothed simplicity, in respect they have an unhappy resemblance to a pair of tongs.

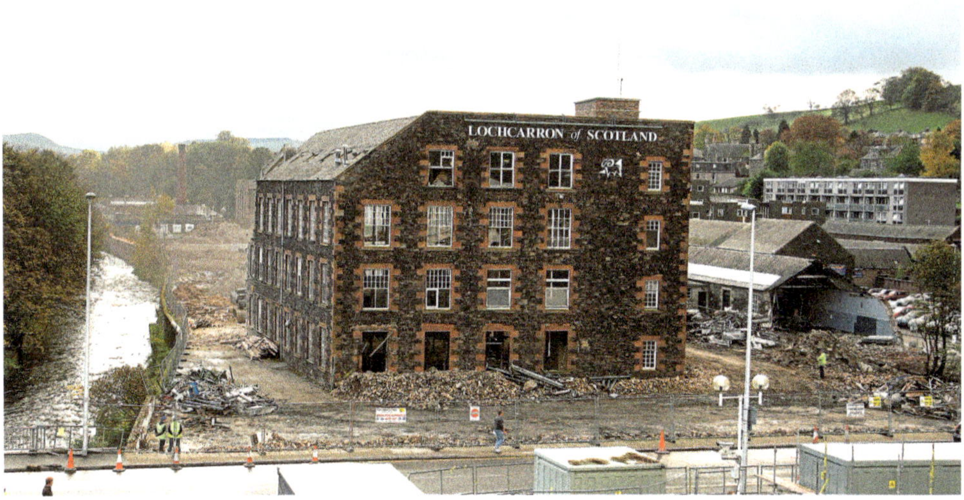

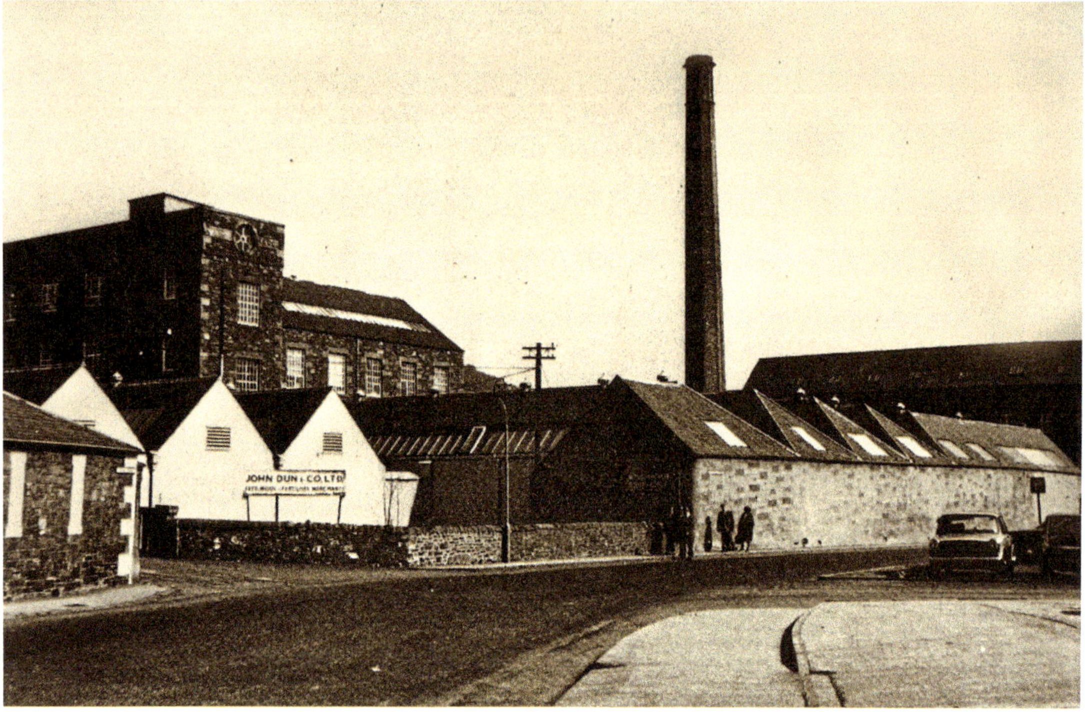

John Dun & Co.

The image above shows the premises of John Dun & Co., Huddersfield Street, (*c.* 1960s) now demolished. The image below shows the same area but with popular High Street stores in its place. To the right on the roundabout – once the entrance to the Burgh Yard – a road gently climbs to join the Abbotsford Road in Albert Place, now known as Braw Lads' Brae.

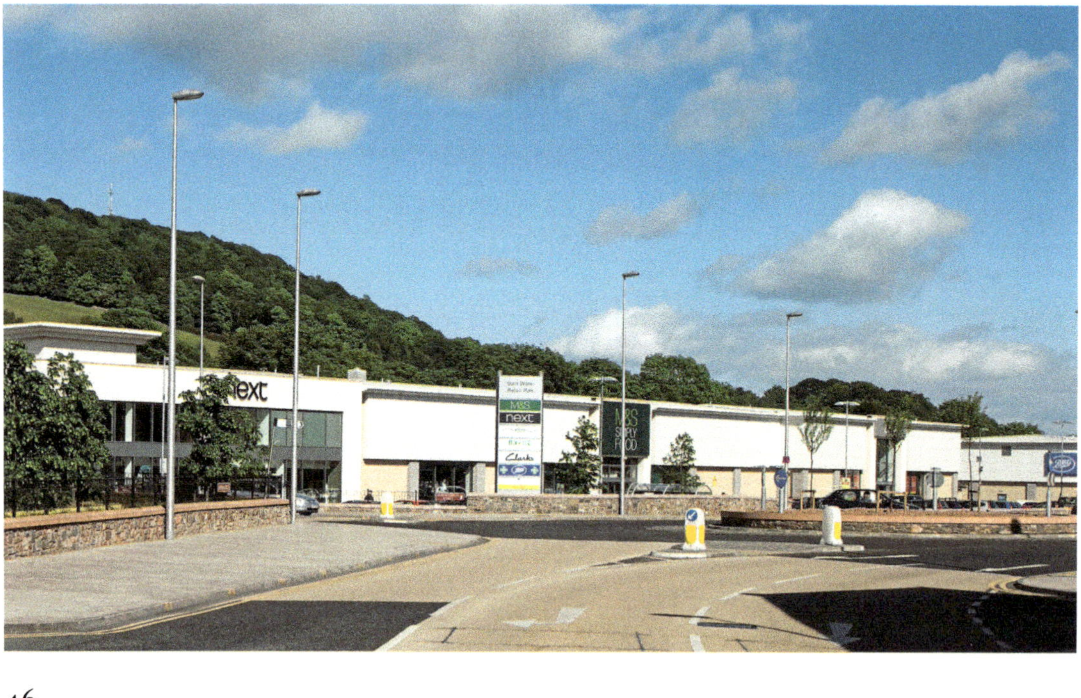

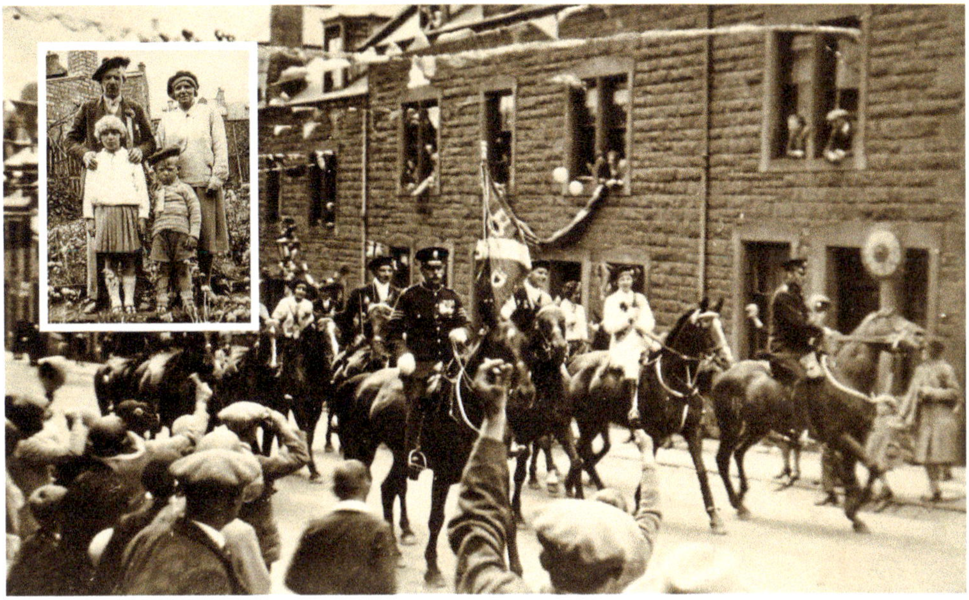

Braw Lads' Day

Burgh Police Sergeant Waugh was the last mounted police officer the town had. He is seen here riding on the first ever Braw Lads' Day in Scott Street in 1930. Today the police mounted section is now centralised in Ayrshire to cover the whole of Scotland. PC Karen Scott (left) and PC Nikki Halliday are seen in Scott Street (2010), checking the road is clear for the main cavalcade. Karen herself had been Braw Lass in 2000 and celebrated this, her tenth anniversary on duty. The inset image shows how my grandparents, mother and uncle dressed in preparation for the first ever Braw Lads' Day.

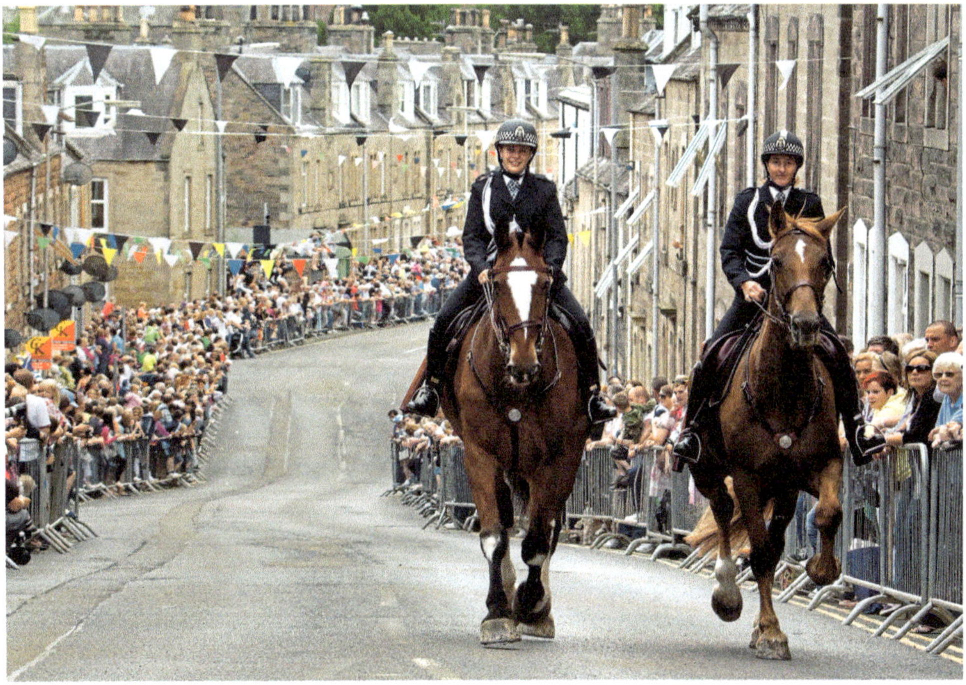

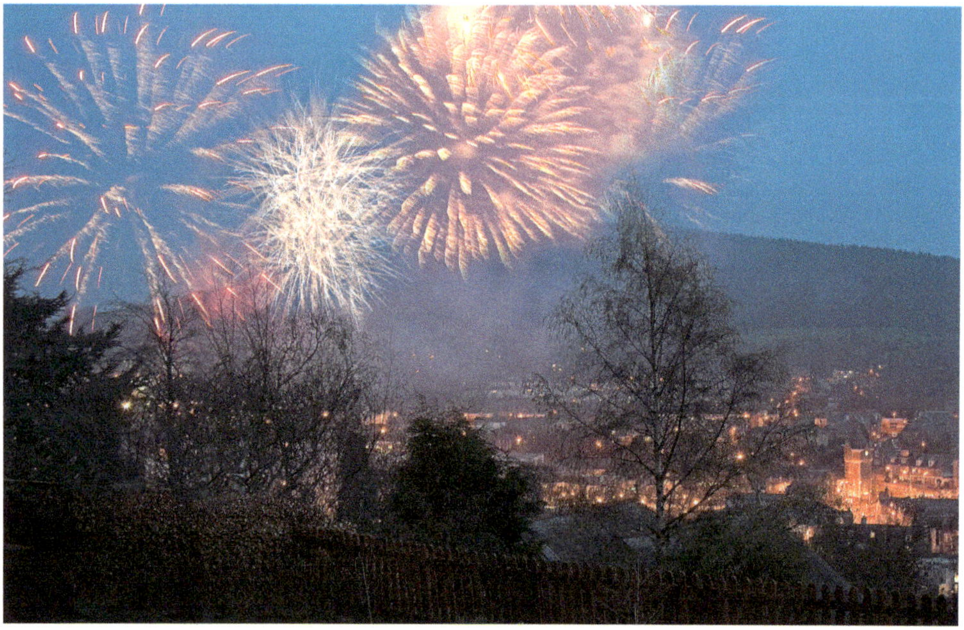

Braw Lads' Gathering

Few things have changed over the years of the Braw Lads' Gathering, but additions such as the fireworks display over the Burgh Chambers in April to announce the new Braw Lad and Lass is one which attracts the crowds. Another is The Big Breakfast. Richie Gray (great-grandson of George H. Tait – page 84), and friends used to gather for breakfast in the 1990s prior to the Braw Lad receiving the flag. Now Richie organises this same breakfast for approximately 300 in the Volunteer Hall. Each person attending is expected to wear the Braw Lads' tie and in recent years the Braw Lad, Lass and Principals have made a short appearance where they get a great reception to start off their day. Inset the 2010 Braw Lad and Lass.

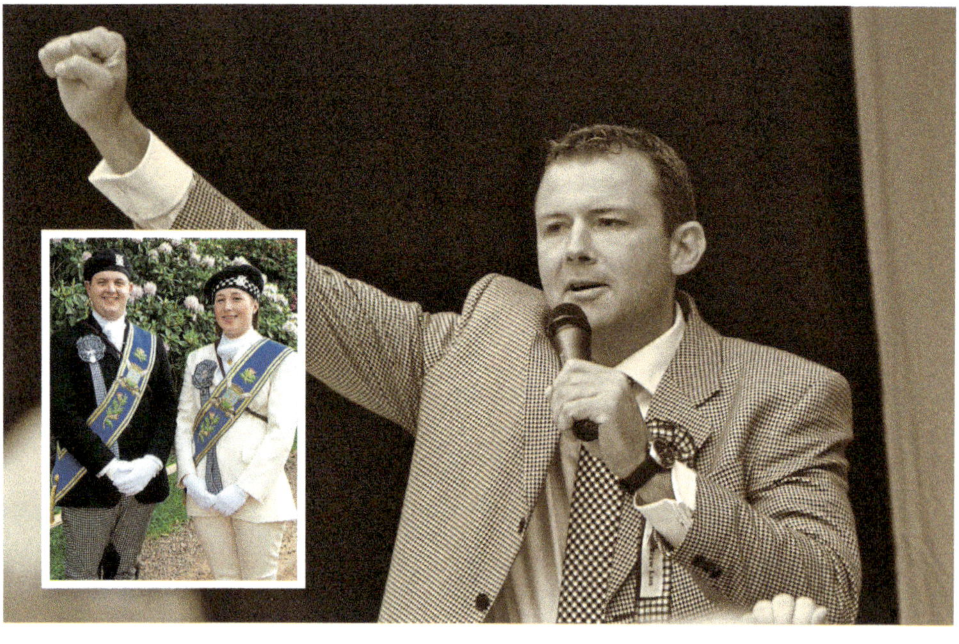

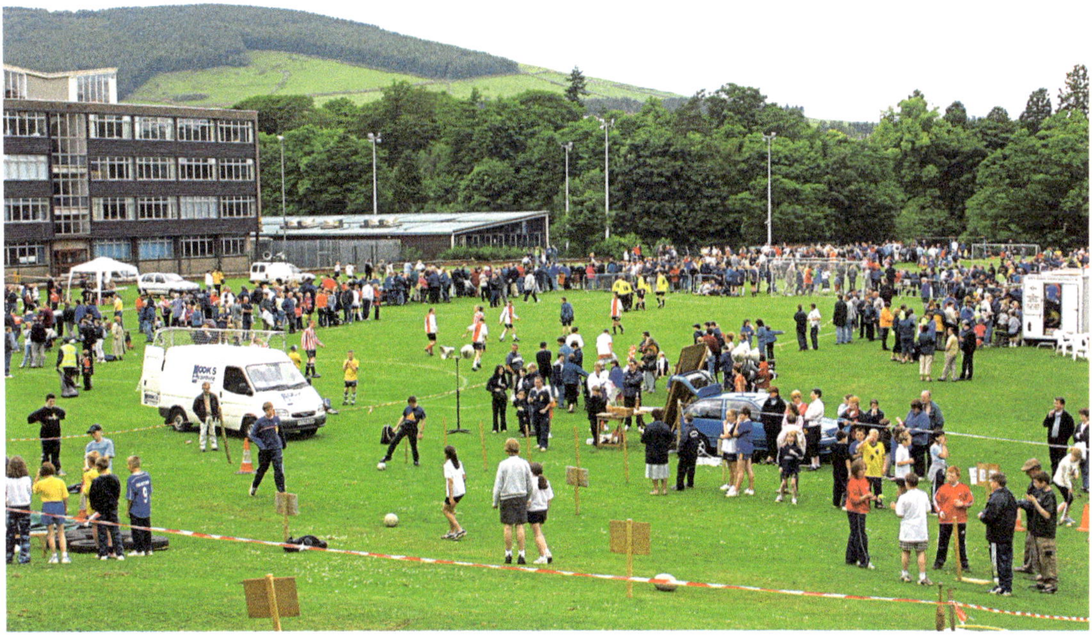

Only Fools Nae Horses

Soon after the Braw Lad and Lass were elected in 2001, the ceremonies involving horses were cancelled that year due to Foot and Mouth Disease. The top image shows the activities which had been arranged in the Scott Park in place of Braw Lads' Day, and below the six principals from 2001, unable to ride to Torwoodlee, took part in the Fancy Dress Parade using the idea from a popular TV series and entering as 'Only Fools Nae Horses'!

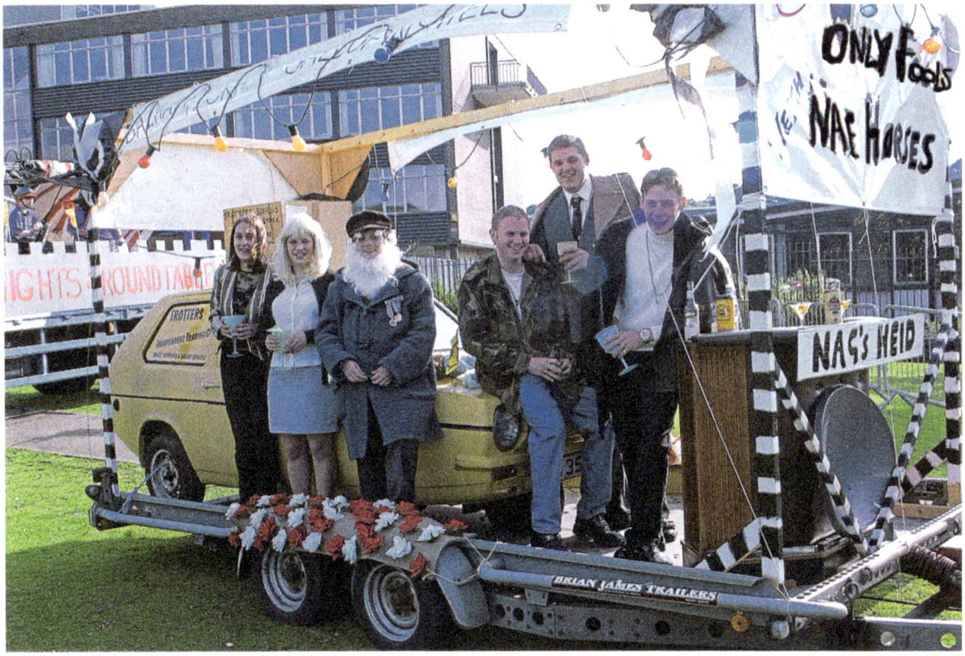

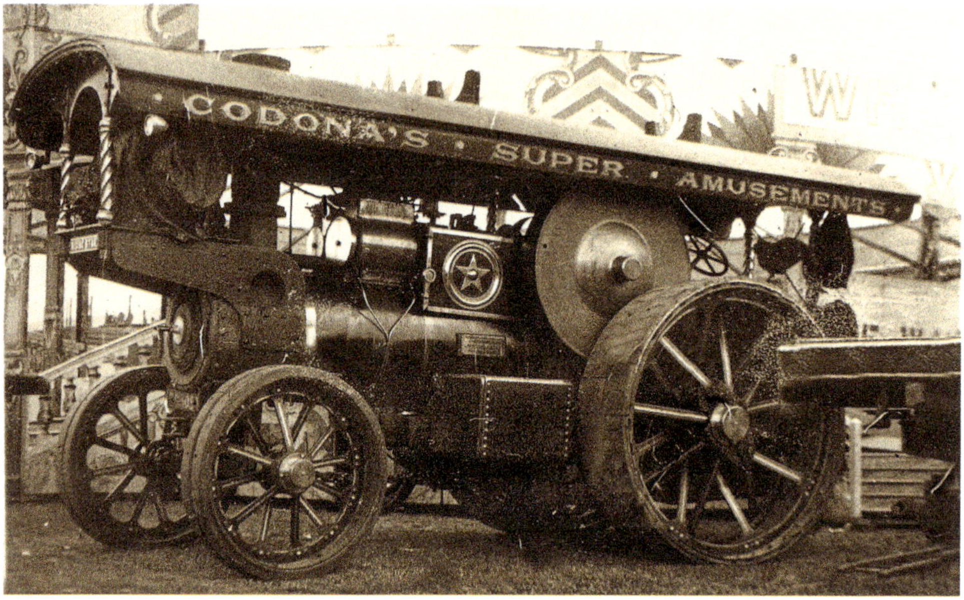

The Codona Family

Another little known custom of Braw Lads' Day is the visit to the shows in the afternoon by the principals. Organised for many years now by Bill Lamb, the Codona family play host to the six principals. Since the start of the Gala Day in 1930, the Codona family take a lease for the park during Gala Week and have continued, each year since, to provide an excellent fun fair. The old image of the traction engine – *Rising Star* – was taken in the early years during one of the Codona family visits to the Gala Week. The image below shows Douglas Codona with friend Bill Lamb. In the inset sisters Margaret and Penny Codona can be seen wearing the black and white checked scarves and rosettes when they met 2010 Braw Lass Katie Scott and Braw Lad Greg Borthwick.

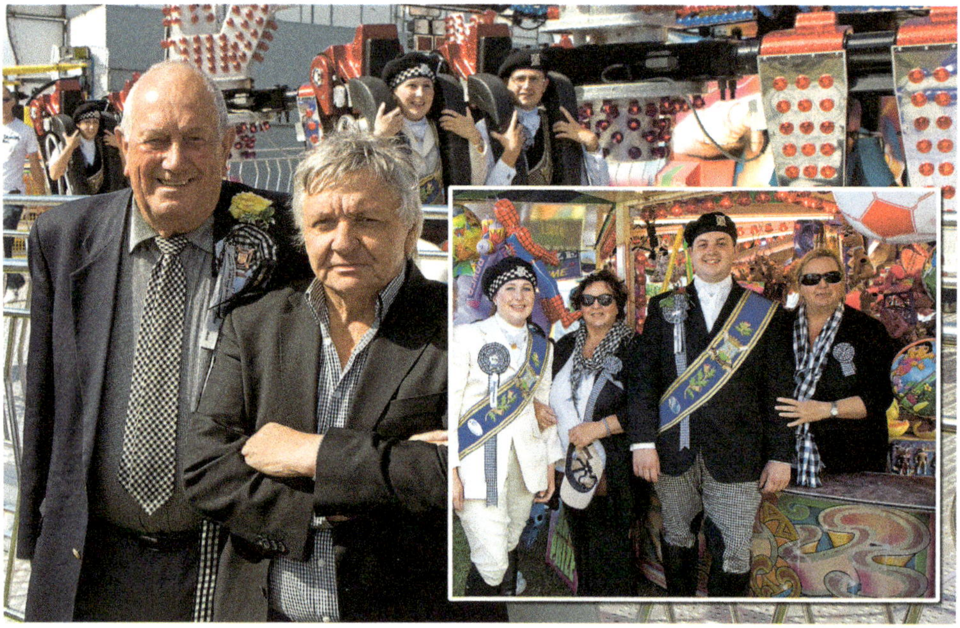

Graham Howlieson

In recent years a Chief Marshall has lead the principals and cavalcade on the Braw Lads' Day. Chief Marshall until 2009 was Graham Howlieson (Huggy), seen leading the cavalcade down Tweed Road in 2005, and also in his early years, less comfortable in the saddle in Balmoral Avenue!

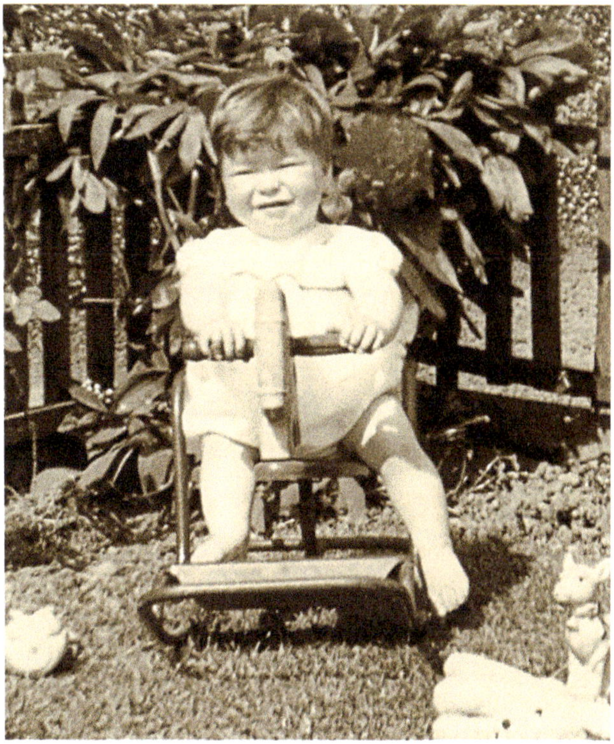

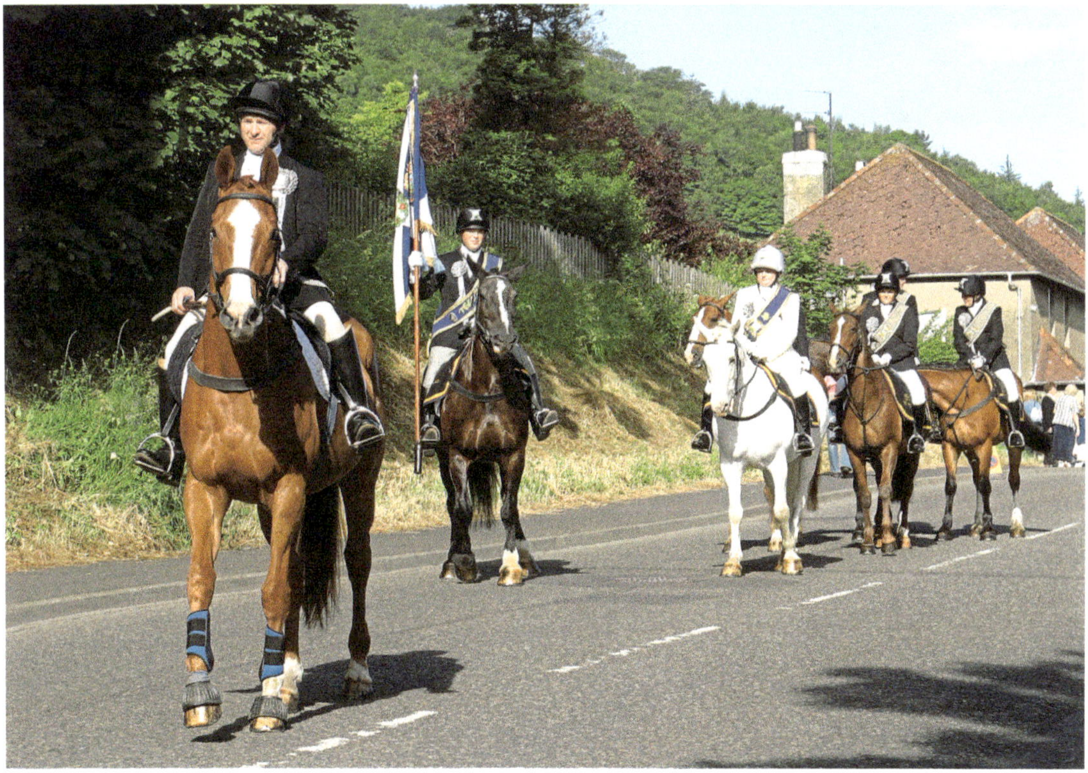

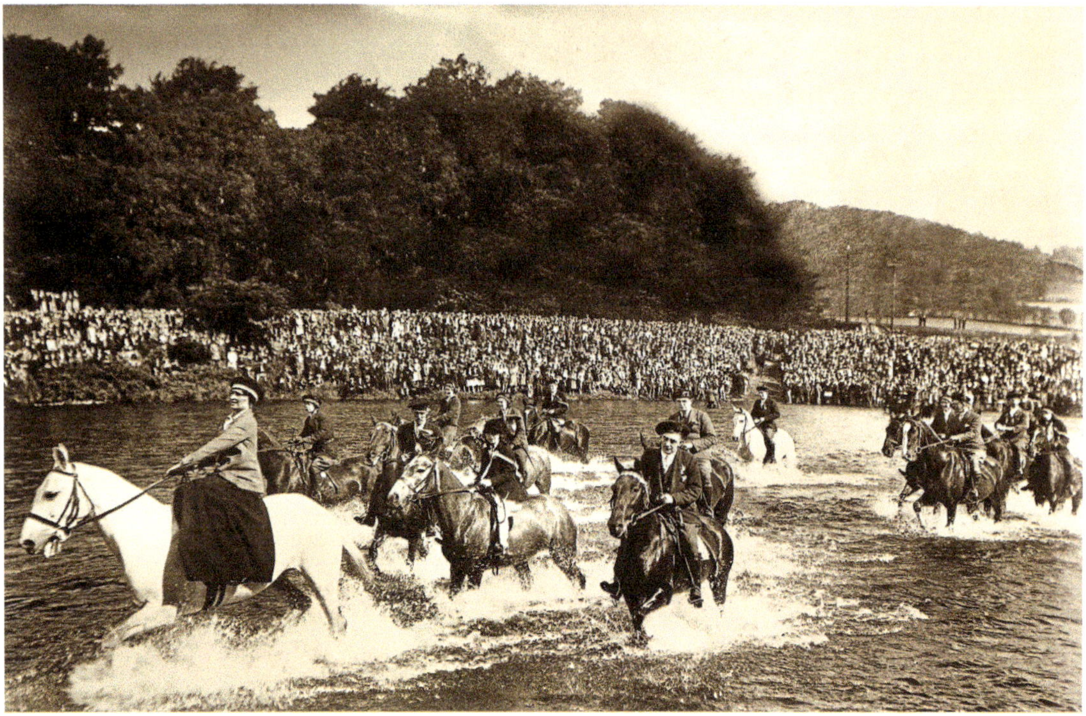

Horses Cross the Tweed

Horses cross the Tweed on a Gala Day with a lady in side saddle leading this group of riders. Below, taken from a popular viewpoint – the bridge over the river at Gala foot – the principals ford the tweed on their way to Abbotsford in 2010.

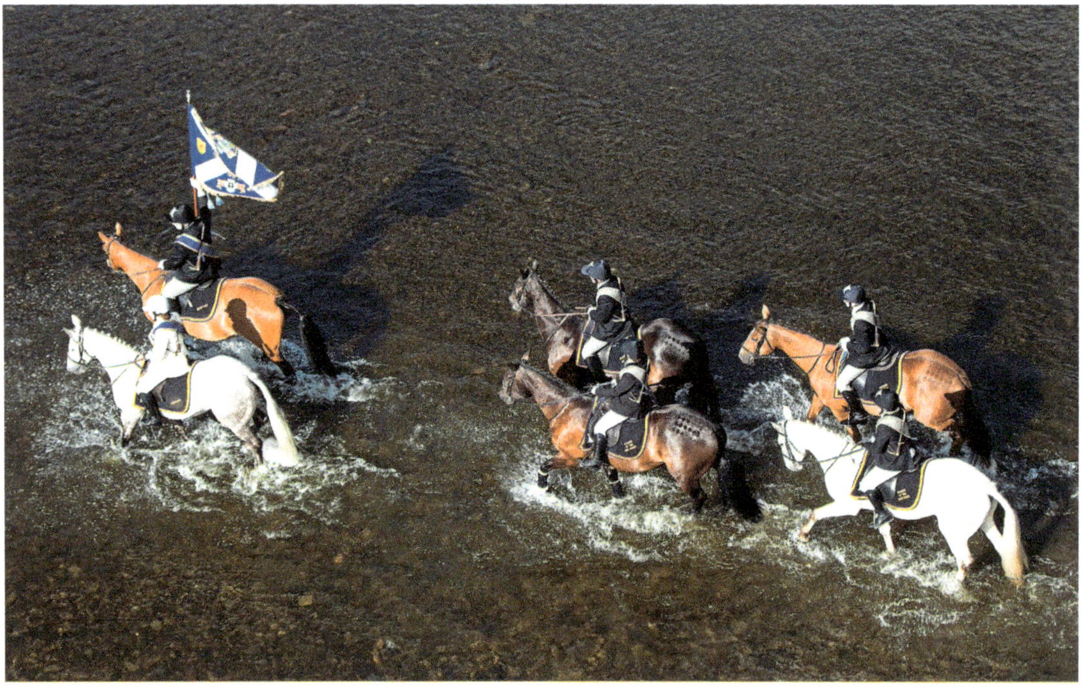

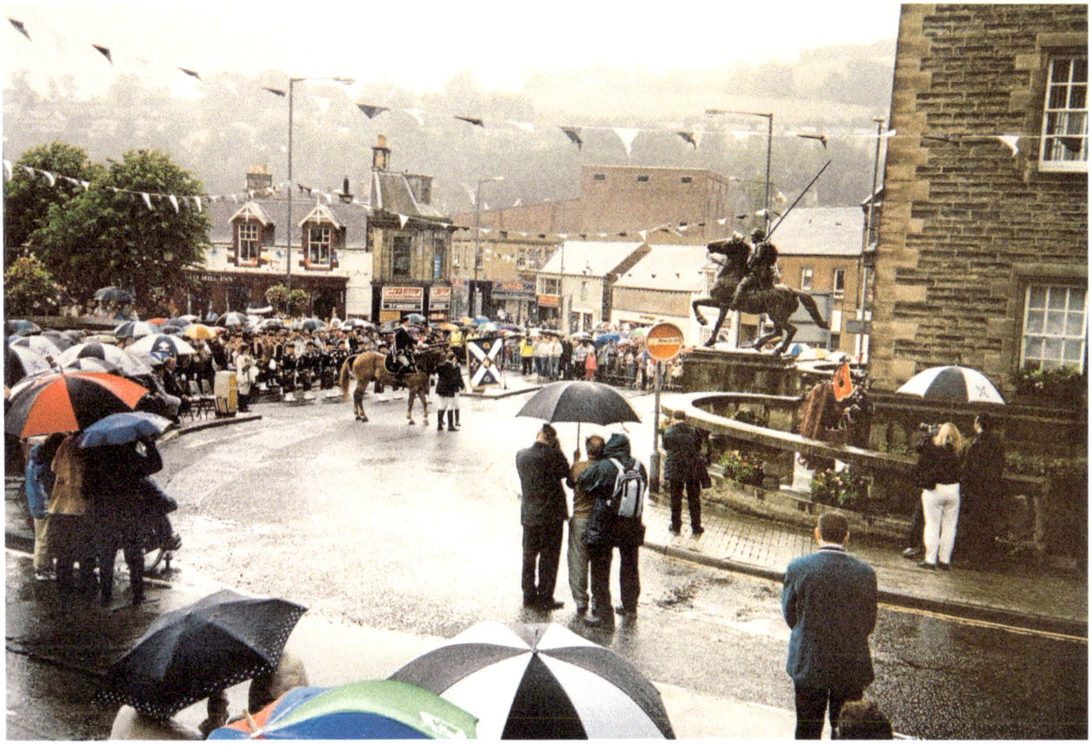

The War Memorial

What started as a lovely sunny day in 2004 ended with a deluge of rain. Ironically a new Gala Braw Lads' Umbrella had been launched and came in very handy for those in attendance at the War Memorial for the final act of homage. Below a close-up taken at night of The Reiver at The War Memorial.

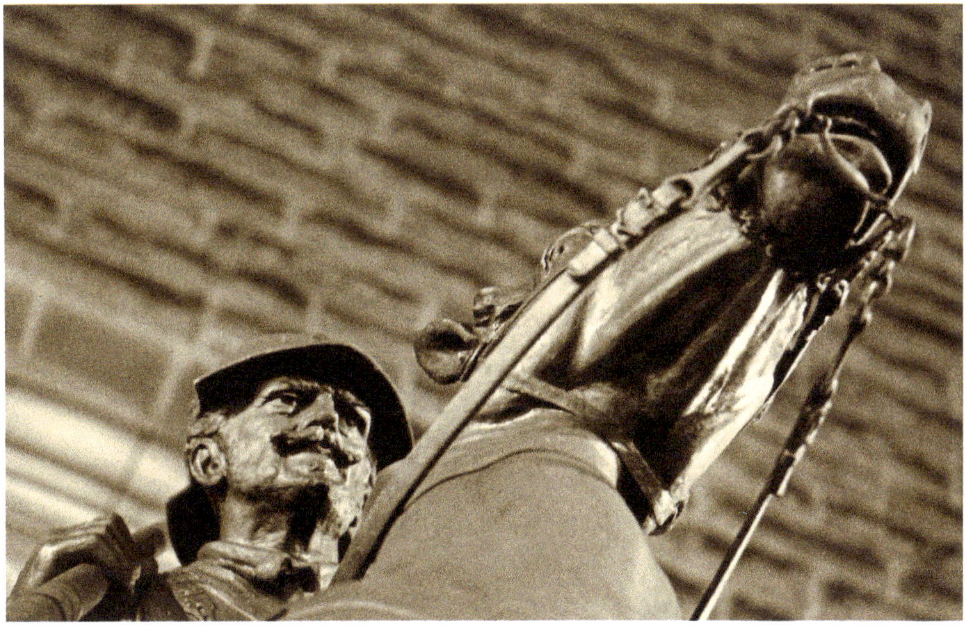

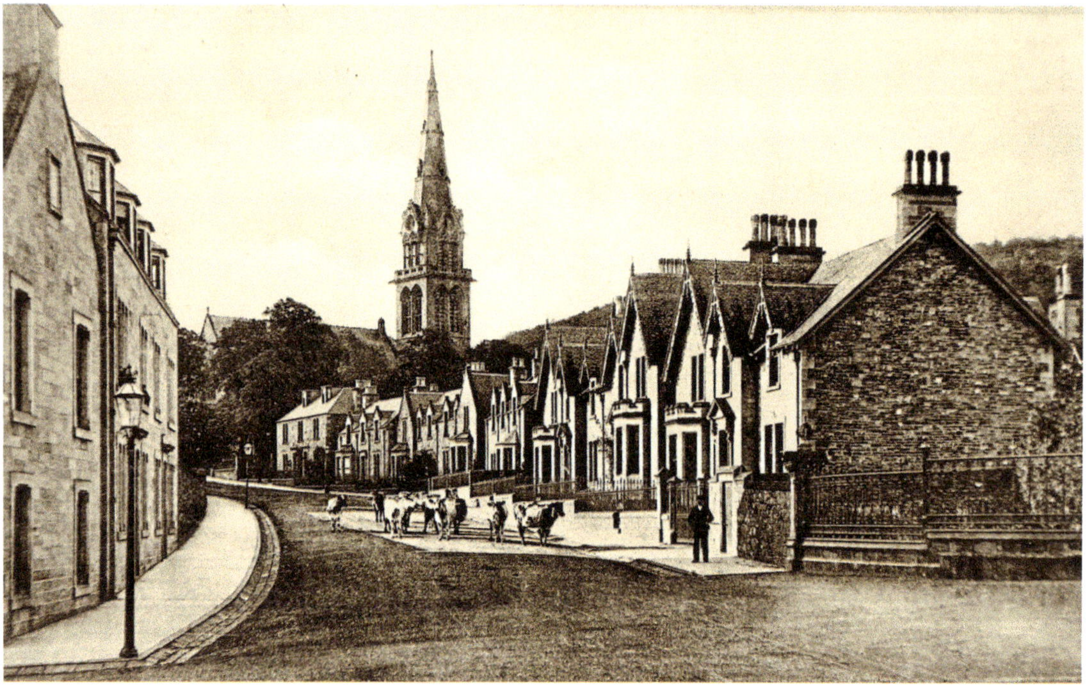

Scott Crescent

In the late 1800s the town had two dairies in Church Street; one belonging to Johnny Cunningham and the other Jock Anderson's. Cows are seen here coming down Scott Crescent, which would if it were to be done these days would require a lot of thought and advanced planning.

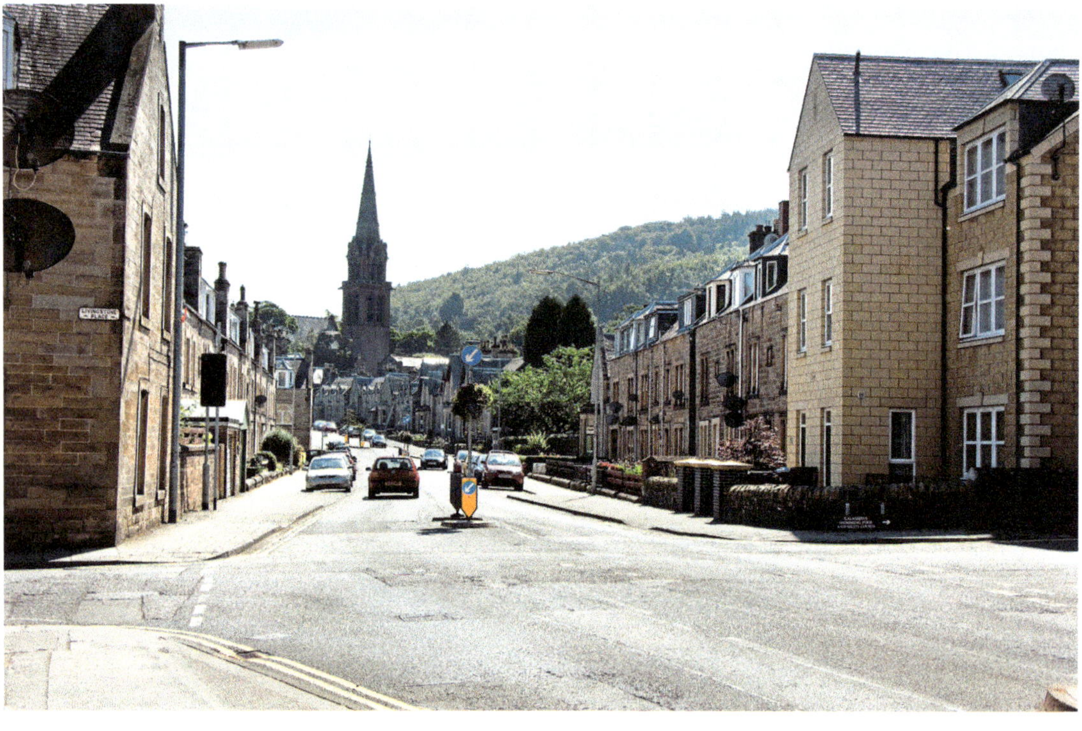

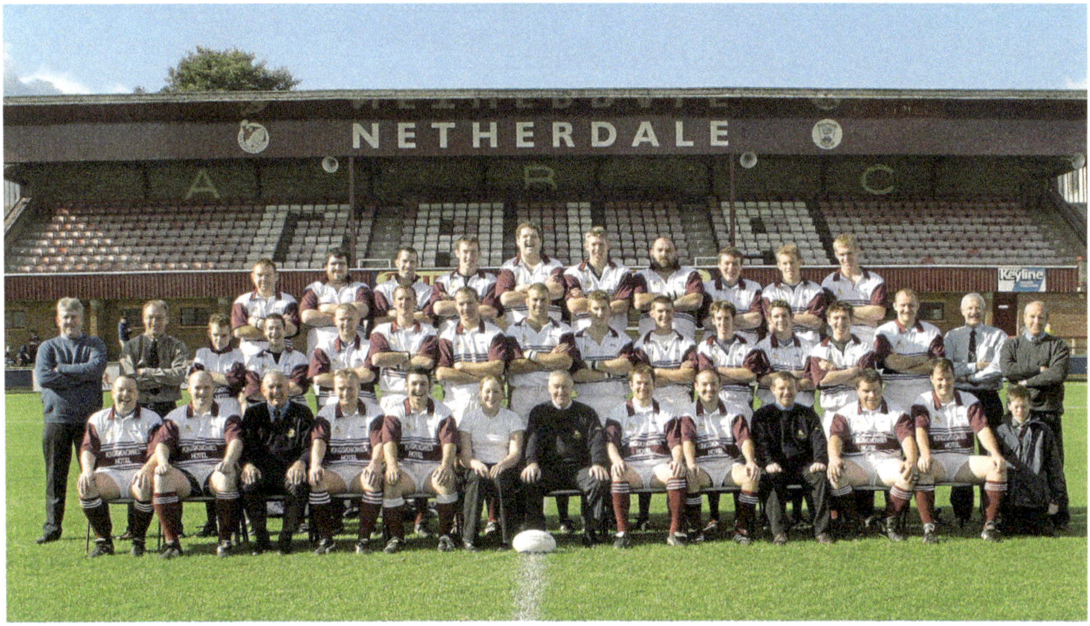

Galashiels Rugby

As with other Border towns Galashiels is well known for its rugby. Gala Juniors are pictured here in front of the Netherdale Stand in 2003. Below the photographer in 1987 capturing this young rugby team at Langlee would not have anticipated how successful these youngers would become. Eight went on to play for Gala RFC, one for Fairydean, one Scotland XV and Capt., one Scotland 7s Int. Capt., two Braw Lads and a Scotland XV Club Captain. Chris Paterson (second from the right in front row) gained over 100 caps for Scotland in International Rugby.

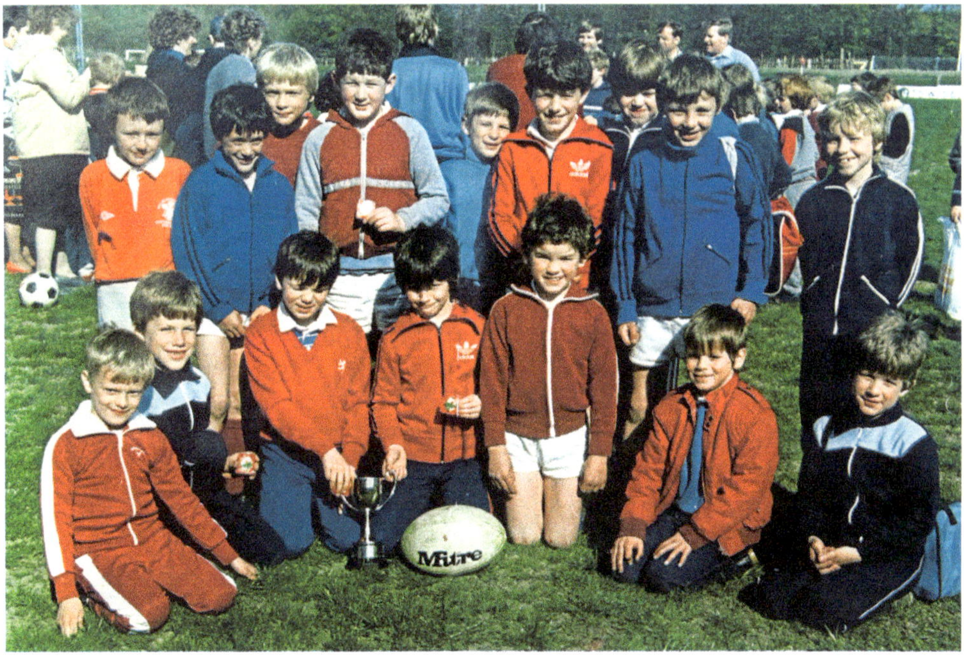

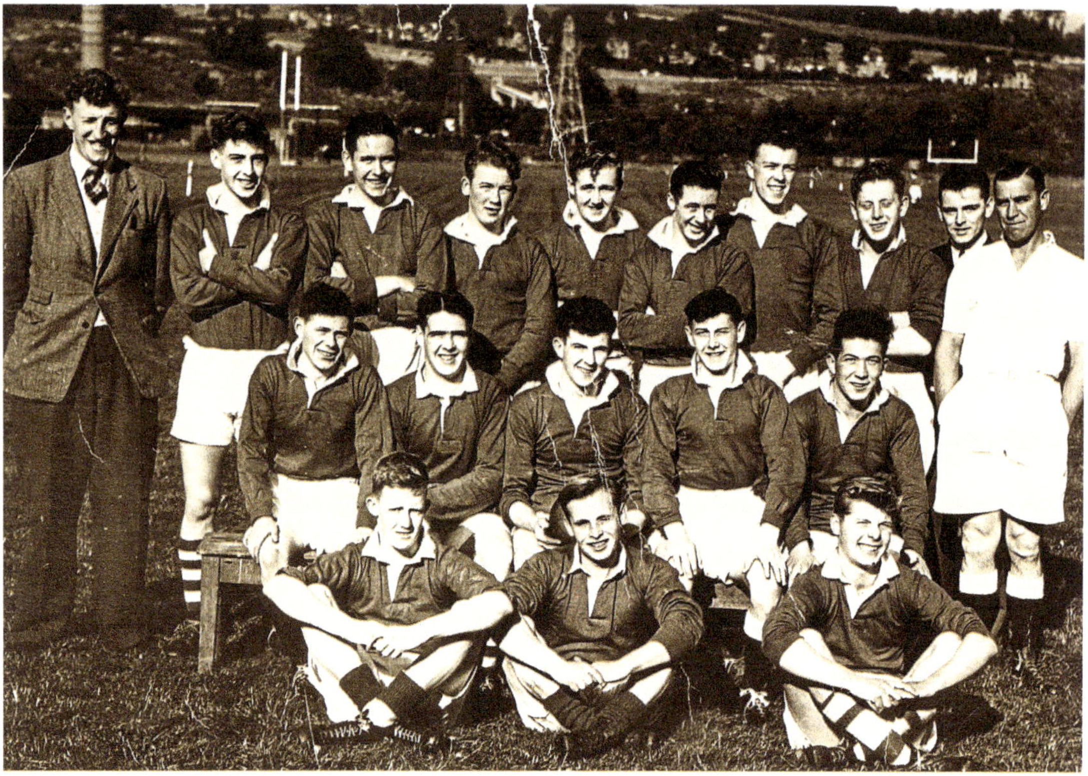

Gala Red Triangle Team
A Gala Red Triangle team of the 1950s era. Also 1st and 4th ward A teams in the under 10 section of Gala rugby boys 7s at Netherdale in 1961.

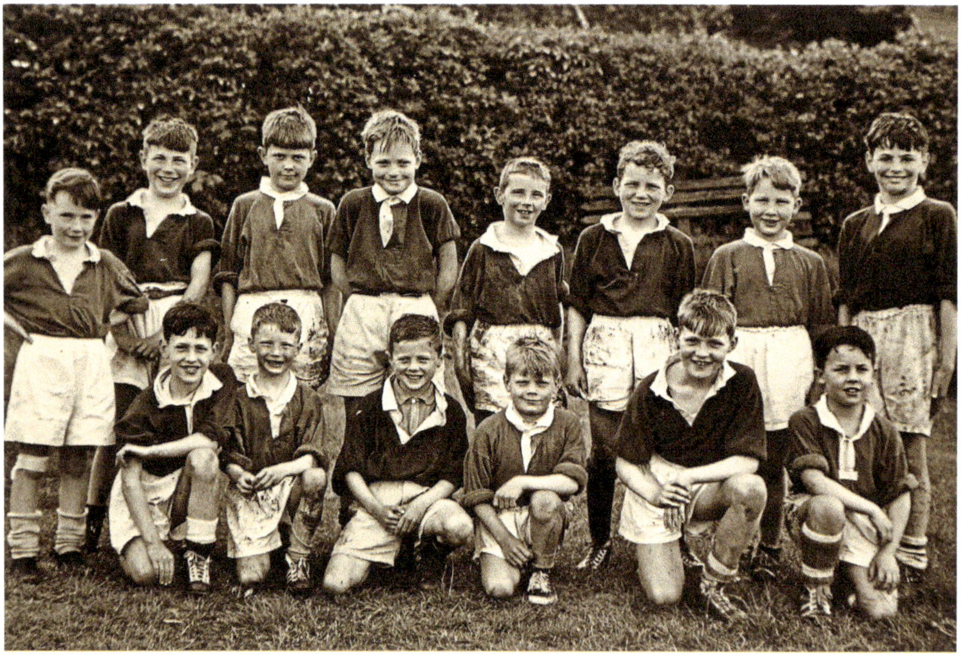

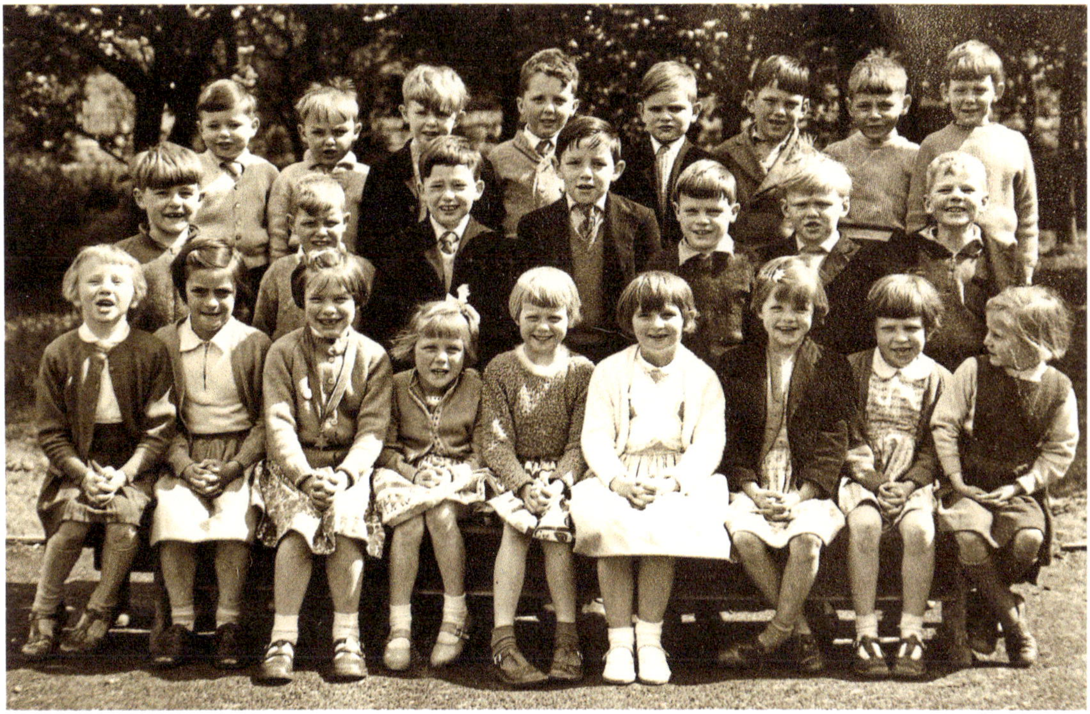

St Peter's School

A St Peter's School group taken in 1961, and another taken in 2008. My grandfather's memoirs recall the custom in the late 1800s of 'barring oot', when pupils stole the keys and locked the teachers out of the school, 'played the pug' up Gala Hill and then paid for it the next day with 'the tawse'.

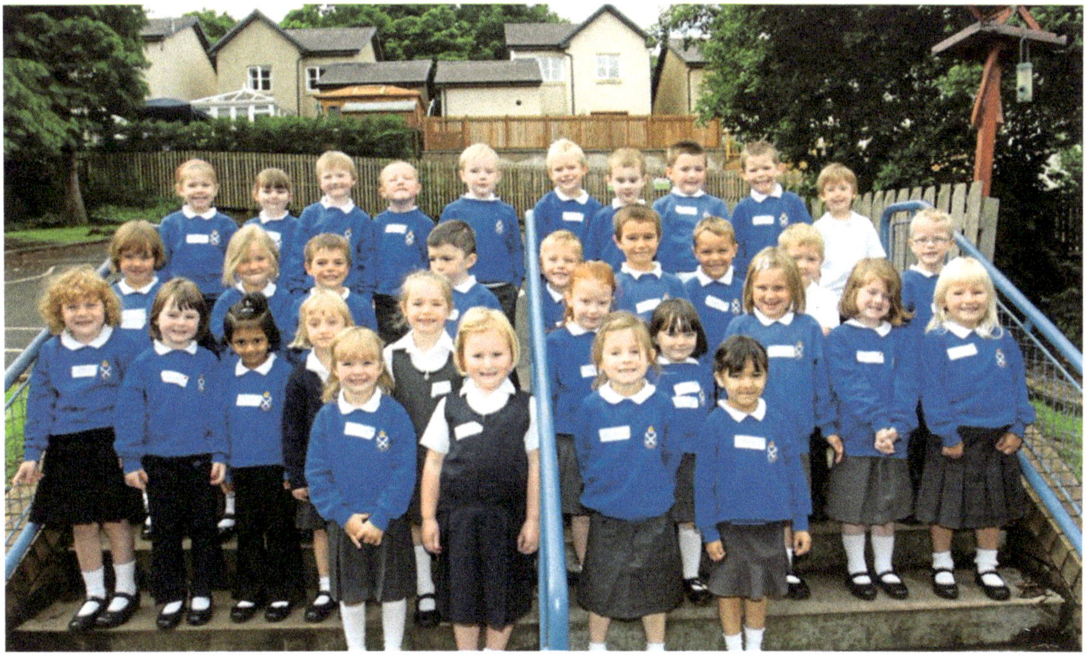

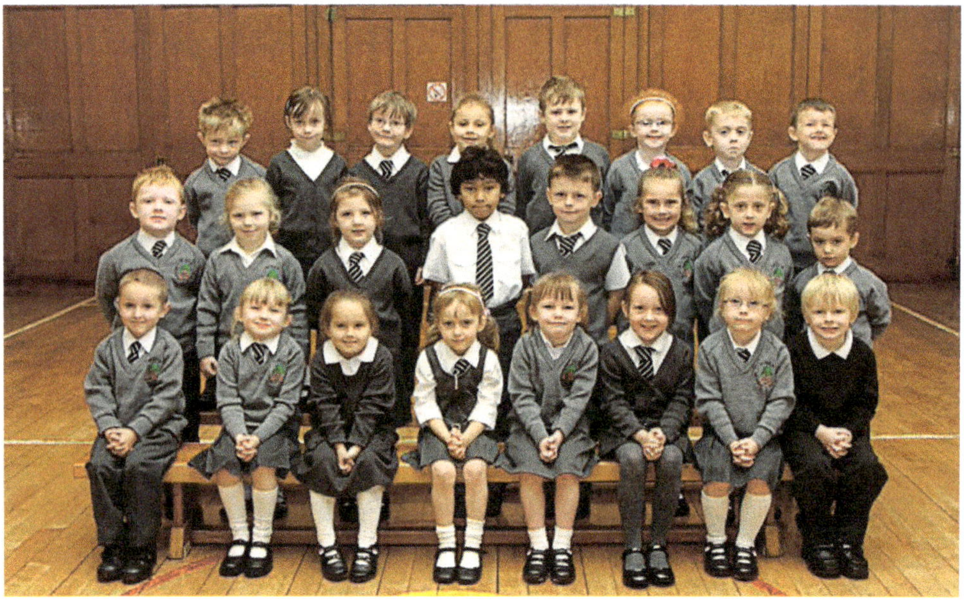

Burgh Primary School
Burgh Primary School group in 2009 and in 1954.

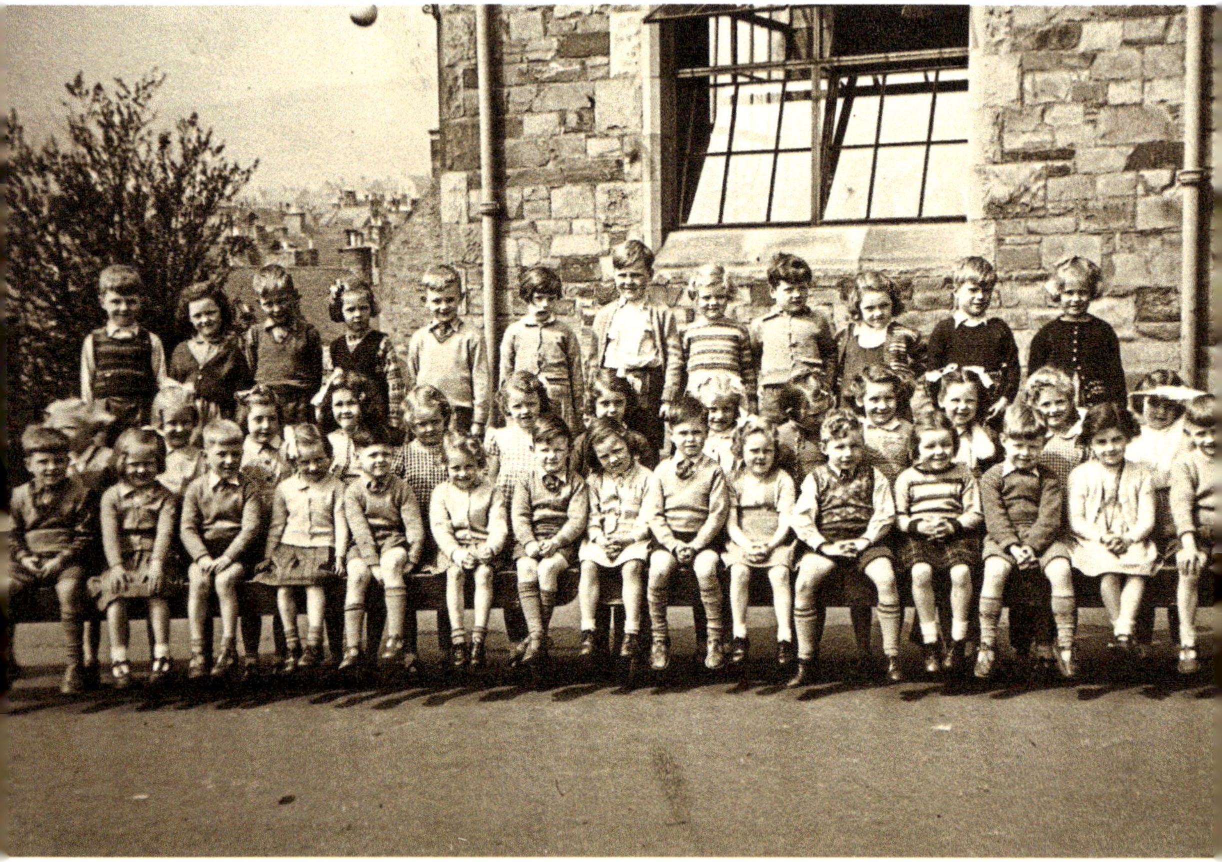

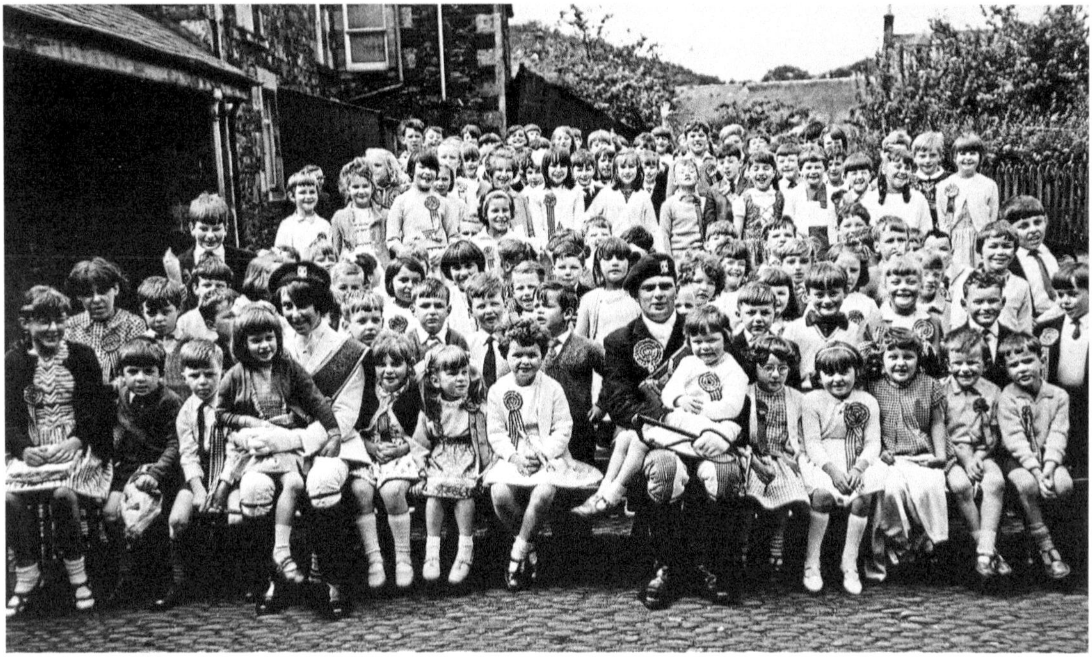

Gala Week Visits

It is customary for the Braw Lad and Lass to visit all the Galashiels schools during Gala Week. Braw Lass Marvyn Clark and Braw Lad Robson Reid are pictured in 1967 with a group of schoolchildren out to wish them well for the Gala Day. Image below – Glendinning Terrace School, *c.* 1960.

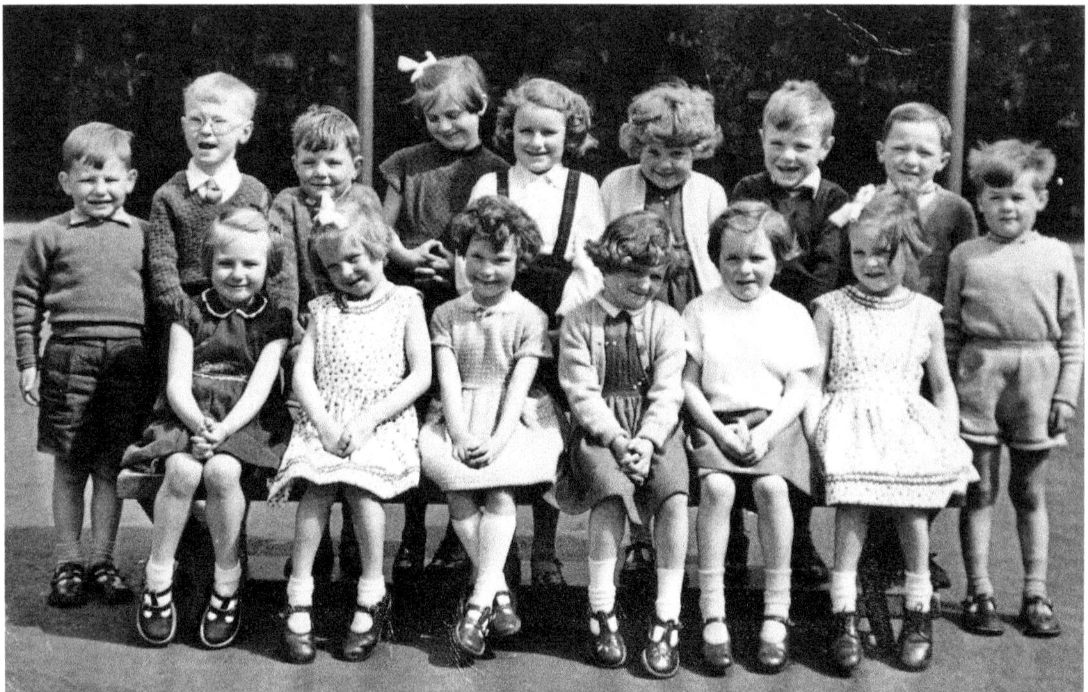

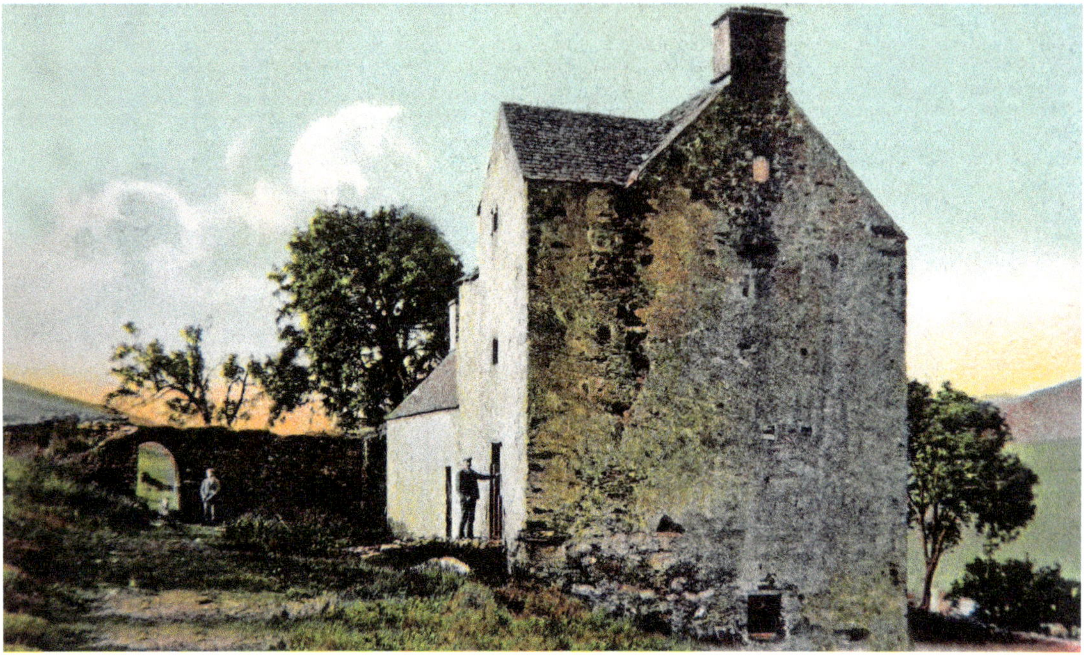

Buckholm Tower

Buckholm Tower was inhabited by one of the Pringles (persecutor of the Covenanters) who suspended his victims from hooks through their chins! Henry Davidson Minister 1714–1749 is reported to have put an end to his 'nightly wanderings' by visiting 'The Deil of Buckholm' and casting out the devil! Buckholm Tower pictured (below) from Meigle Hill is now a ruin.

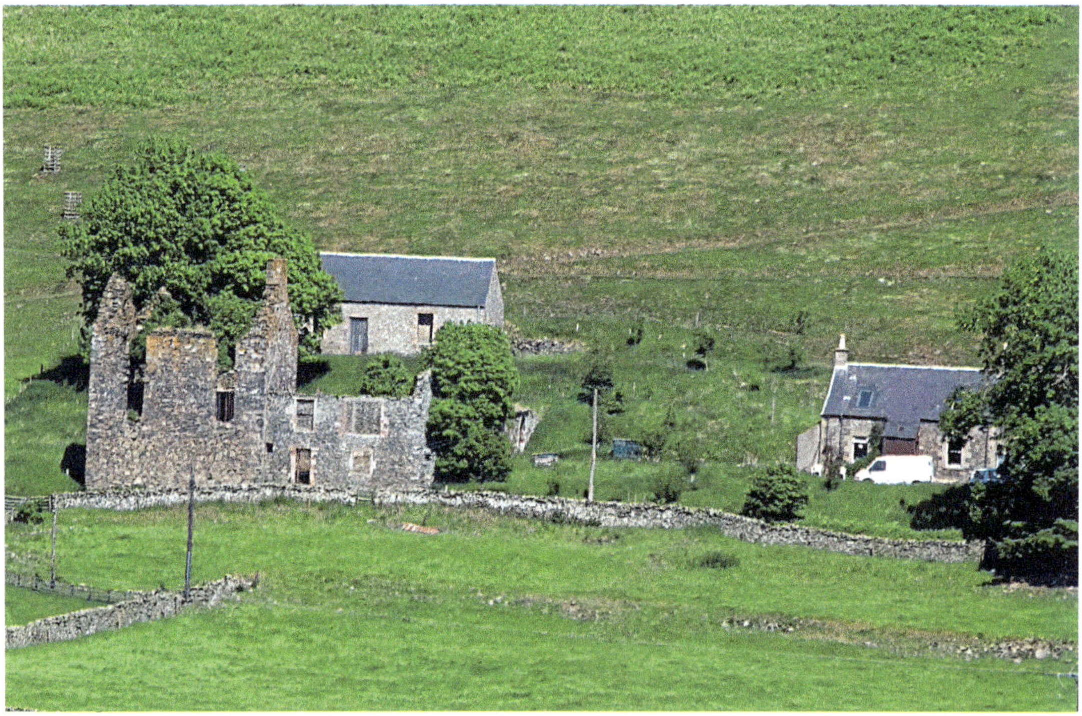

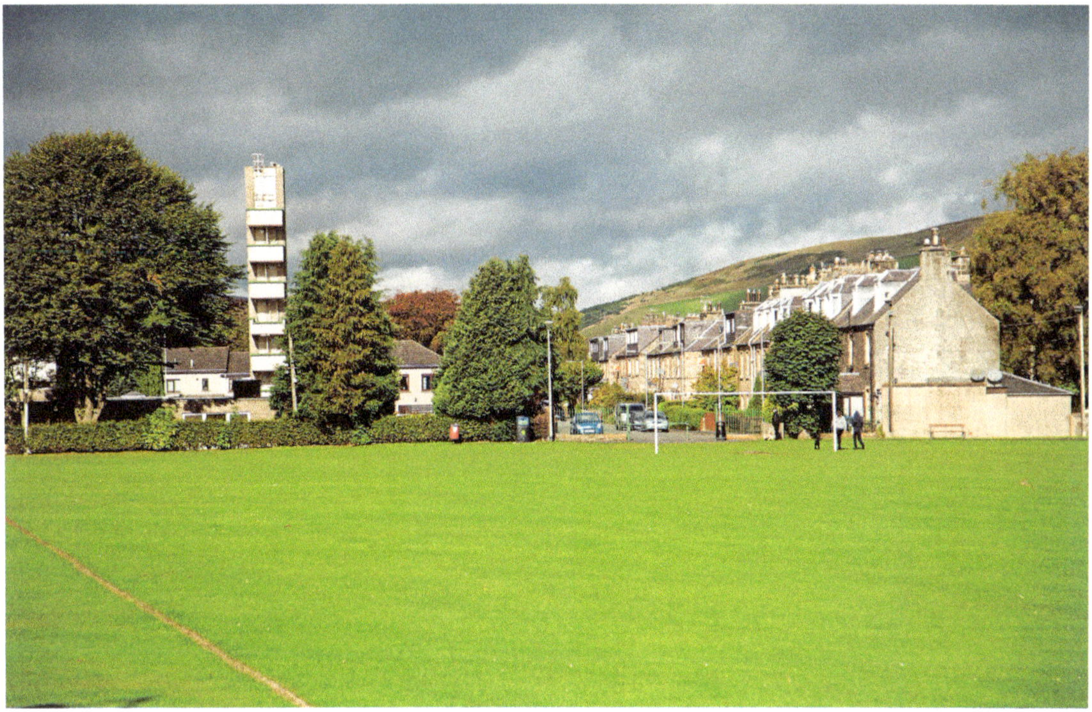

The Public Park

The image above shows the public park now with a football pitch and a fire station just behind the trees. The old image on the left shows a plane, *c.* 1916, in the same area. Interested onlookers watch from just above Croft Street, something which must have been a very unusual sight.

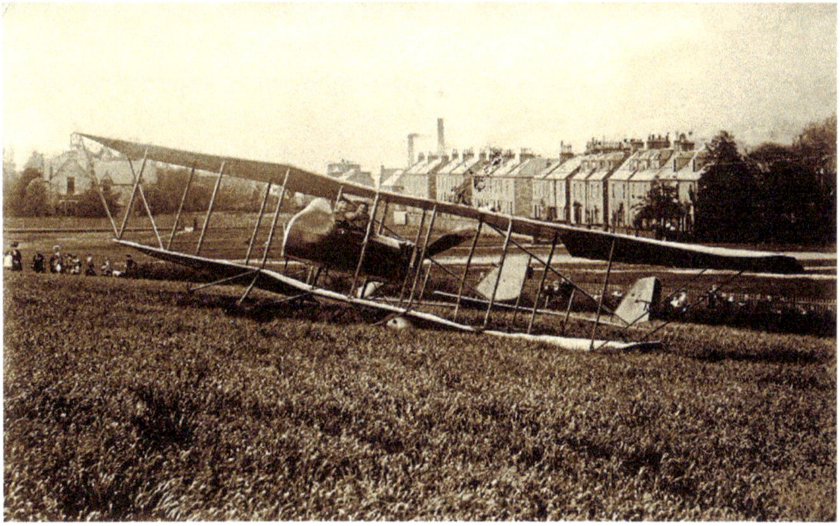

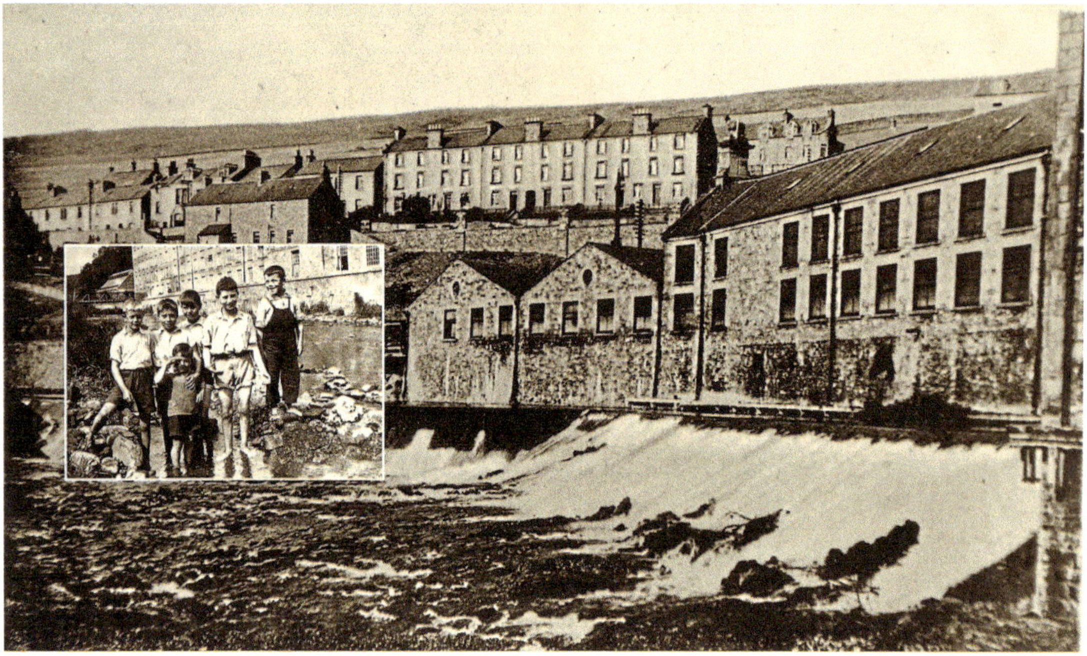

The Mill Laid

Situated in the Wilderhaugh area the Mill Laid is difficult to view as it was. The inset image shows young Sinclair Chalmers, James Davy, John Morrison, Jackie Kennedy, and Arthur and Ronnie Ballantyne in the late '20s having fun in the water. Due to access the new image taken from Low Buckholmside, shows some of the original houses in the trees on the right-hand side.

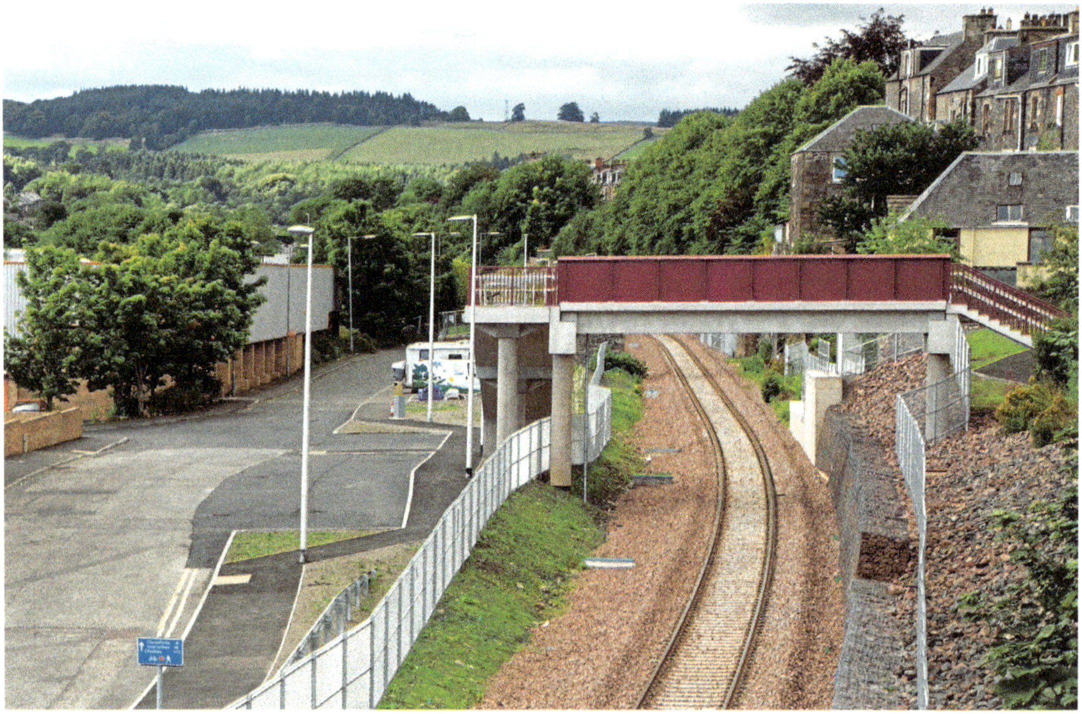

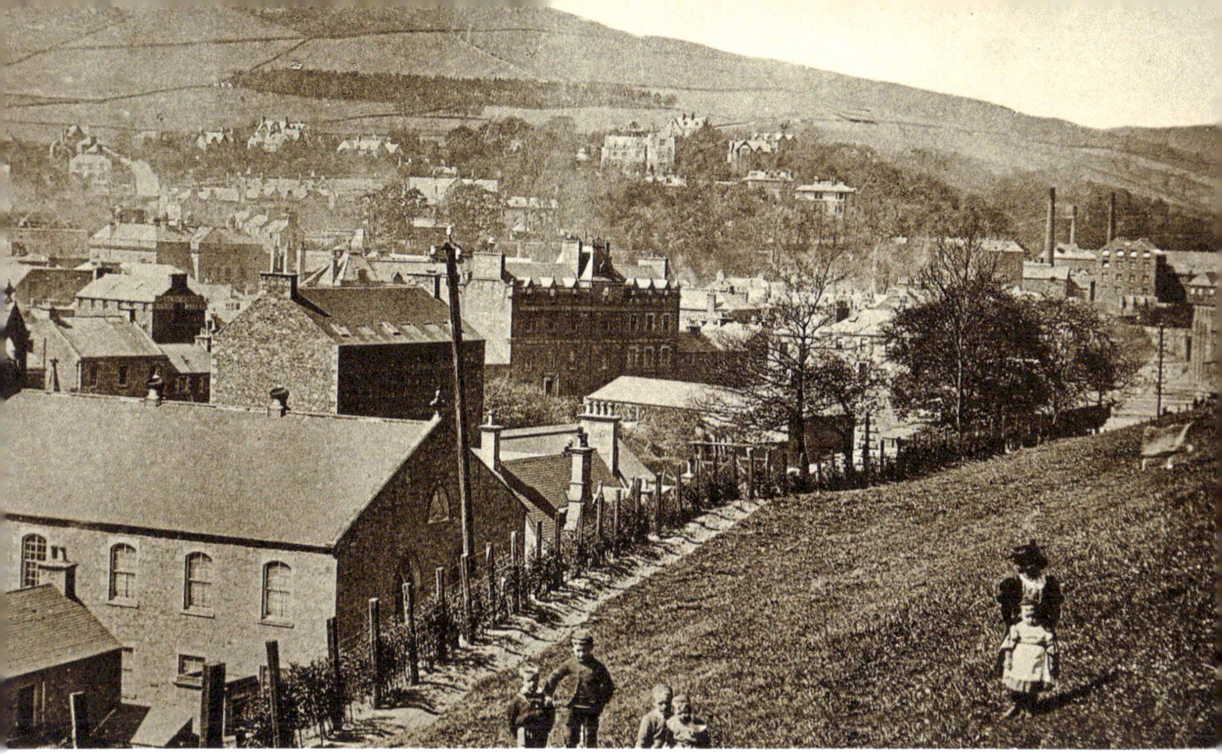

High Road Park

The High Road Park is still a popular place to walk or sit, despite the tree growth which now restricts the views over the town.

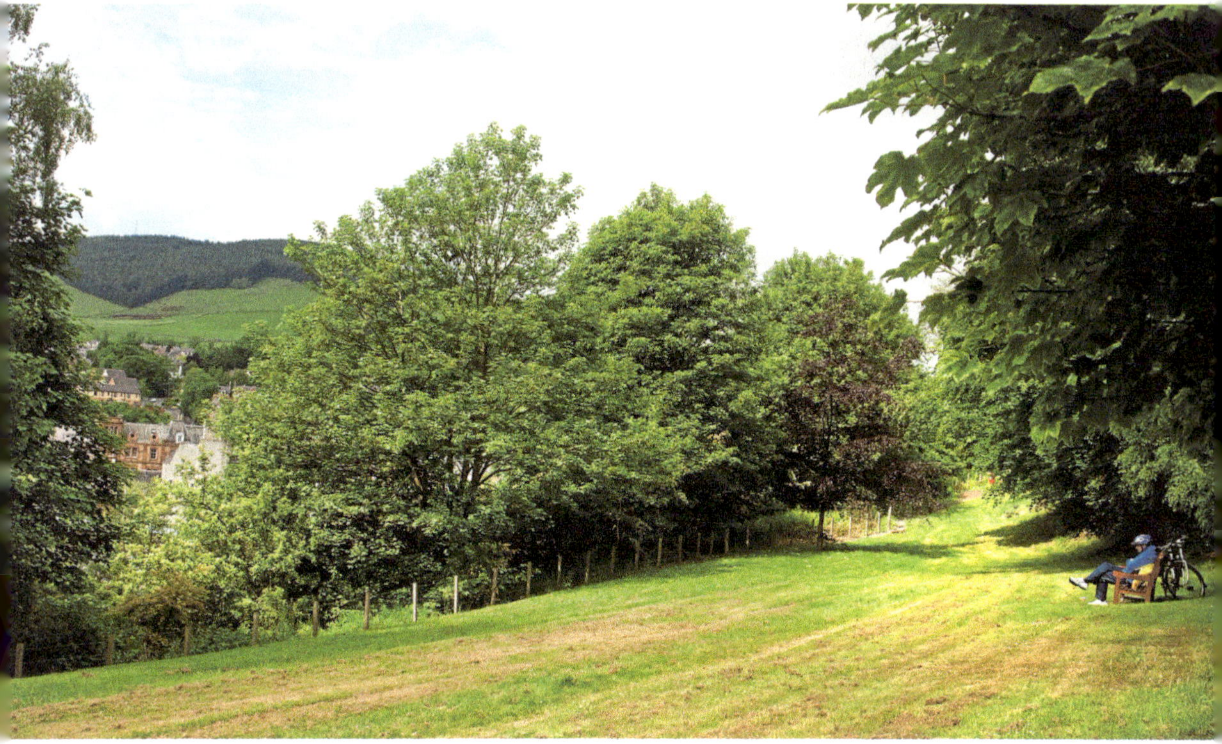

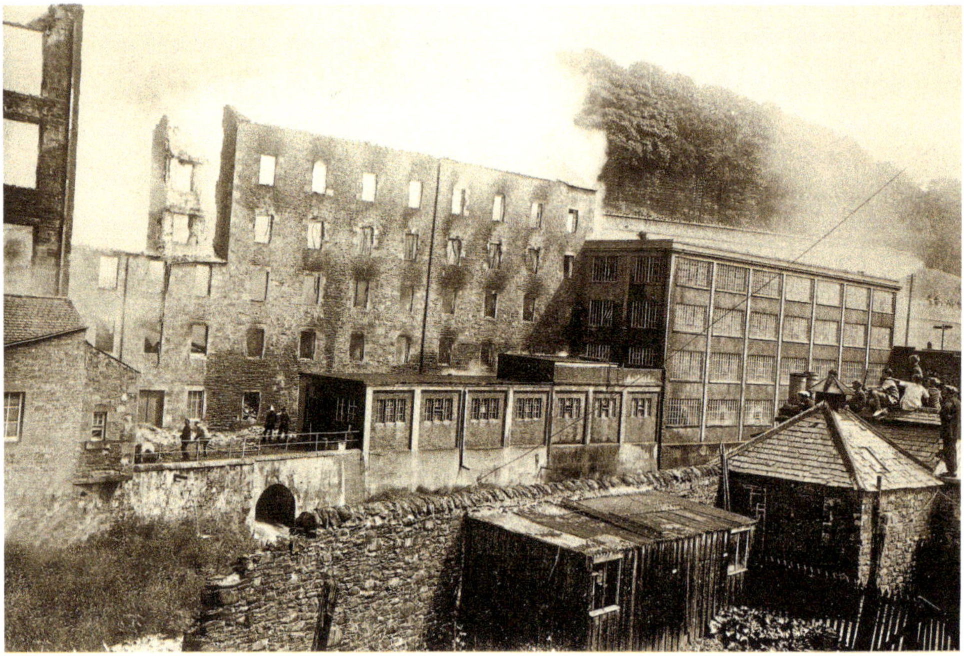

Fire at the Mill

The image above of a mill fire in 1928 shows the site of where Laidlaw & Fairgrieves Mill was recently demolished to make way for a new housing complex. This is now best viewed from the opposite direction, in the High Road. The spot where hundreds of onlookers can just be seen in the old image on the top right of the picture, lining the wall to view the fire in the mill.

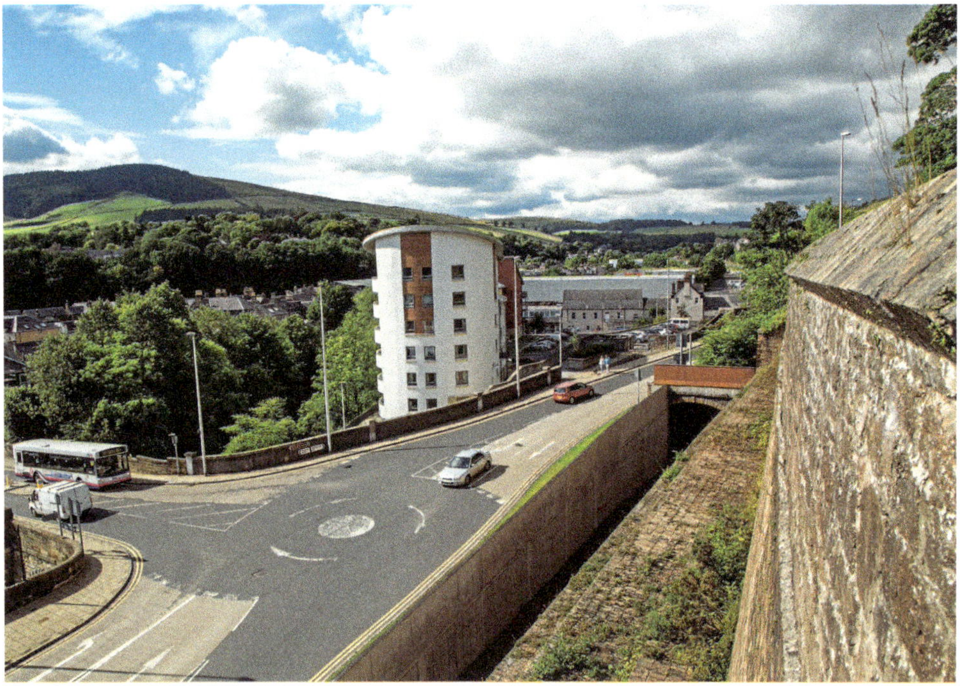

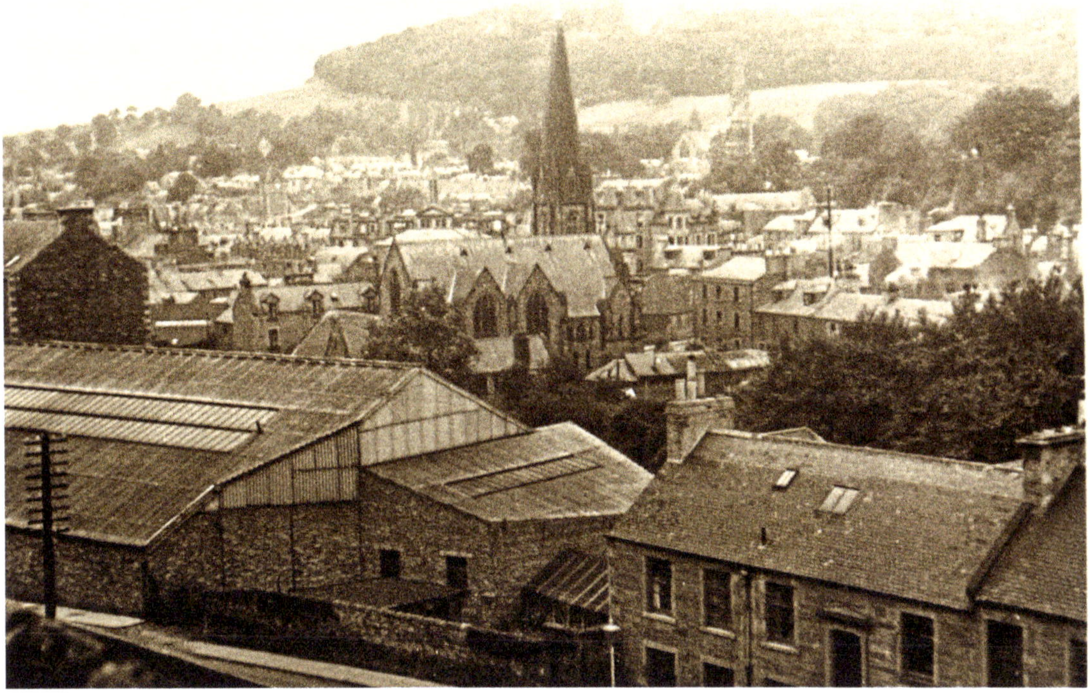

Ladhope Vale
Looking over from the High Road onto Ladhope Vale and in the distance to Gala Hill. In the old image the church spire of St Andrews Church in Bridge Street can clearly be seen. This was removed in 1985.

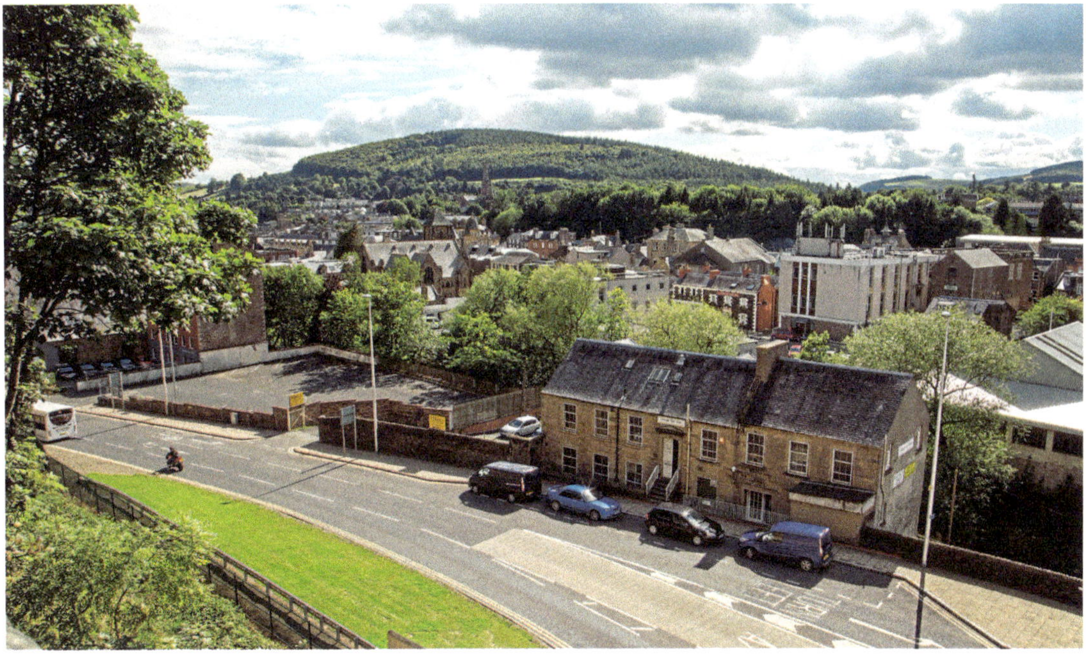

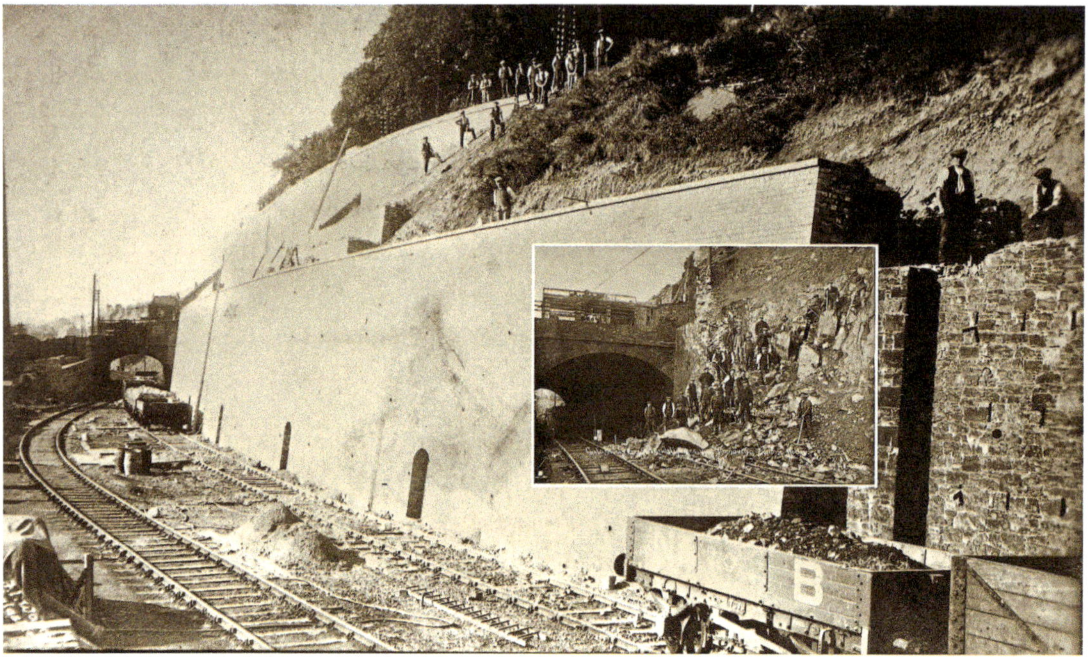

Ladhope Tunnel

In December 1916, the retaining walls at Ladhope Tunnel collapsed and had to be rebuilt. Workmen are seen in the inset image posing for the photographer on the steep embankment. Today the walls at the tunnel have been strengthened to take the reinstated rail line.

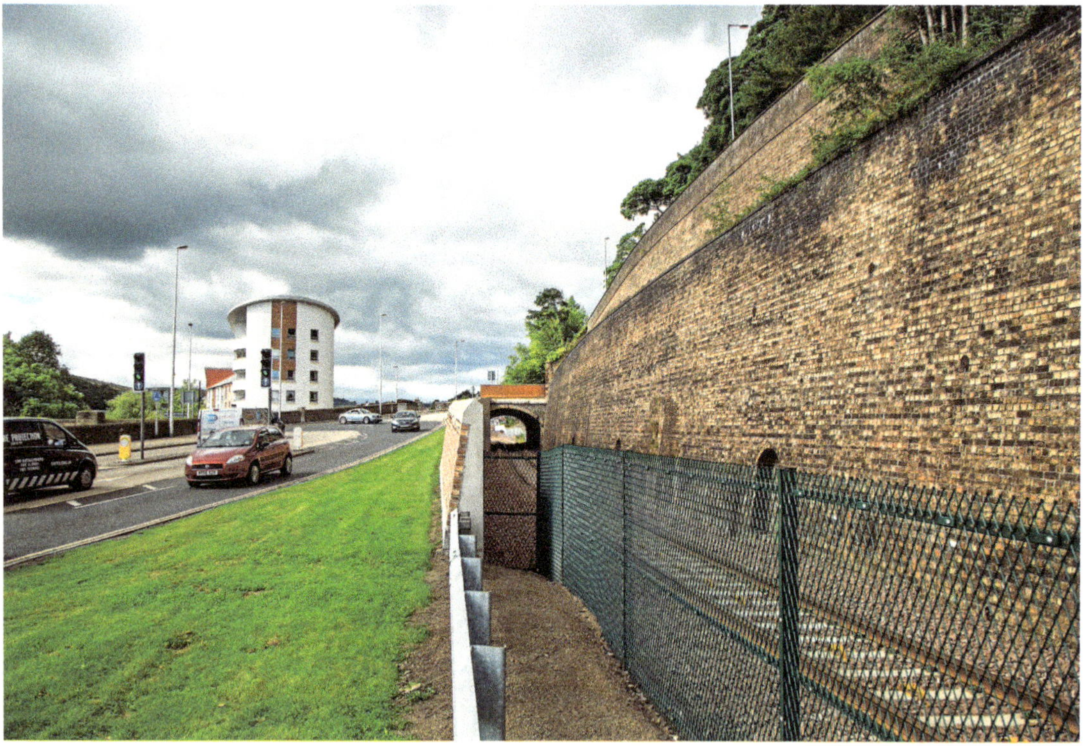

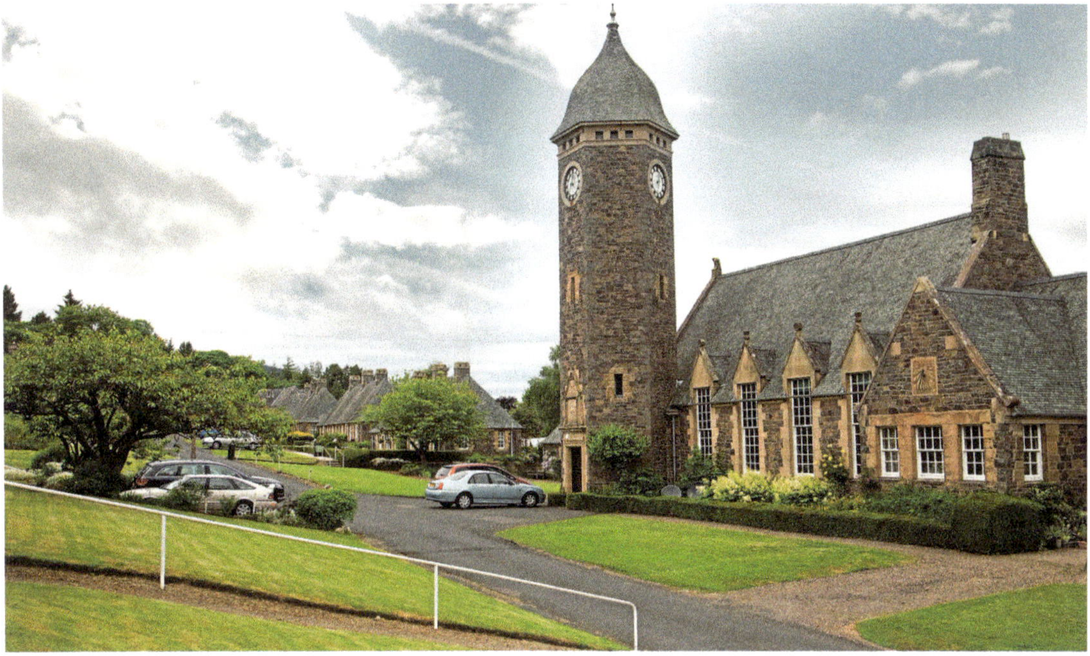

Lucy Sanderson Homes

A lovely residential area opened in 1933. James Sanderson and his wife Lucy had no children and when James died in 1927 he left funds for the building of sixteen semi-detached cottages for folk who had done good work in the town. The murals around the walls in the community hall were painted by William Rawson Lawson, who studied at Edinburgh College of Art under Robert Burns, and M. R. Caird, in 1936.

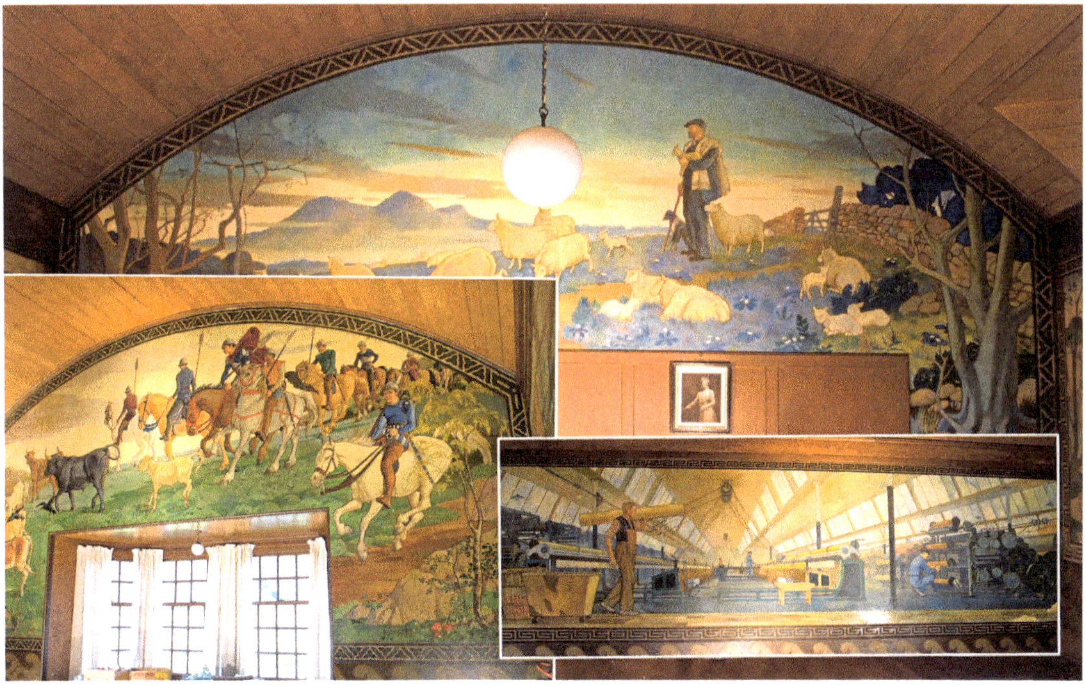

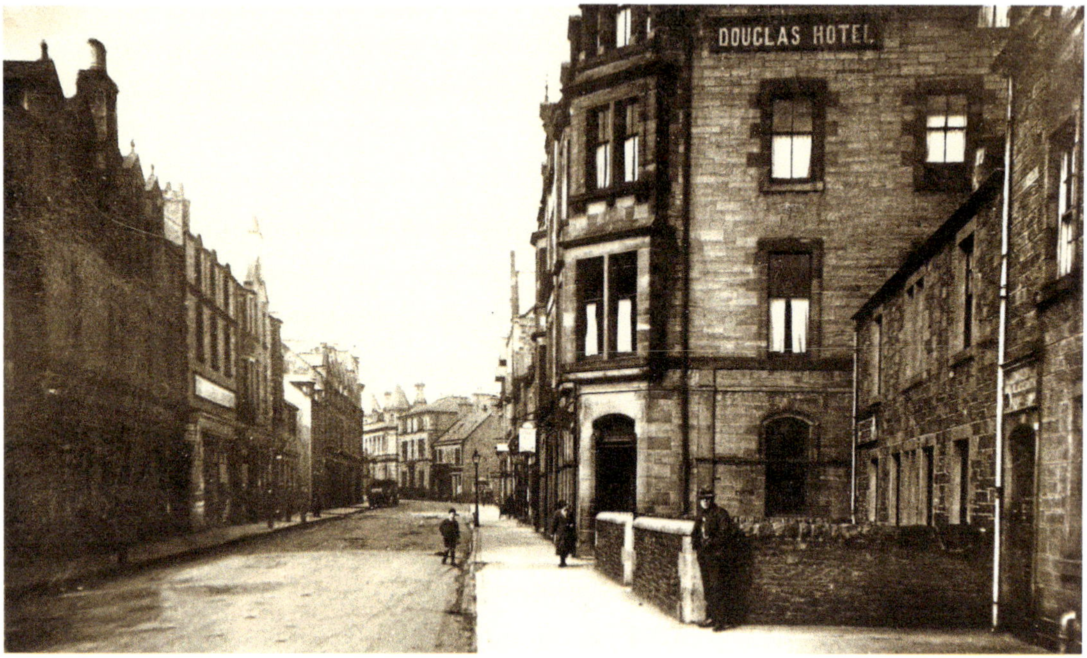

Channel Street

Four photographs showing the contrast in Channel Street. Noticable is the amount of 'For Sale' and 'To Let' signs in the street. Many of the small independent shops now find rates prohibitive in the town centre, on top of the the lack of trade in the recession present at the moment.

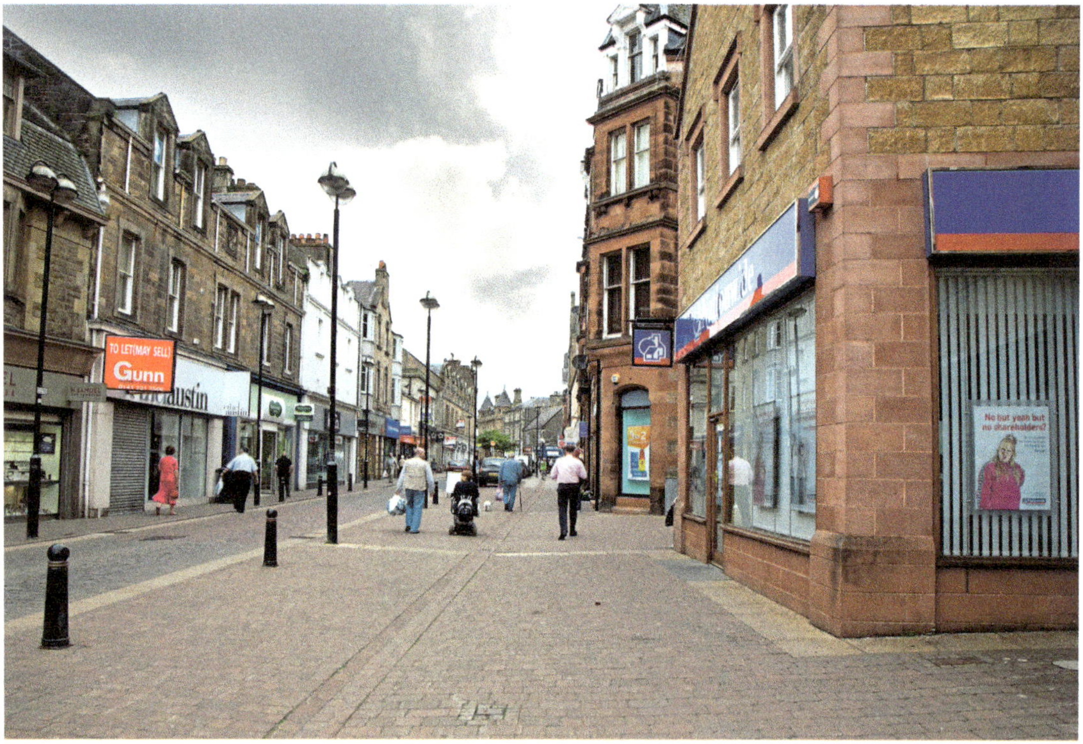

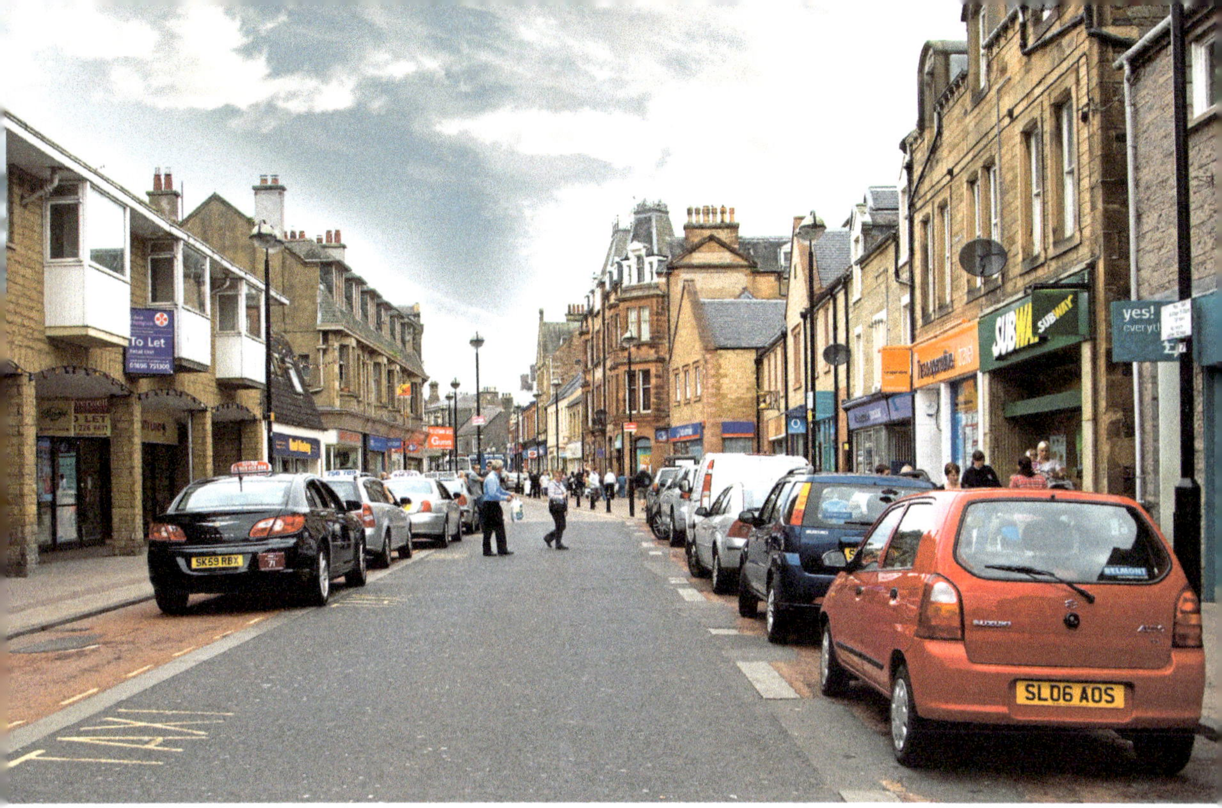
To Let
SUBWAY
yes!
SK59 RBX
SL06 AOS
TAXI

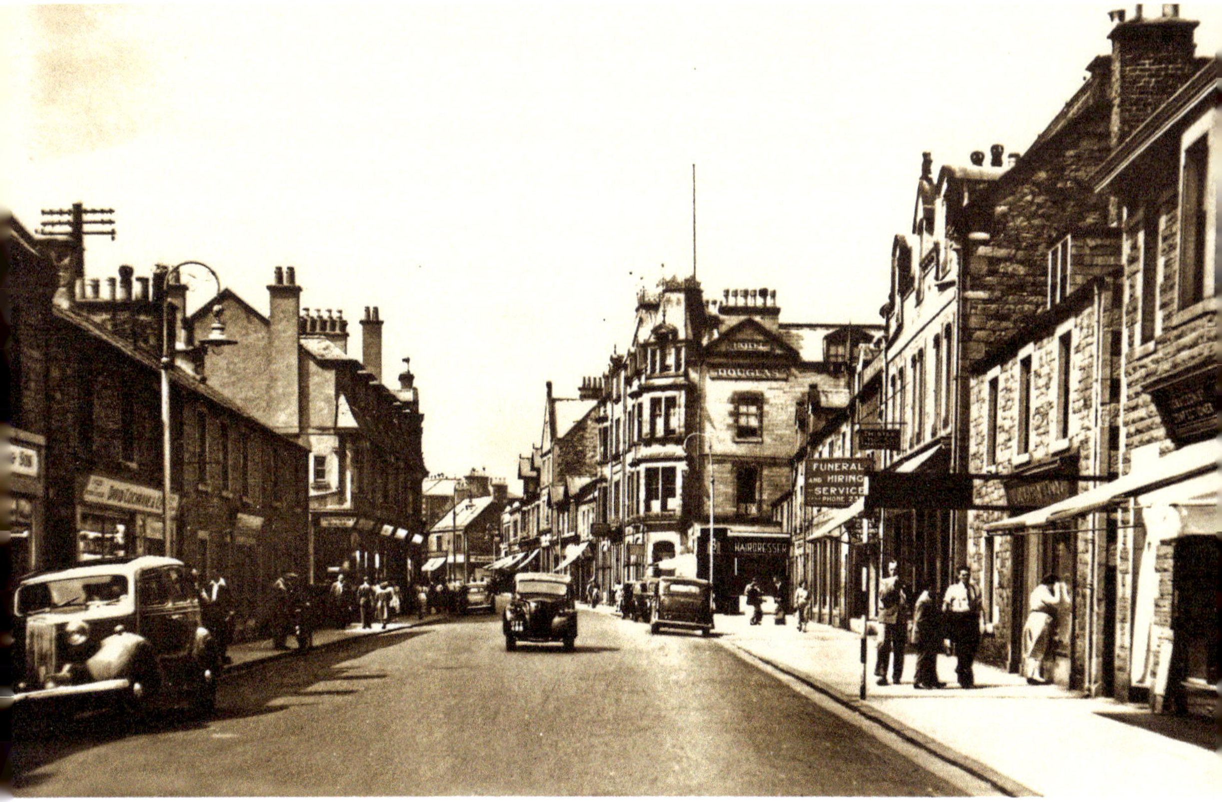
FUNERAL
AND HIRING
SERVICE
HAIRDRESSER

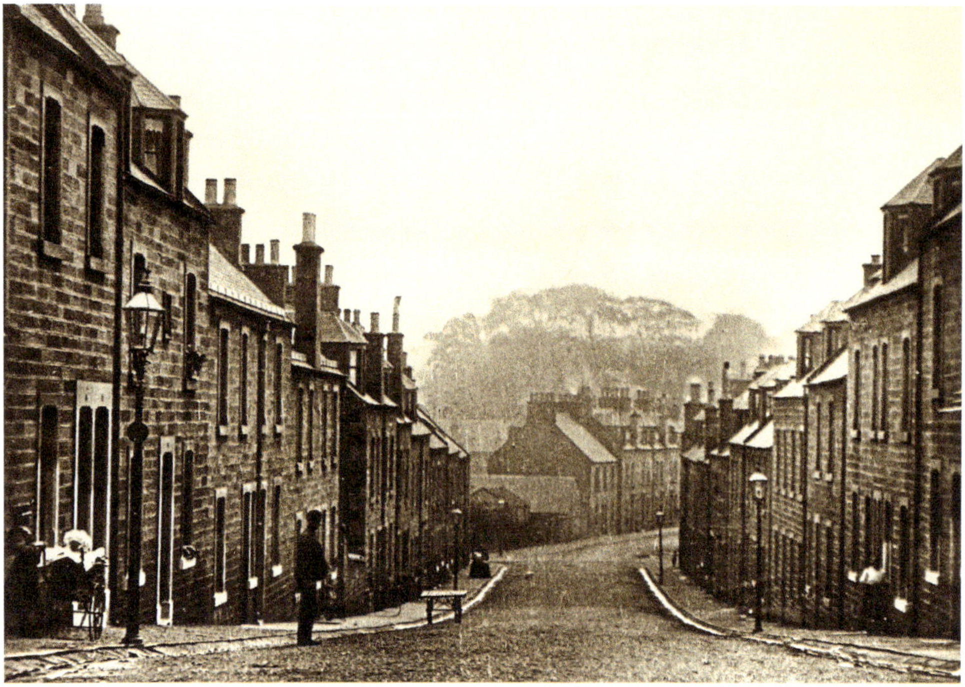

St Andrew Street

For a number of years St Andrew Street has been a popular area for first-time house buyers. It is much busier in the way of traffic now and has satellite dishes aplenty!

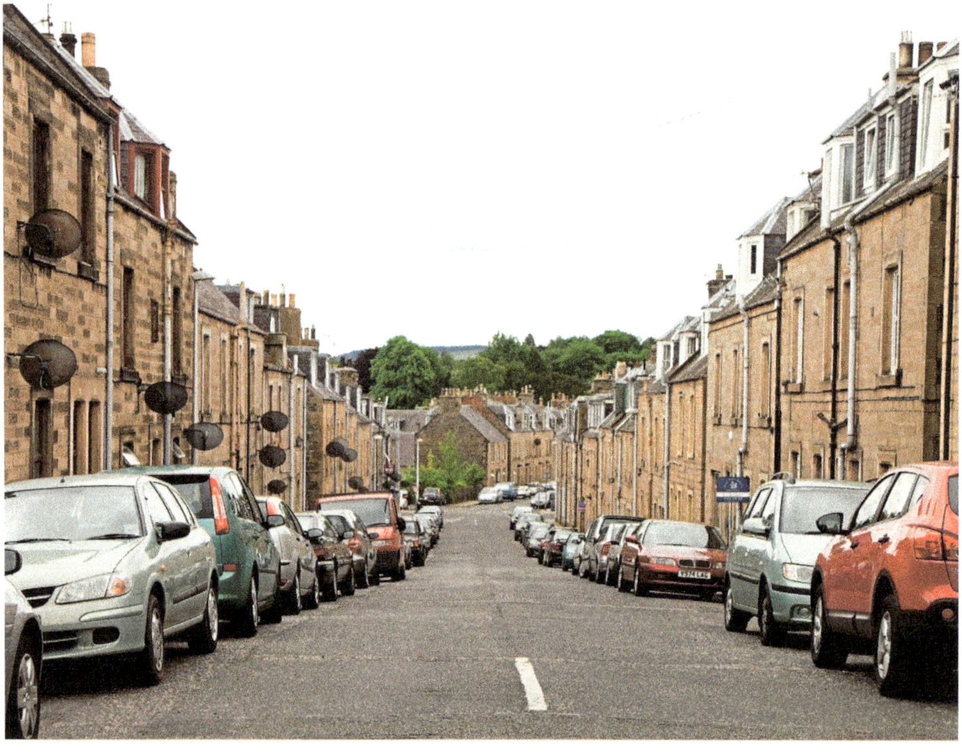

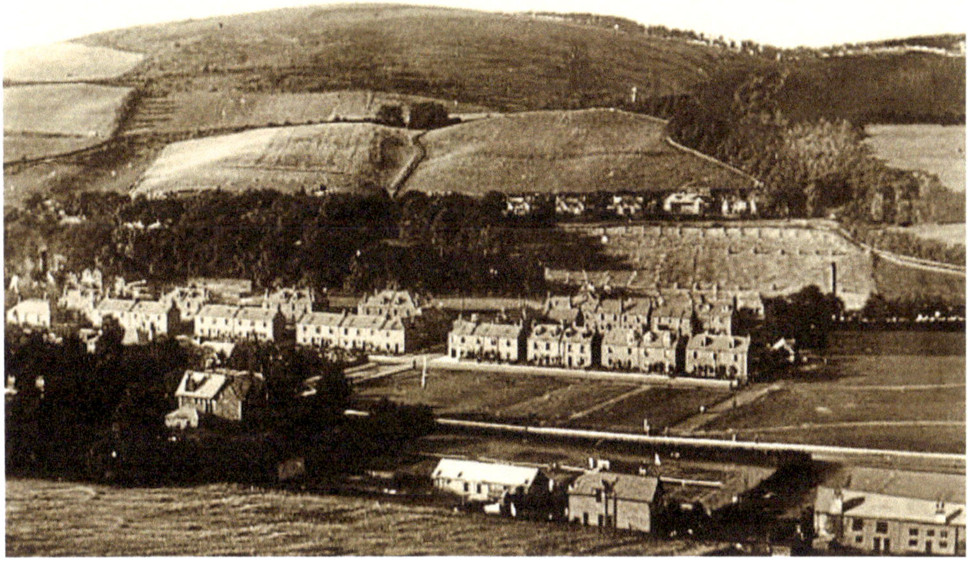

Fields and Houses

Looking over from Gala Hill long gone are the penny and twopenny putting greens and the fields are now filled with houses – now Glenfield and Langhaugh housing estates. The fire station, which opened in 1974, can be seen with its training tower in the new image. Robert Bros. Circus seen here visiting the public park in 2010.

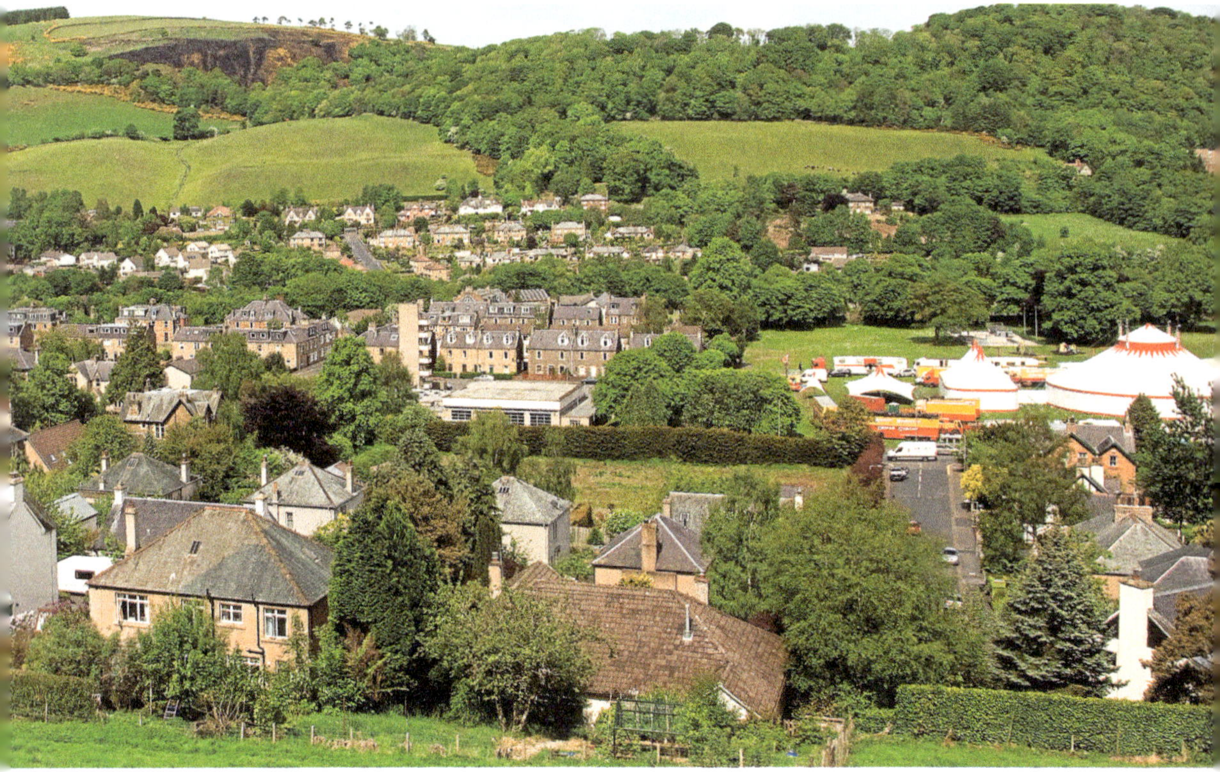

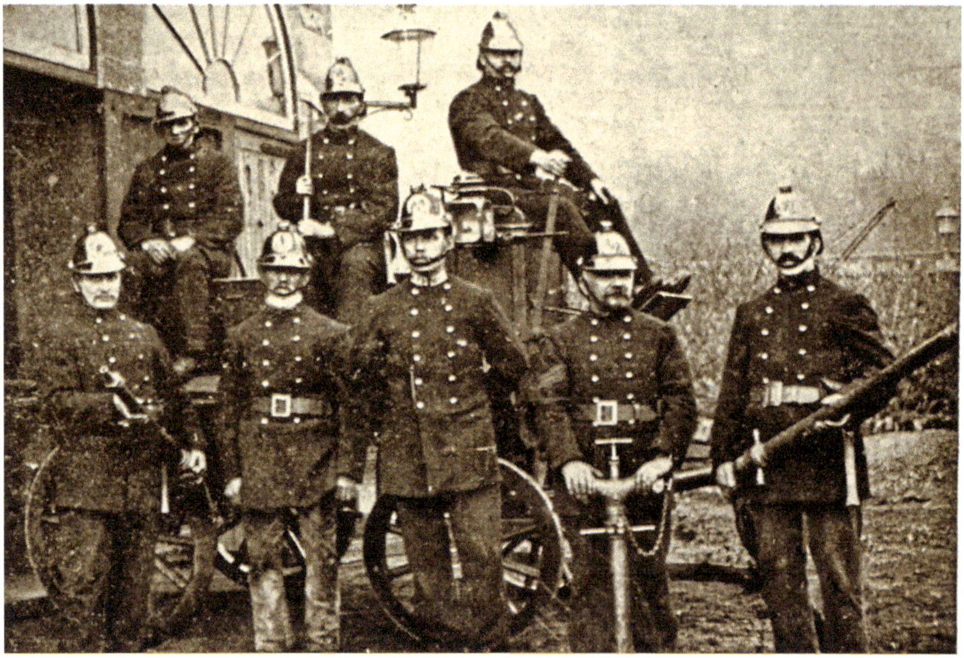

Galashiels Fire Crew

This photograph of an early Galashiels fire crew proudly displaying their equipment certainly is a contrast to the image below taken in early 2000. Firemen Brian Aitchison and Bruce Swan demonstrate new personal equipment and protective suits which could be used at chemical and other major incidents.

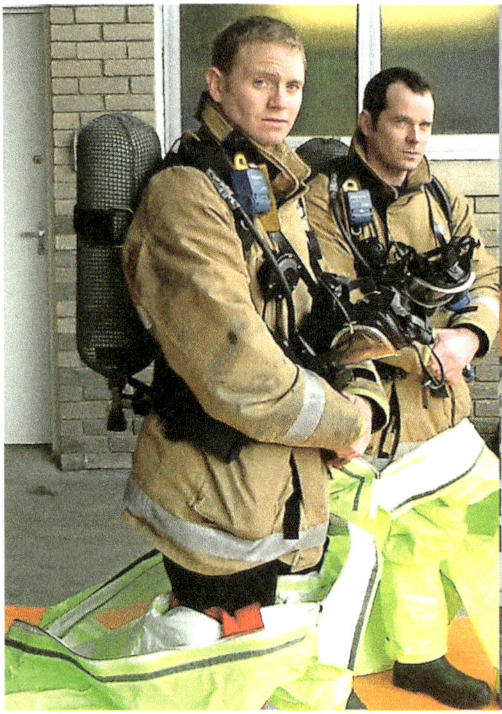

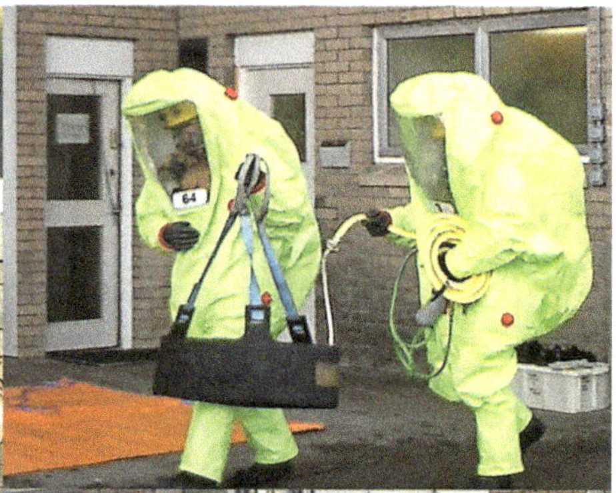

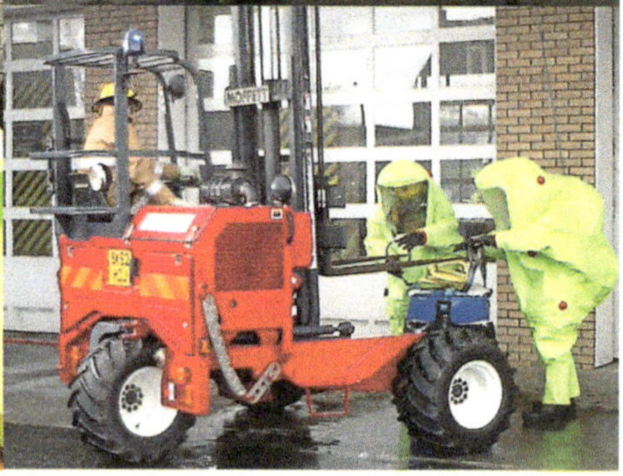

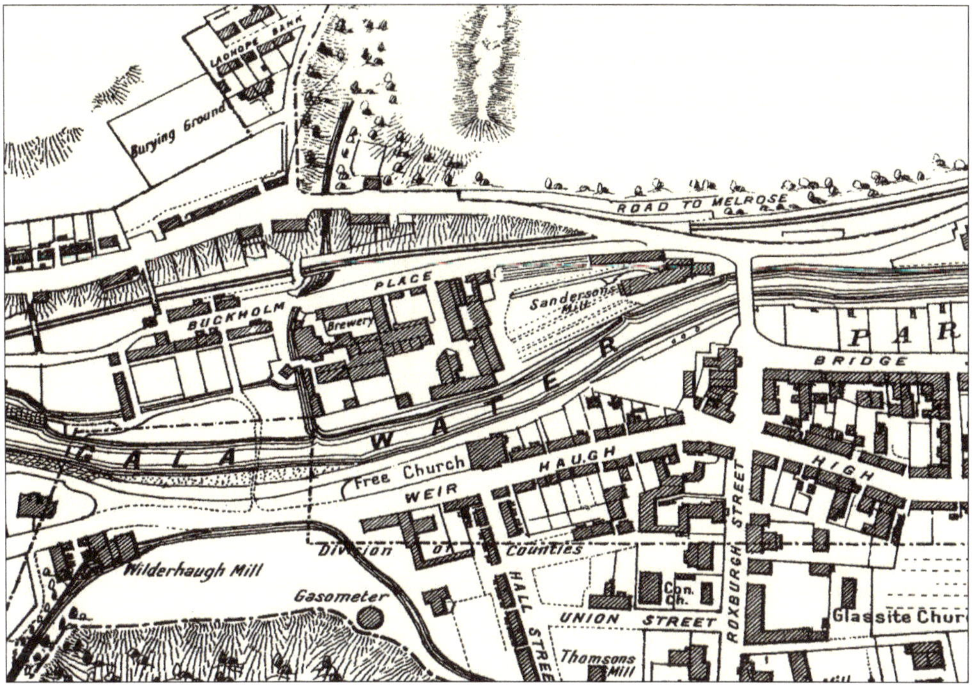

Galashiels Brewery

Galashiels Brewery commenced in 1804 – started by a group of five men including the Revd Doctor Douglas in Low Buckholmside for the 'production of London porter'. A copy of a letter from one James Dalrymple of Edinburgh in 1807 to Gallowshiels Brewery'complained 'that the ale was never of any use and it soured on his hand!' This particular brewery closed in 1809 which suggests he may have been right! The new image shows The Ladhope Inn today which sits above the area where the brewery once was. It bears a plaque outside 'Established 1792', proving it much more of a successful venture!

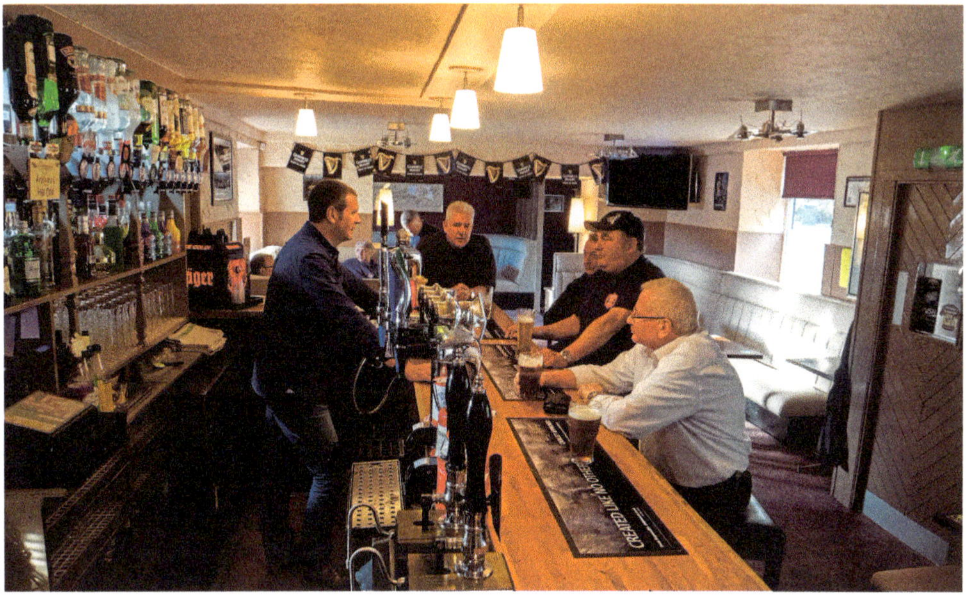

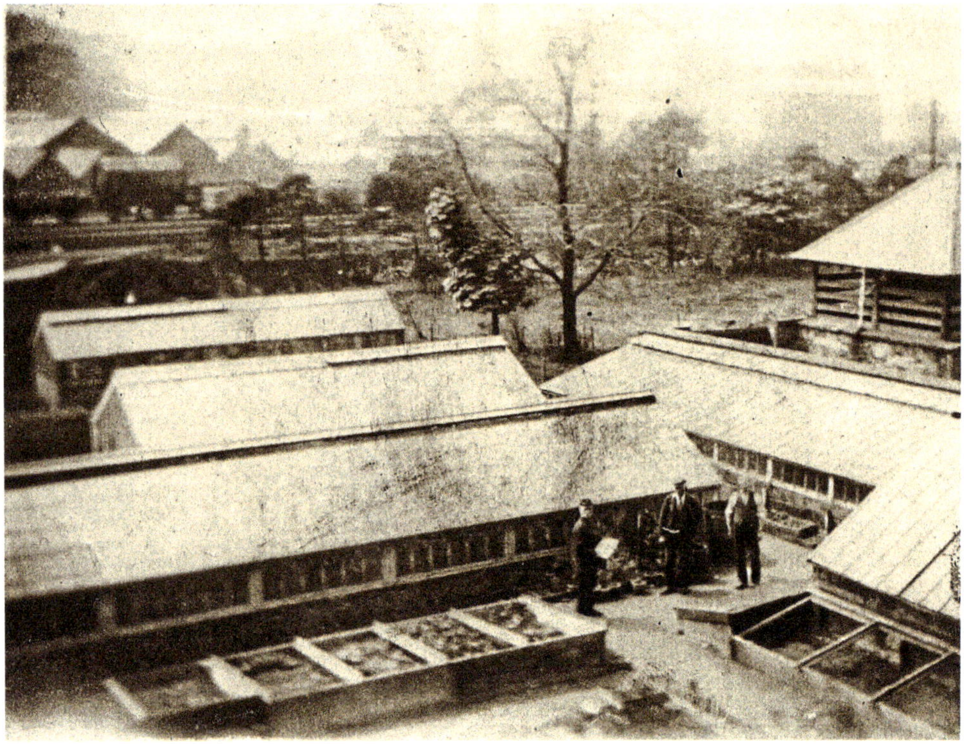

Curry Road Industrial Estate

This market garden stood on the site of what is now Mitchells in Curry Road Industrial Estate. The old railway line can just be seen beyond with signs of Huddersfield Street and Peter Anderson's Mill.

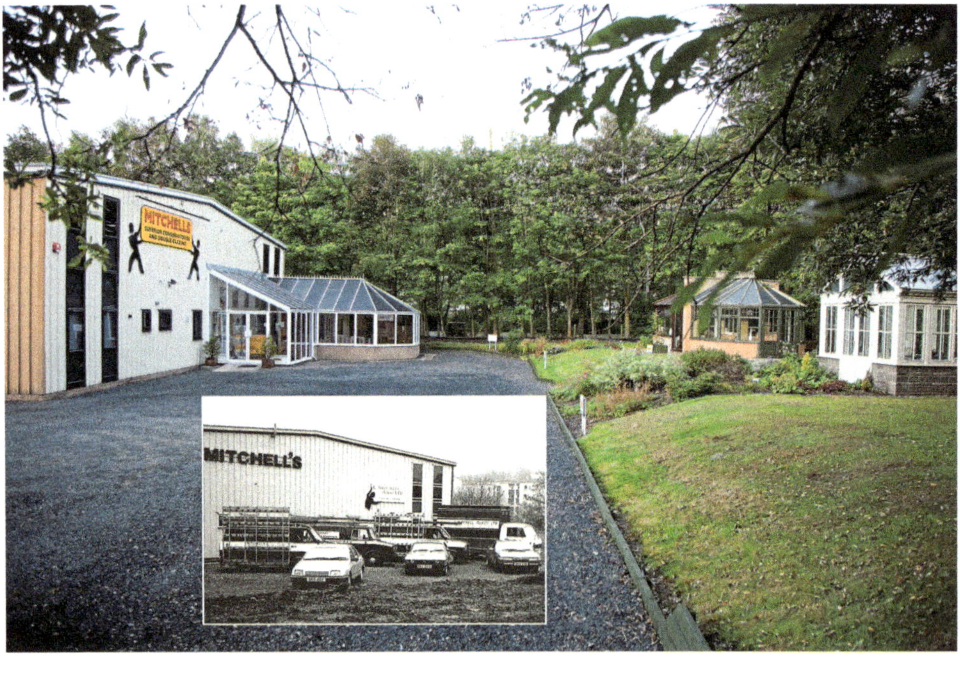

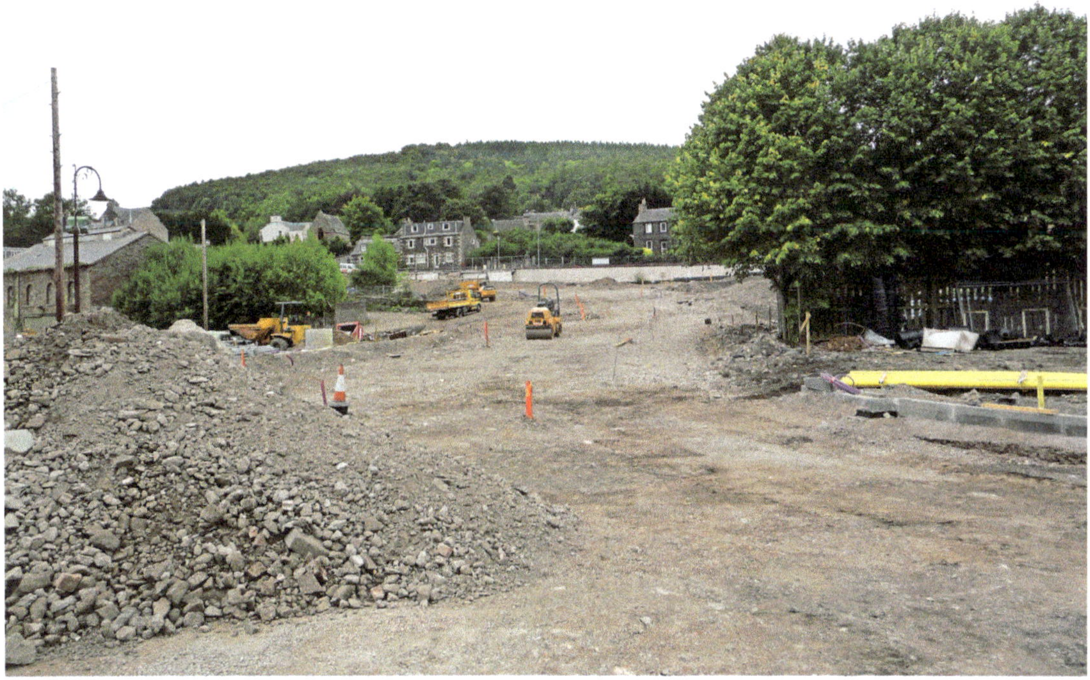

Braw Lads' Brae

The clearing of the old burgh yard in 2006 when the old garage premises, previously occupied by Chalmers McQueen, was demolished to make way for the new 'Braw Lads' Brae'.

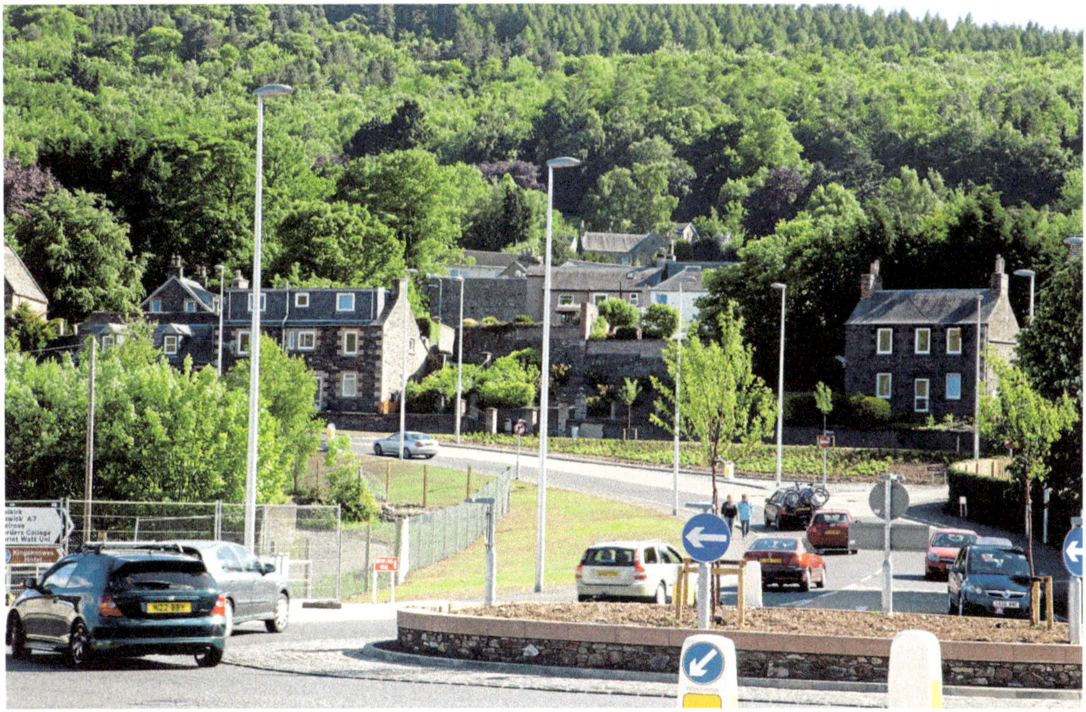

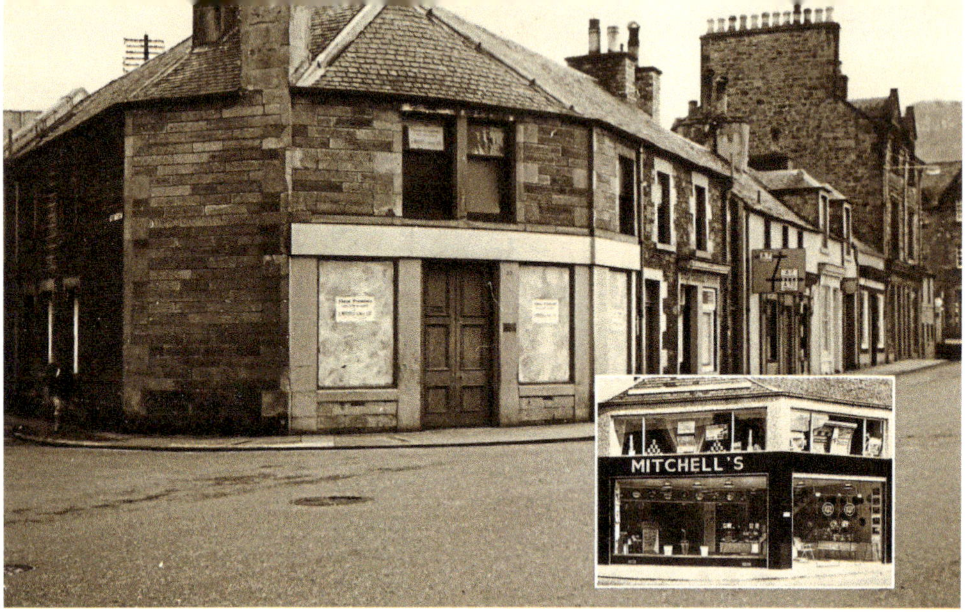

James Beveridge Ltd

This old image shows the premises of what was James Beveridge Ltd, Licensed Grocers. The premises were taken over by Mitchell Glass in 1960, and having changed hands several times since, is now occupied by Quins Restaurant and Coffee Shop, named after Roger Quin, the poet who wrote 'The Borderland' – one of his best-loved poems.

"From the moorland and the meadows
To this City of the Shadows
Where I wander old and lonely, comes the call I understand;
In clear, soft tones enthralling,
It is calling, calling, calling –
'Tis the spirit of the open from the dear old Borderland"

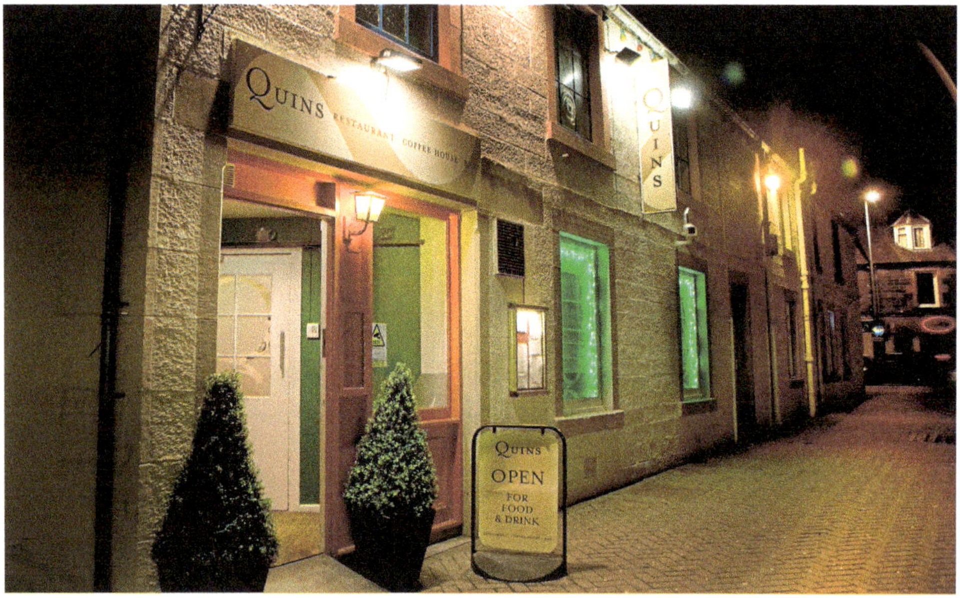

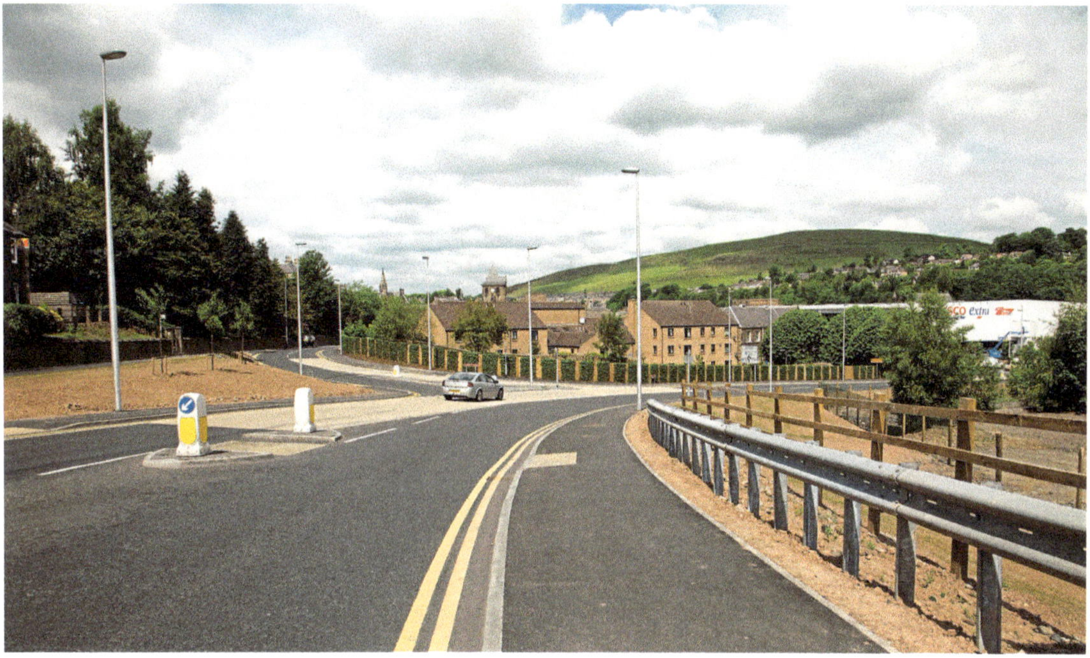

Braw Lads Day' Cavalcade

The Braw Lads' Day photograph in the late 1960s shows the cavalcade heading out along Albert Place after passing the old garage forecourt. The new route taken since 2010 will involve a right turn on the Gala Day for the riders coming from the Burgh Chambers, not something which is permitted for traffic.

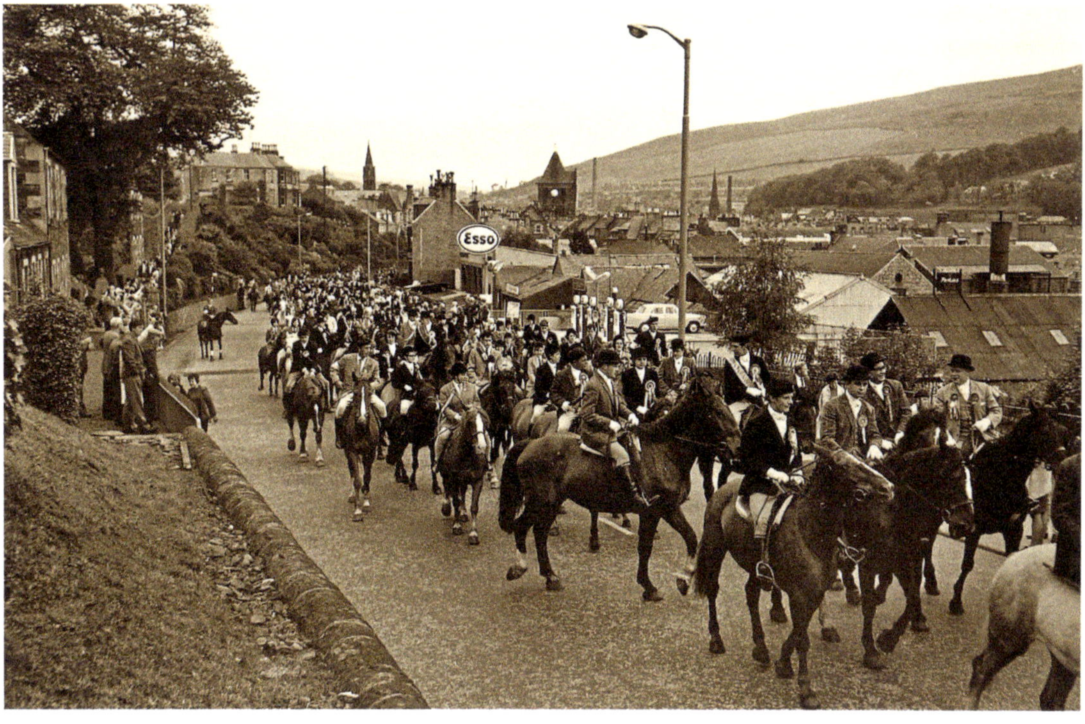

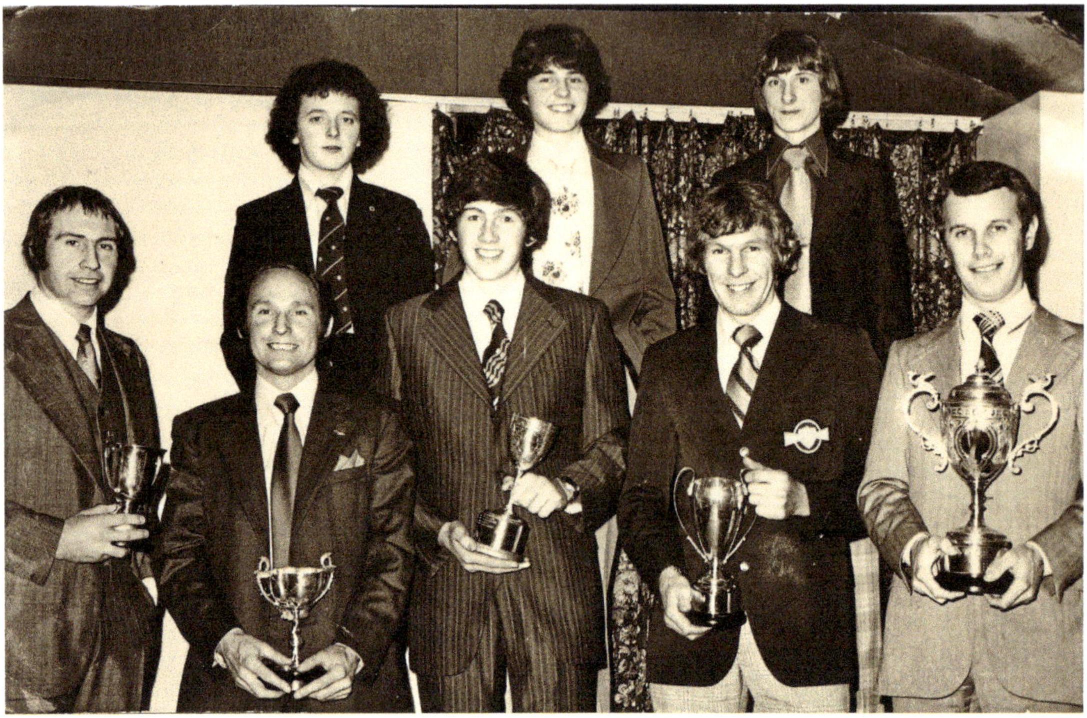

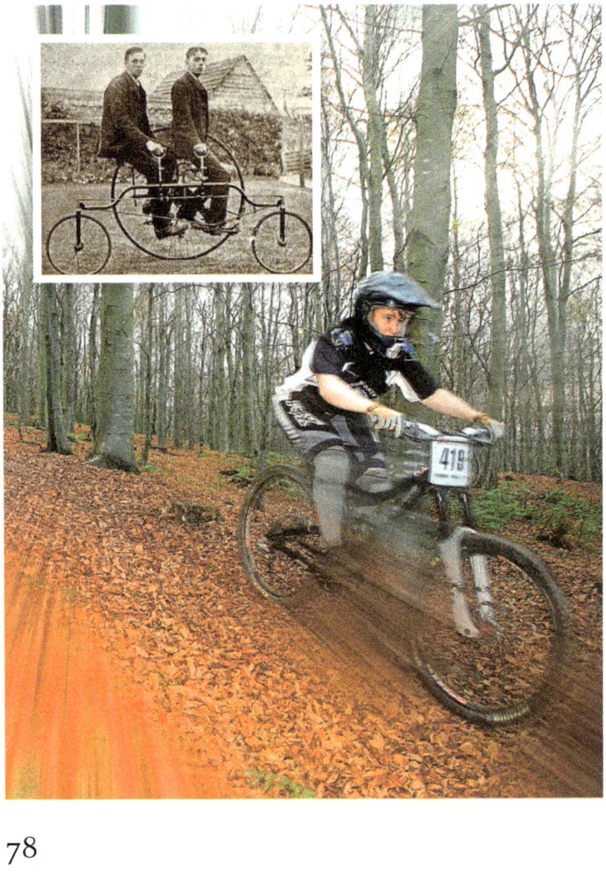

Gala Cycling Club

Gala Cycling Club trophy winners seen in a group picture from the late '70s. In the new image Lynne Aitchison, daughter of Don Aitchison (extreme left in the older image) practises on Gala Hill. Lynne won a second place in the Worlds' Masters Downhill Championship in Canada in 2006. She now does stunt work with schools. Inset an early 'bicycle built for two' photographed at Ladhope House.

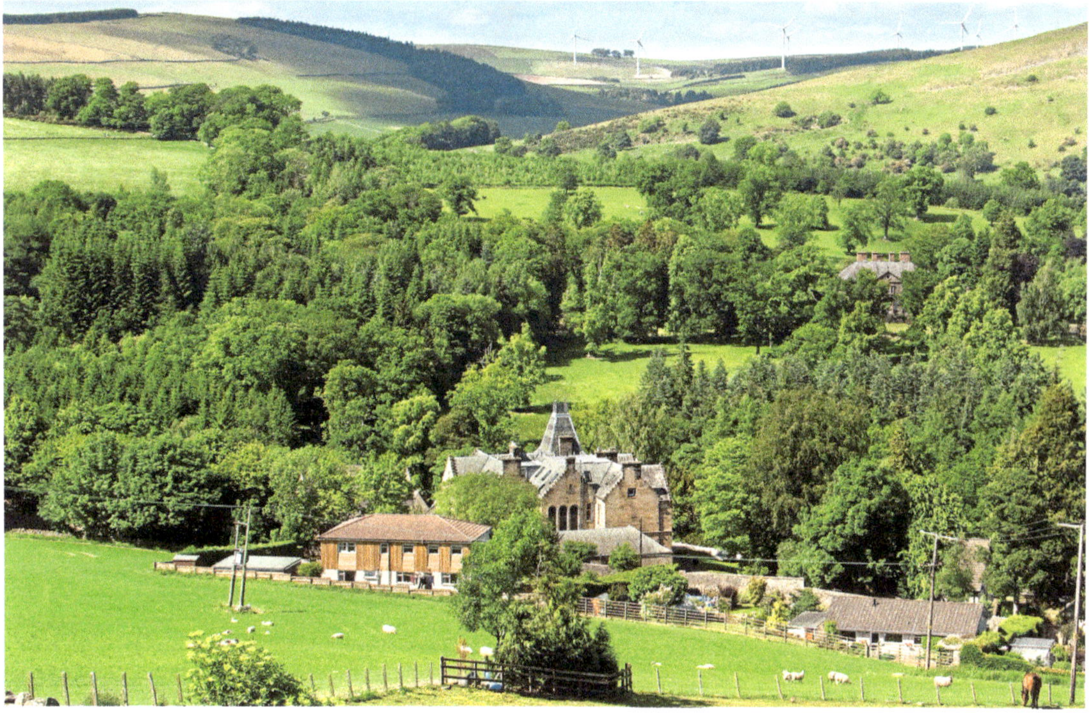

Balnakiel House
Viewed from Meigle Hill, Balnakiel House is lost among a new housing estate. The Sisters and staff of St Mary's Balnakiel ran the house and centre from 1949 to 1991 for women with learning difficulties. The property had been acquired in 1948 by The Poor Servants of the Mother of God. The house, which also had a lovely chapel building with walnut wood panelling is now being sold as private accommodation.

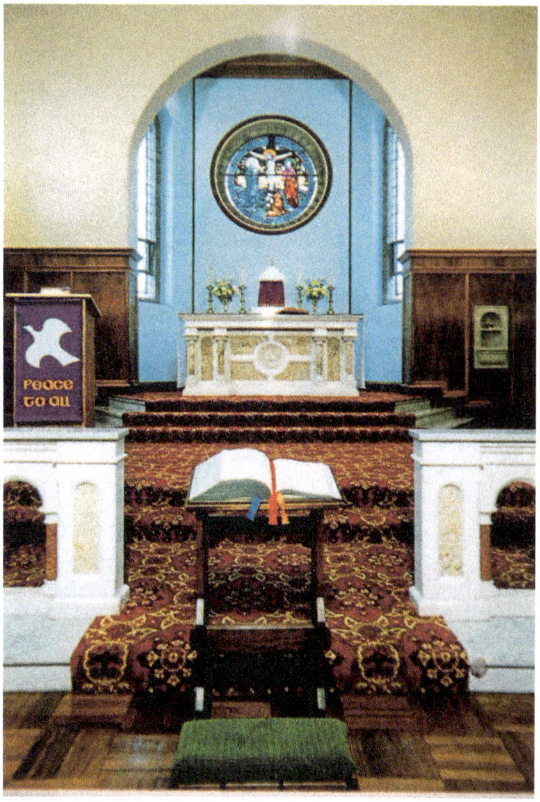

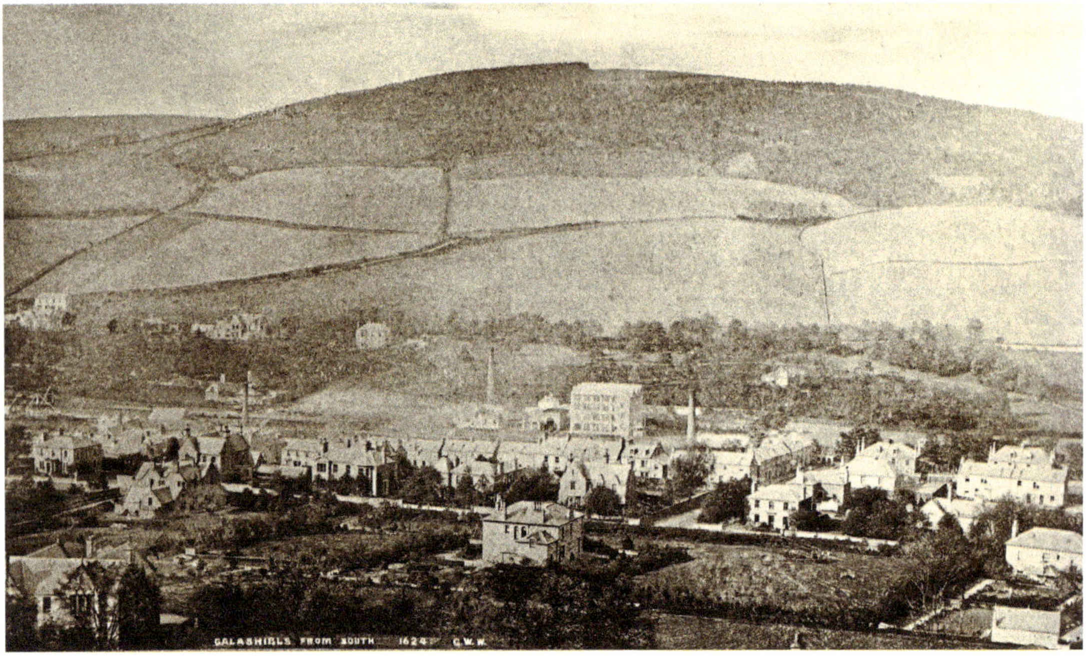

Old Town View

From Gala Hill the old view, *c.* 1880 shows a very sparse town with Abbotsford Road in the foreground. My grandparents' home until 1965 – Eastneuk in Parsonage Road, can be seen on the left. The house had previously been owned by Dr Sommerville, who in the winter months would turn his carriage into a sled to be pulled by his horses. Langhaugh Mill, centre was built in 1875 and burnt down in 1911. The density of the houses now in Melrose Road and Forebrae Park area is quite noticeable.

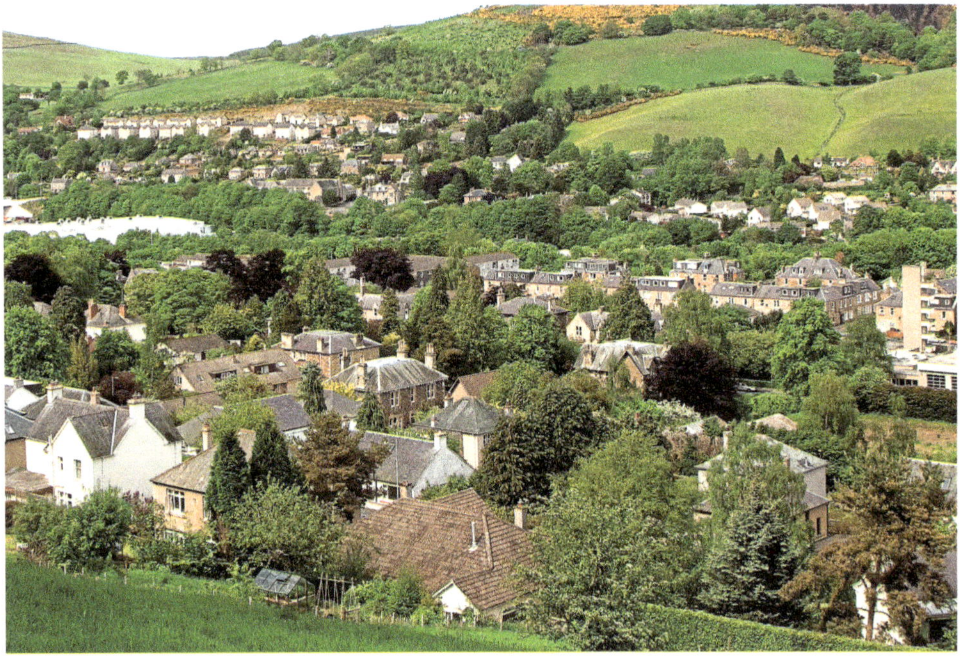

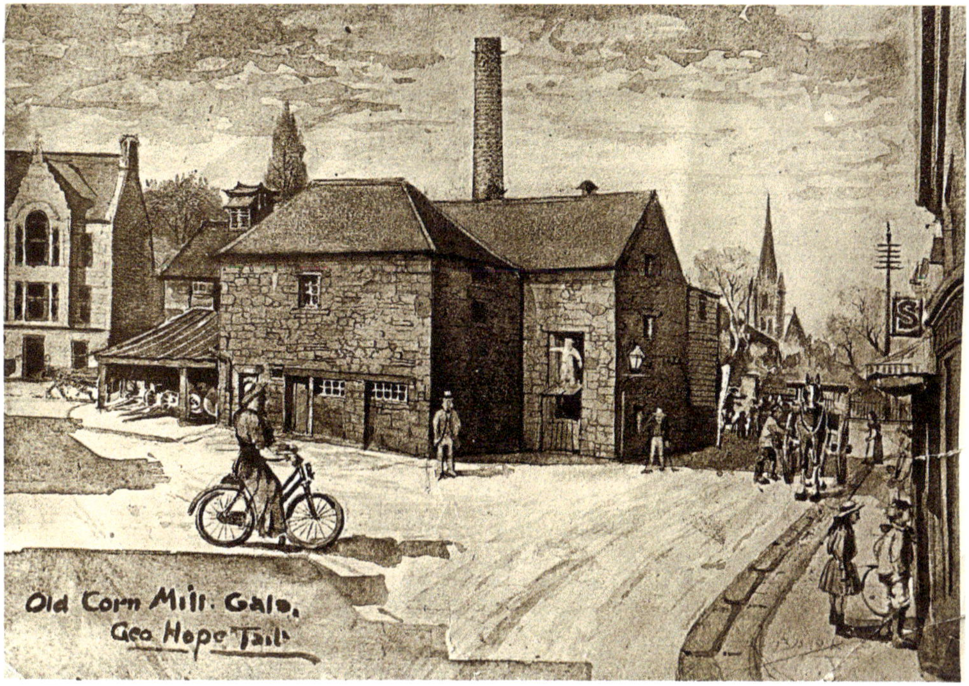

Old Corn Mill

A pencil sketch by George Hope Tait shows an early view of the old Corn Mill. Some artistic licence would appear to have been used, but the library building and the small shops can easily be seen, around the old mill. The latest image shows the appropriately named The Auld Mill pub which is situated in Cornmill Square.

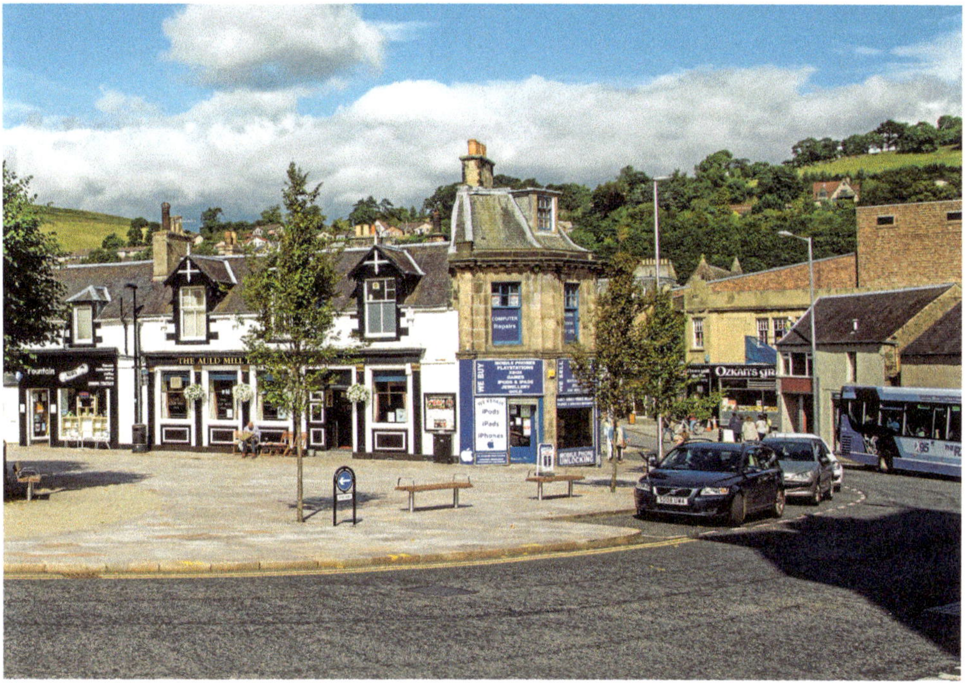

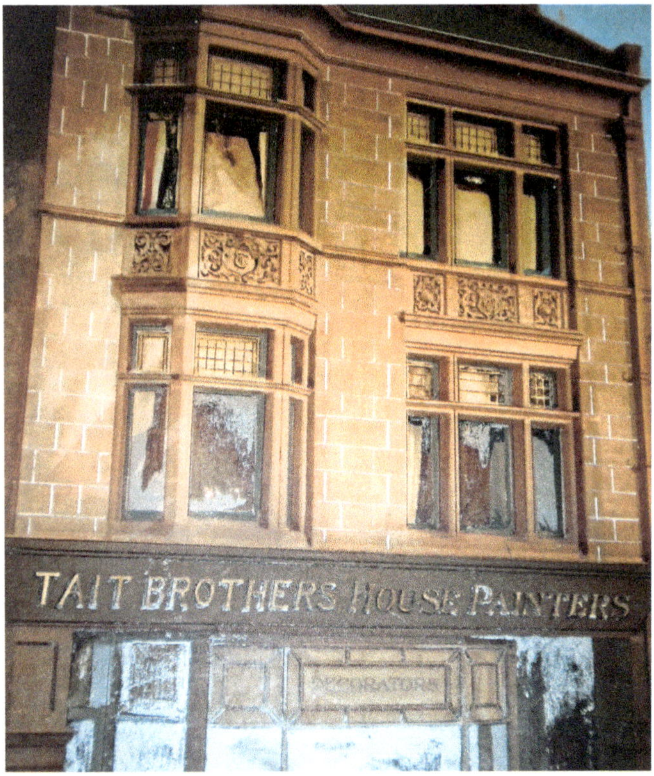

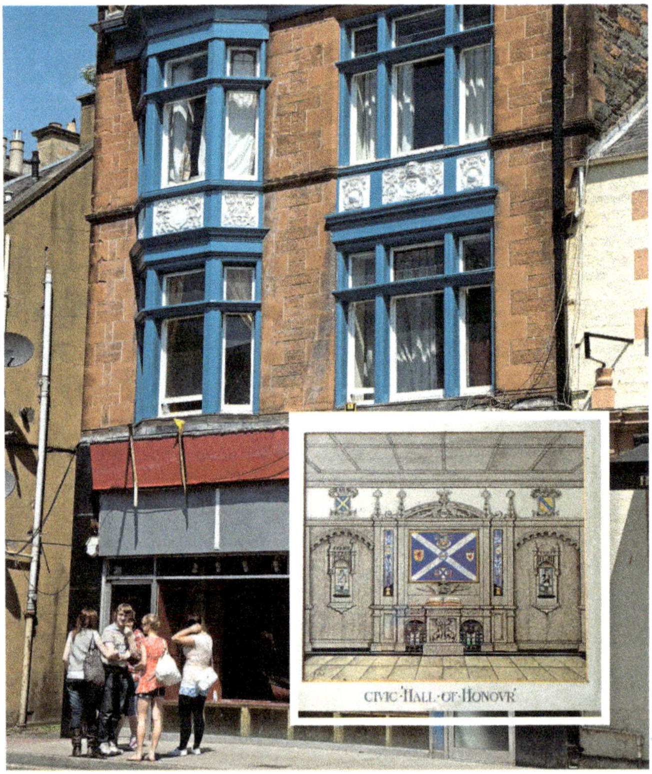

George Hope Tait

Born in 1861, George Hope Tait came to live in Galashiels before the time of the first Gala Day. This is a painting he did of the family house and business which he and his brother built at No. 26 High Street. Inset a copy of one of several large, detailed framed plans, which were never used in the town. The plaques on the Old Town Cross were designed by George Hope Tait and would lead us to imagine he may have had some influence in the first Braw Lads' Day. Records would seem to suggest that he was instrumental in doing research which then had some bearing on the formation of the ceremonies we now see on Braw Lads' Day.

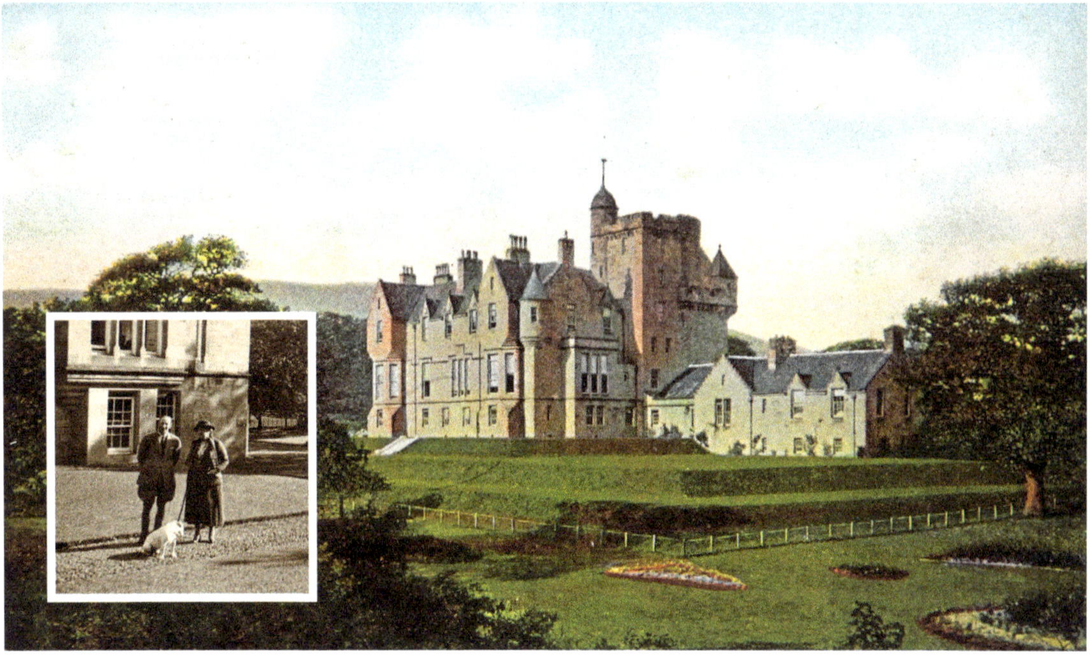

New Gala House

A picture of Mrs Scott MacDougall and her son Hugh Scott (who died at Dunkirk) outside New Gala House, which was demolished in 1987. Built in 1877, it was situated in Gala Policies. after it was vandalised it was then sold in 1978 for £7,000. Old Gala House, standing in Scott Crescent, is a popular gallery, museum and meeting place with lovely gardens and facilities.

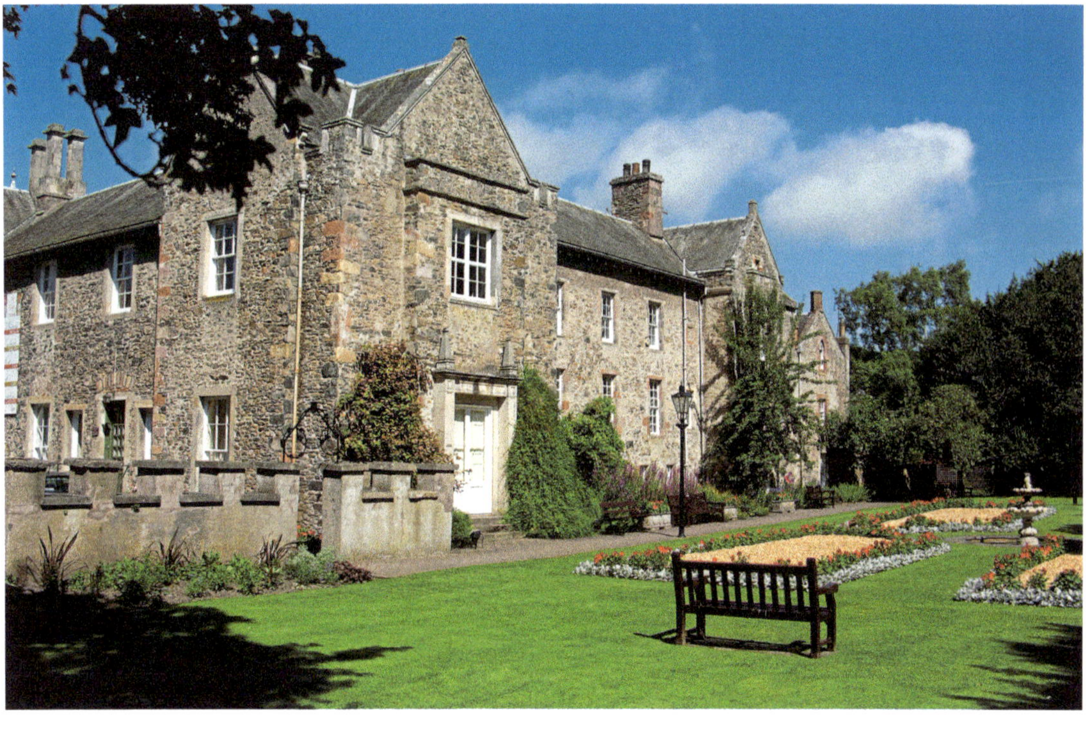

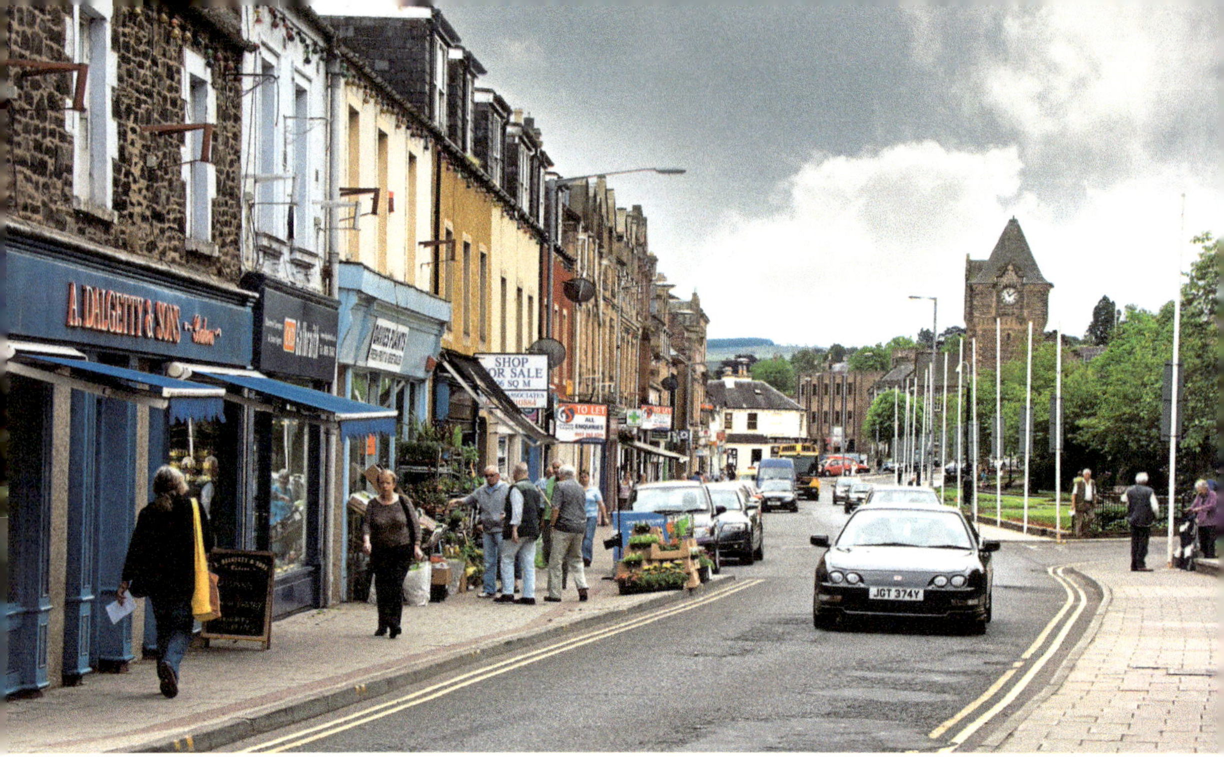

Bank Street

The views from the top end of Bank Street looking down show a similar layout despite there being a 100 year difference, and a missing War Memorial. Like channel Street, although appearing busy it sadly shows the state of the economy with the many 'Shop For Sale' signs.

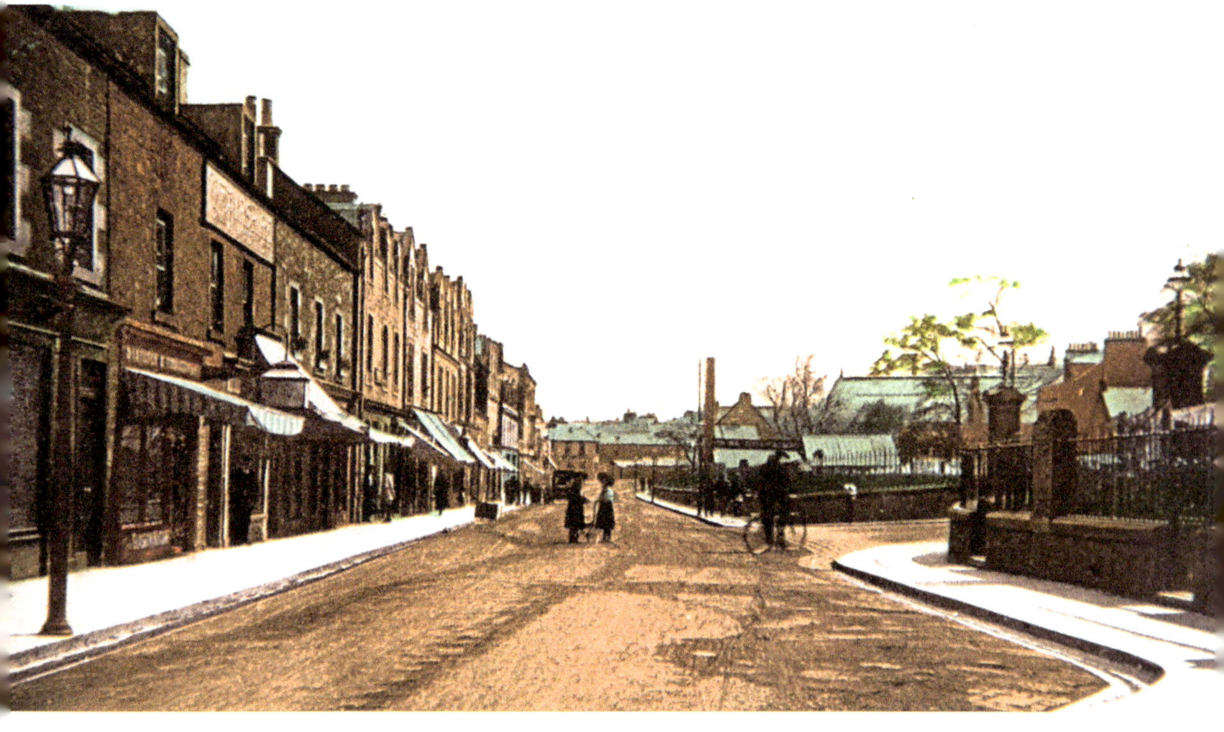

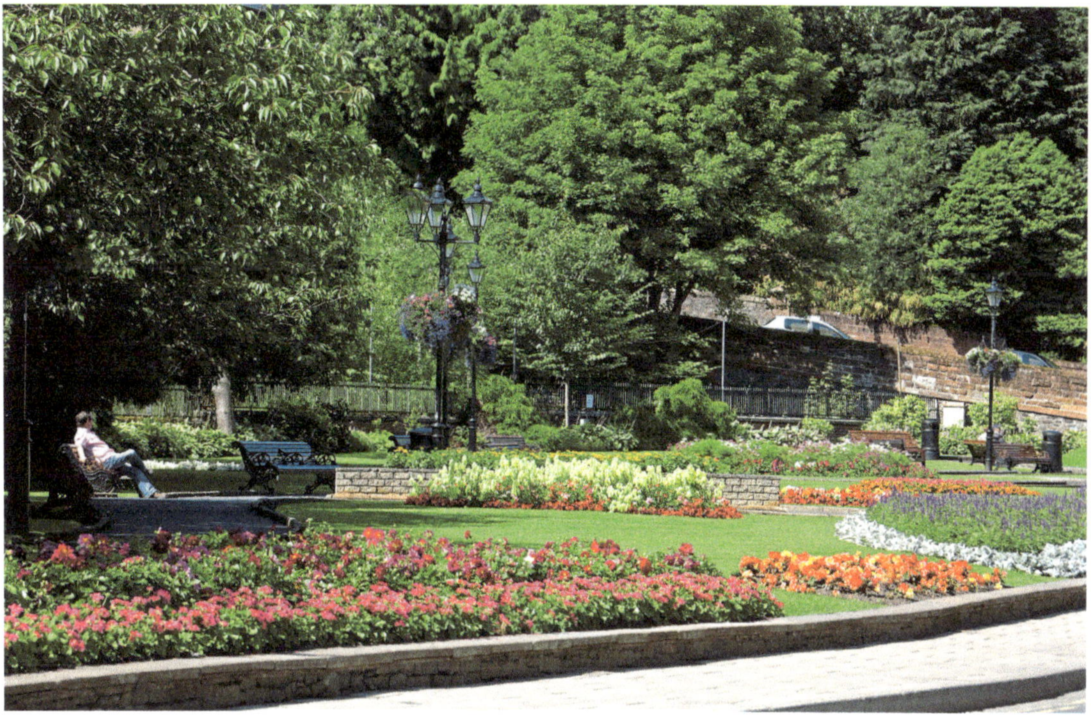

Bank Street Gardens
On the opposite side of Bank Street, the gardens are constantly maintained to a high standard by the park's department and throughout the year provide a lovely floral display for visitors and locals alike.

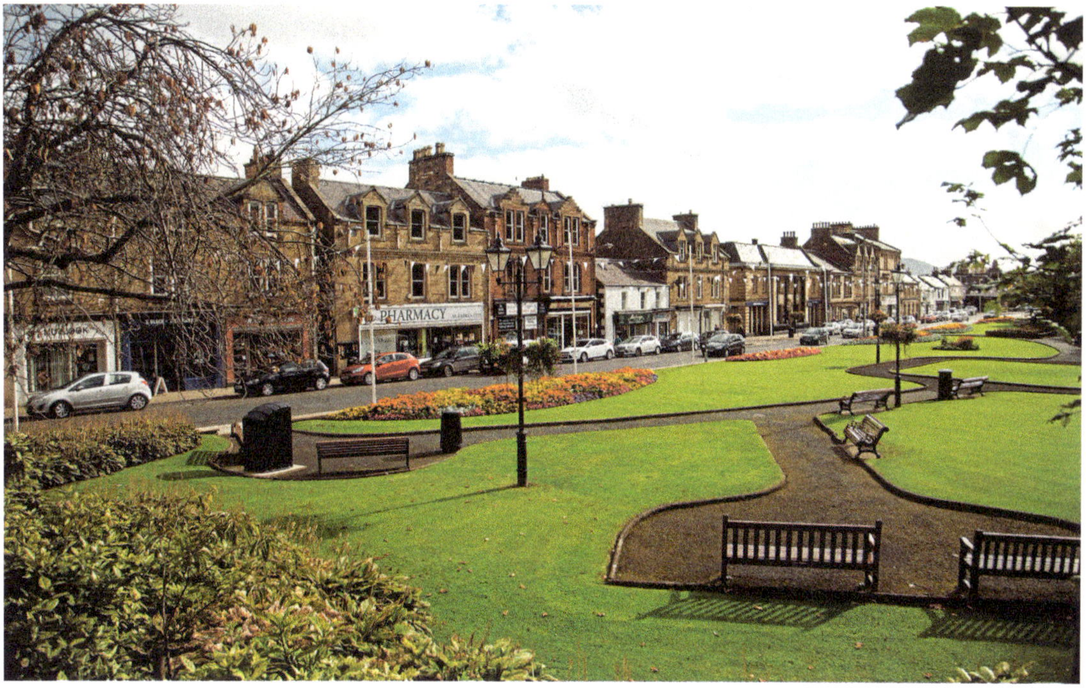

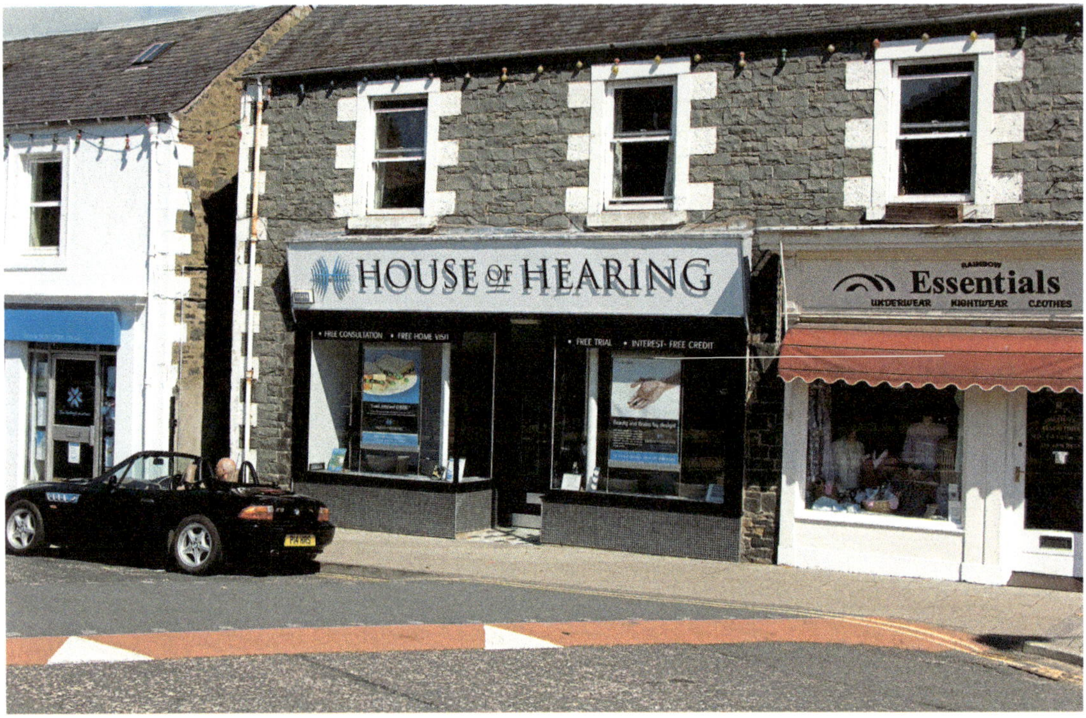

Lipton's Teashop

Bank Street showing what was the Lipton's Teashop and Grocers, around 1930, now the House of Hearing. The old image shows Mr Peters, centre, along with Dick Prosser, George Ramsay, Ella Liddle and Arthur Hancock.

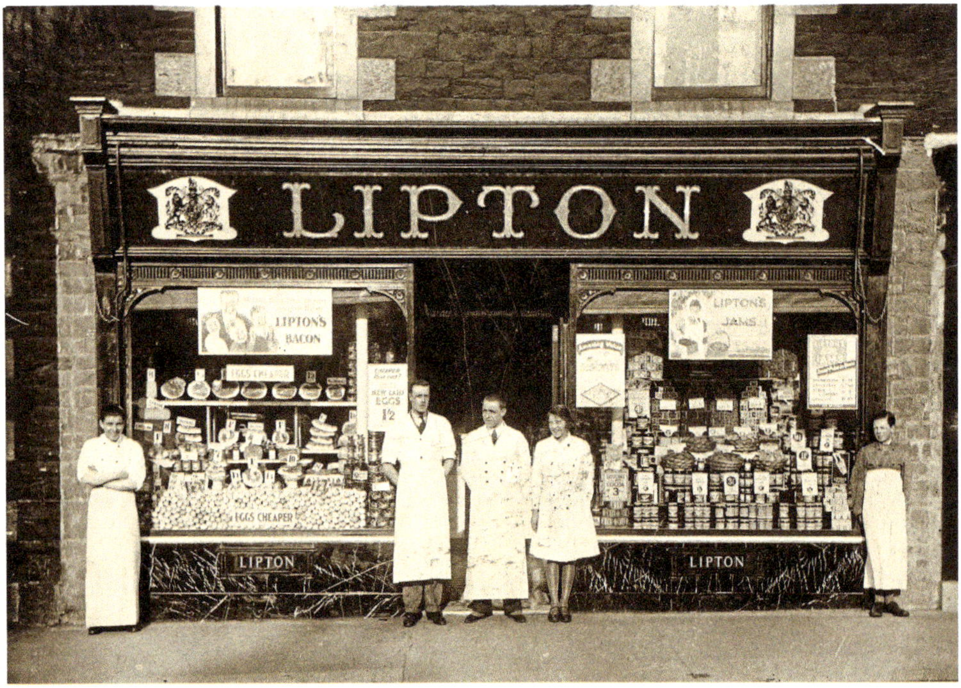

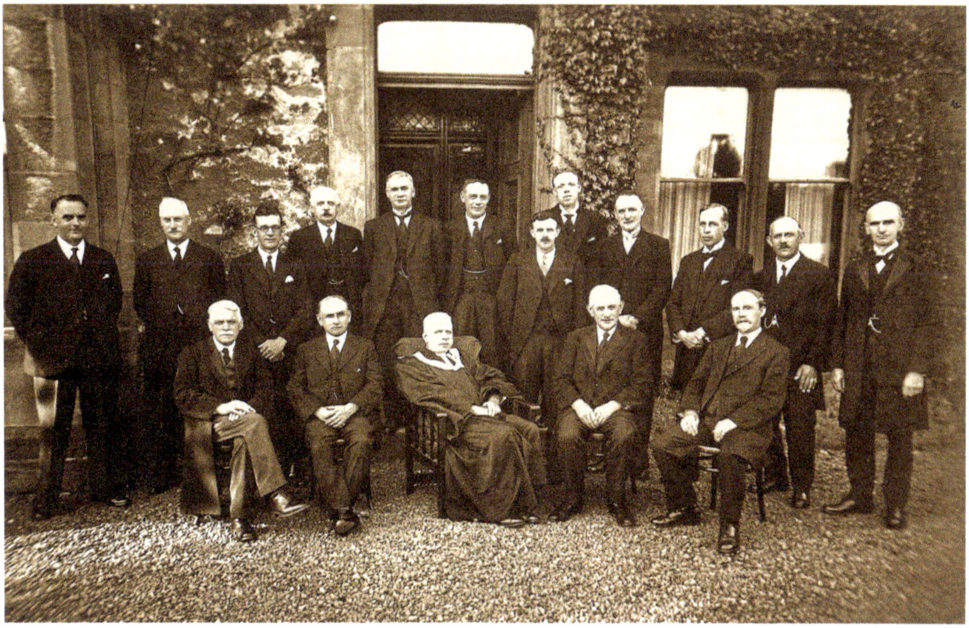

Galashiels Churches

Two quite different Kirk Session photographs. A very austere South United Free Church Kirk Session outside The Manse. At one time there were five united free churches in the town. Trinity Church combined with the South United Free in 1936 and became known as St Cuthbert's. Situated in Gala Park it then became Ladhope St Cuthberts and in the early eighties St Aidans. It united with the congregation of St Ninians in the High Street in 2005 and the two congregations took the name of 'Trinity' once again. The more recent image shows the Trinity Kirk Session and Congretational Board with Minister, Revd Morag Dawson.

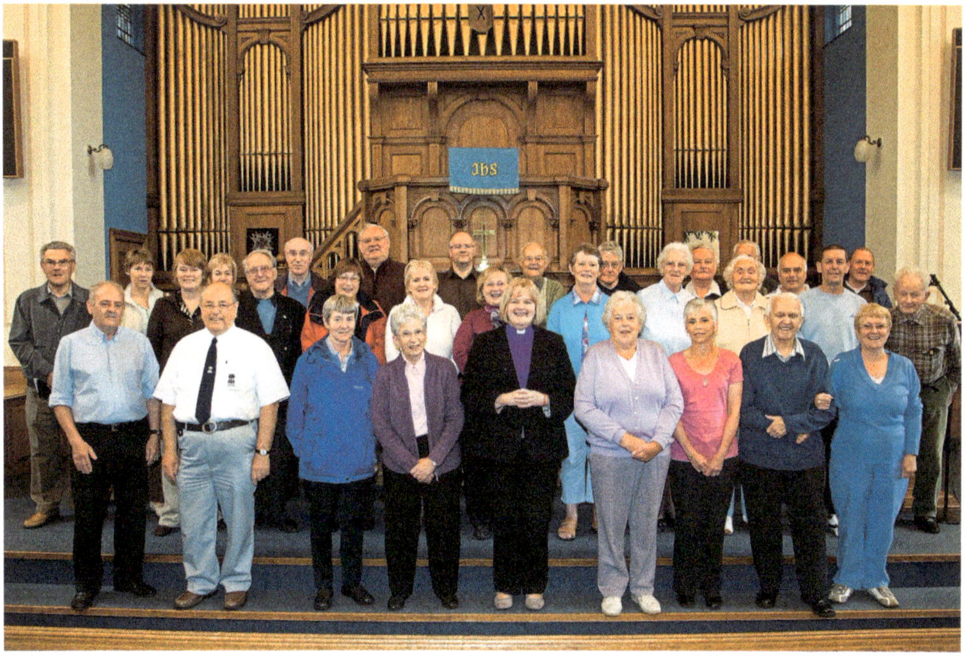

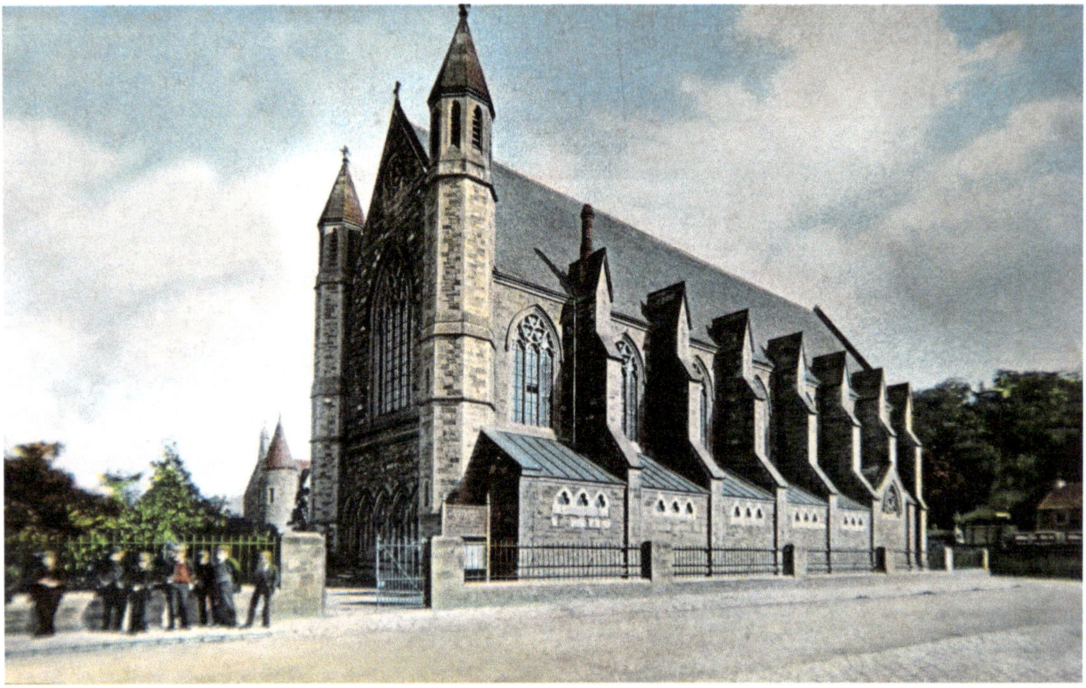

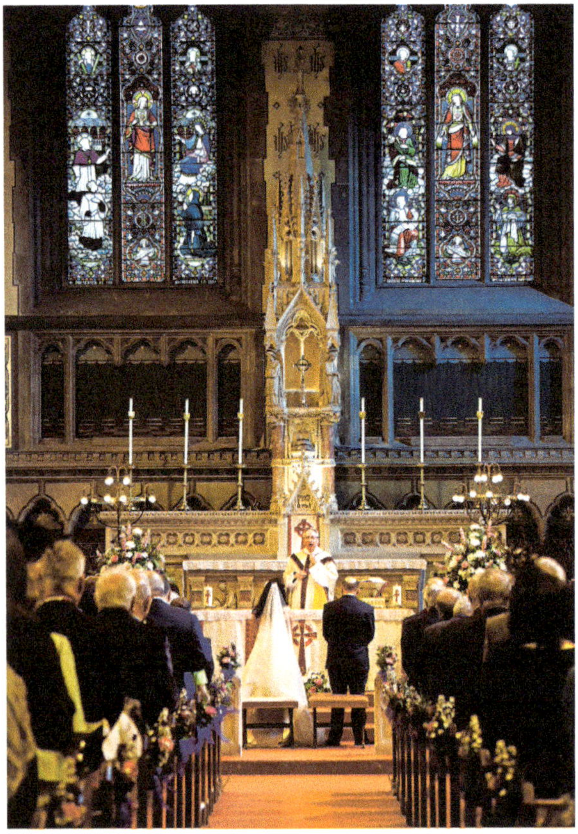

Church of Our Lady & St Andrew

Church of Our Lady & St Andrew, completed in 1858 and extended in 1870. This exterior remains almost unchanged today, however the gentlemen in the old image would get quite a shock at the amount of fast flowing traffic if they suddenly were transported back to that particular corner. The new road which comes along the front gates of the church carries traffic into the town centre and beyond. The interior of the church, with lovely stained glass windows and altar is a joy to use for a wedding photographer. The bride in the wedding shown is Celeste Mitchell, a descendant of the Macari family mentioned on page 24.

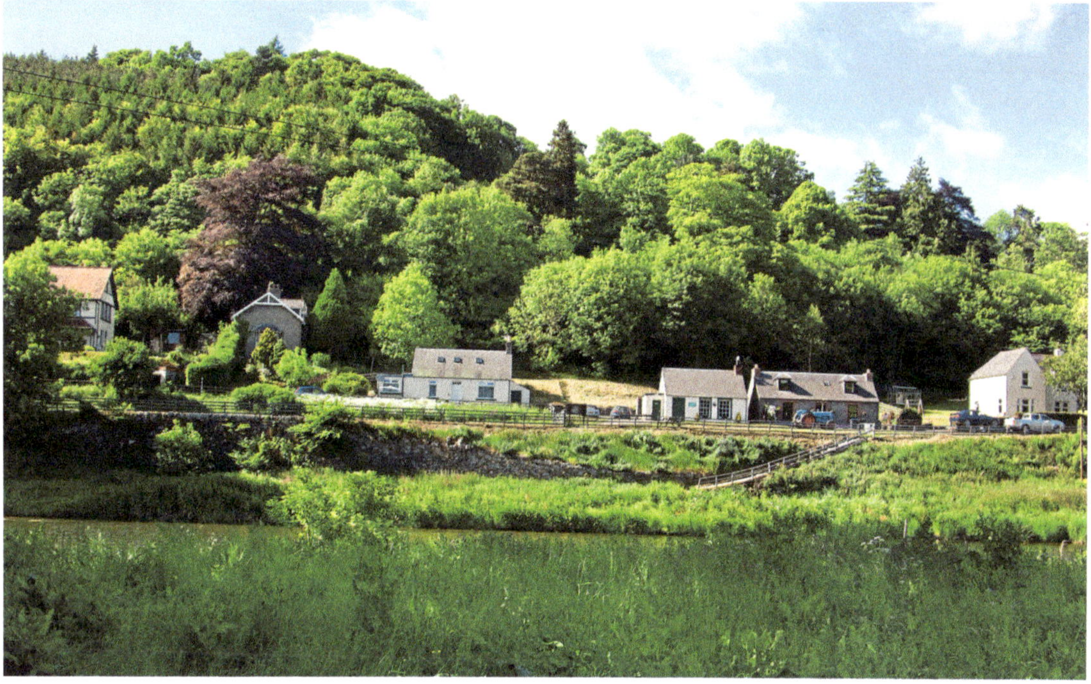

Crossing the Tweed

Once a busy ferry crossing carrying passengers across The Tweed. The train would stop at Abbotsford Ferry Station allowing passengers to catch the ferry to Abbotsford. The mock-Tudor style houses, built in the early 1900s by Adam Grieve, can still be seen. In 1723 a boat, carrying a number of people and a horse, broke free from moorings opposite Abbotsford and travelled to Galafoot before overturning, drowning eighteen people. It is reported that 'The Session considered this a token of the Lord's anger!'

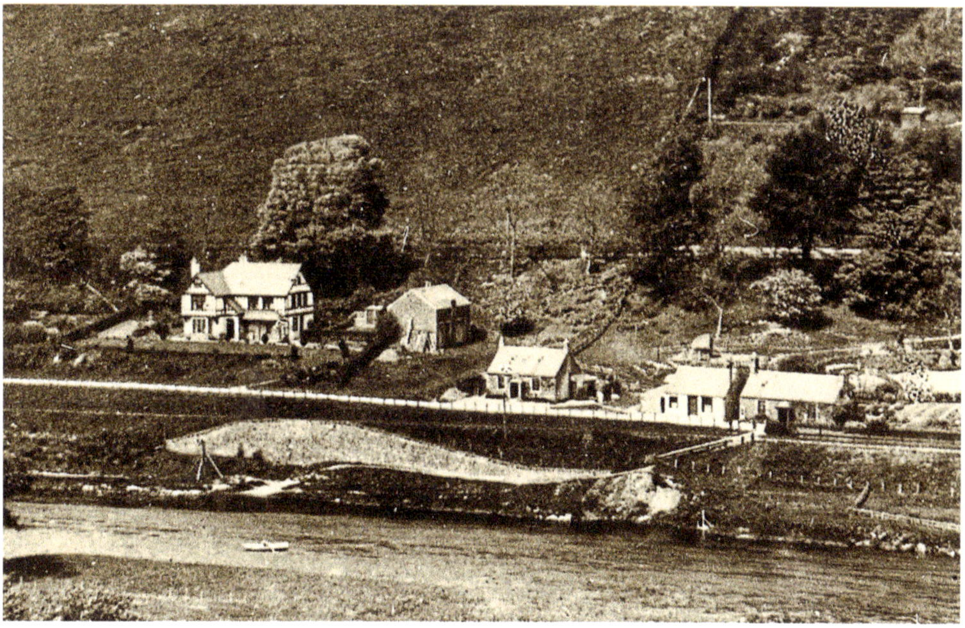

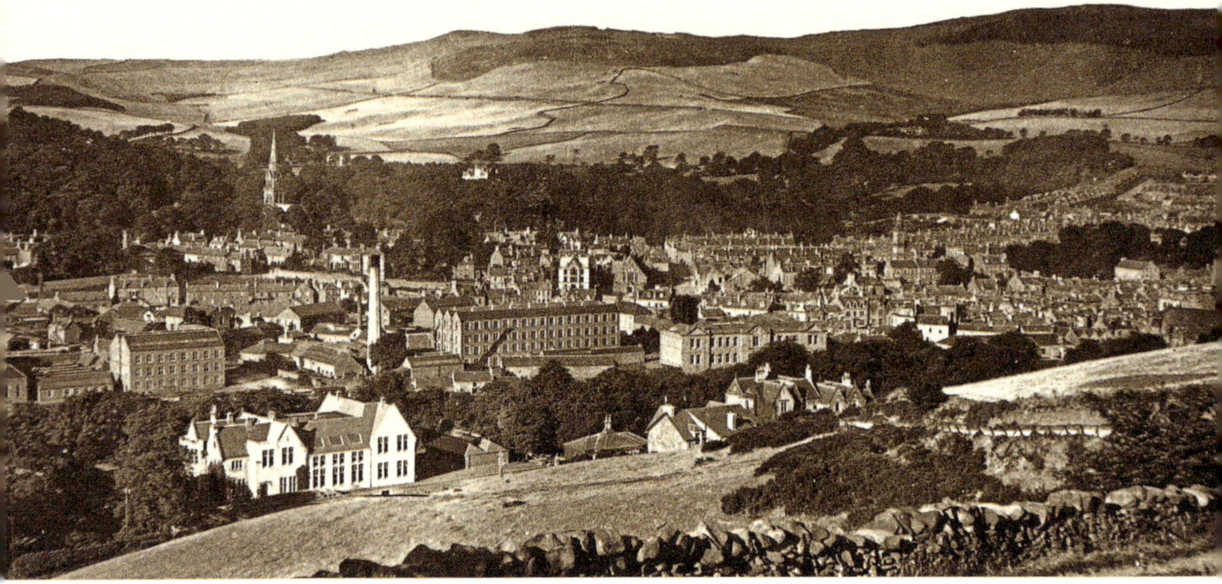

Bruce's Hill
From Bruce's Hill with a view quite changed now in 2010, and being dominated by the white roofs of Tesco and Next.

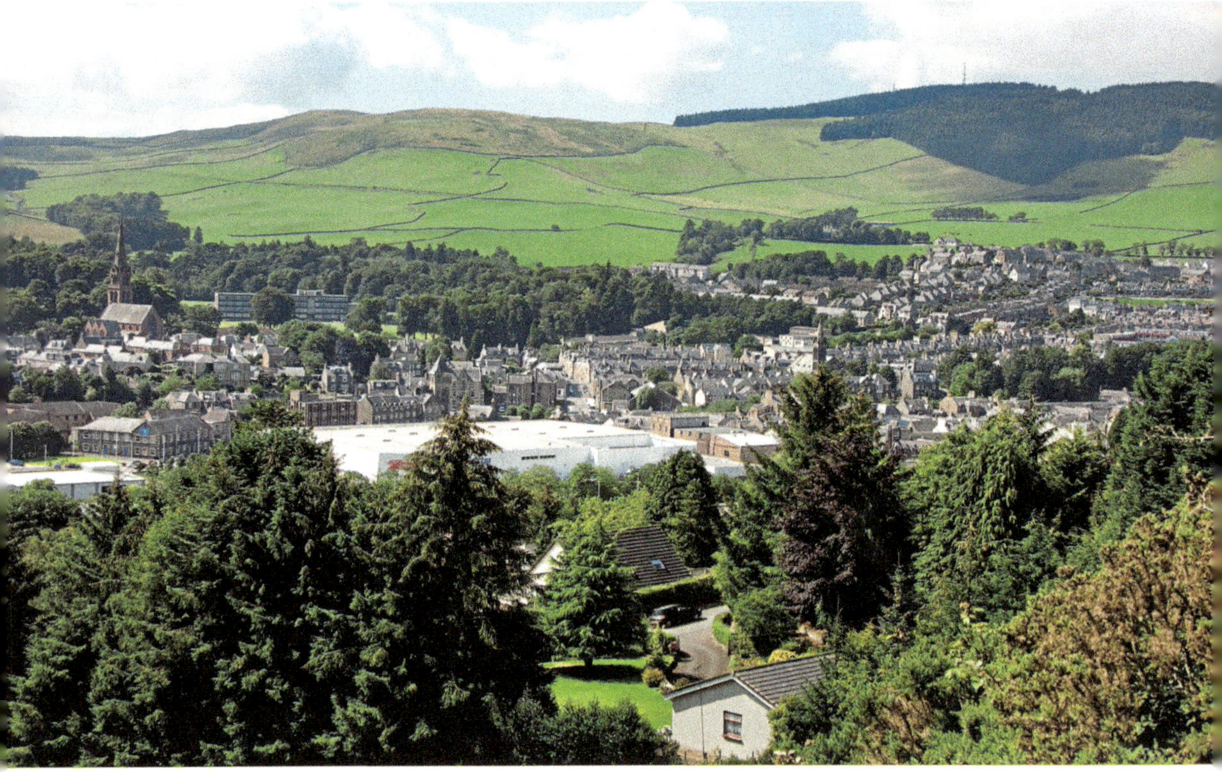

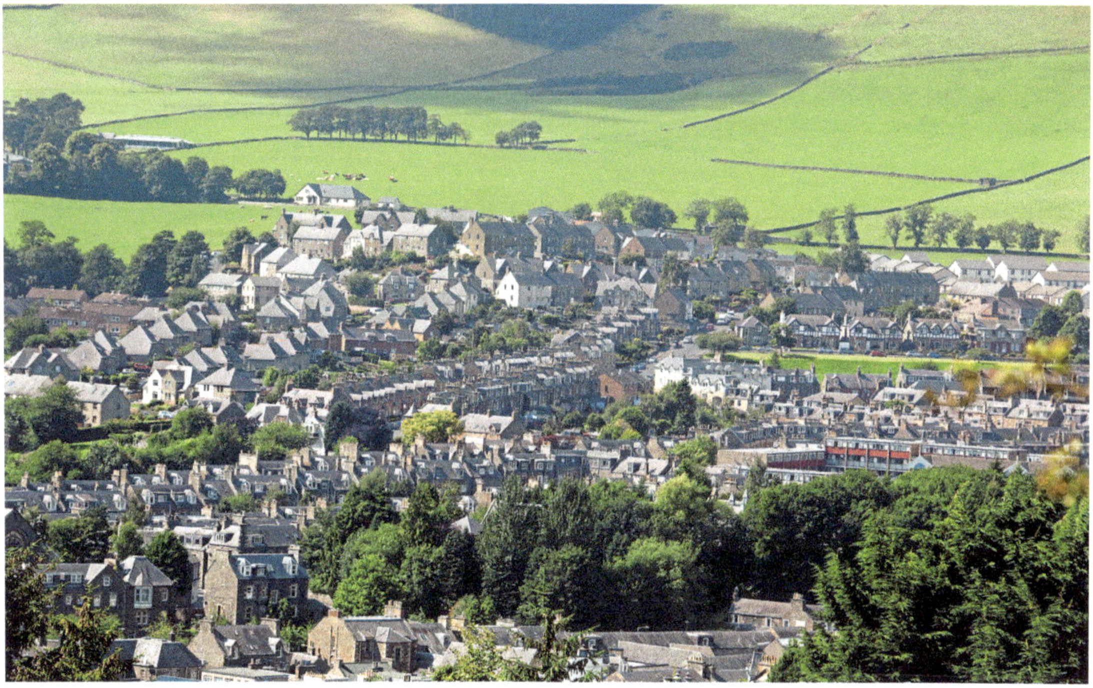

Modern Views

These two 2010 views from the same spot show the town nestled among trees and showing views across to Eildon Street, Meigle Street and Mossillee in the top image and Huddersfield Street, Parsonage Road and St Peter's Church in the other.

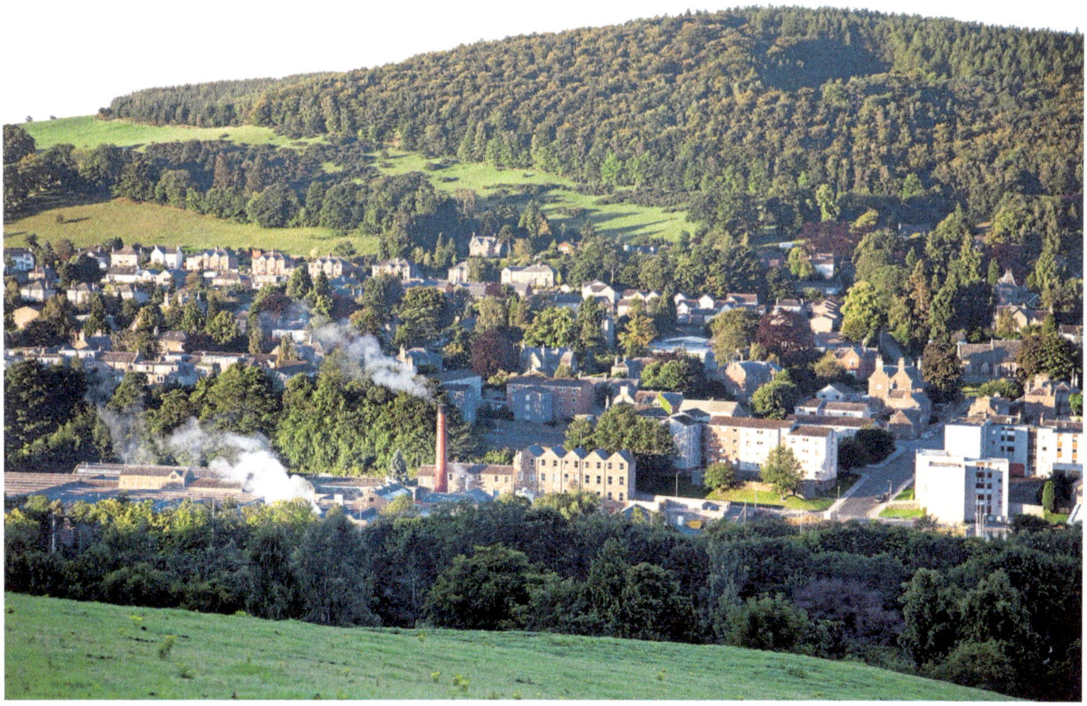

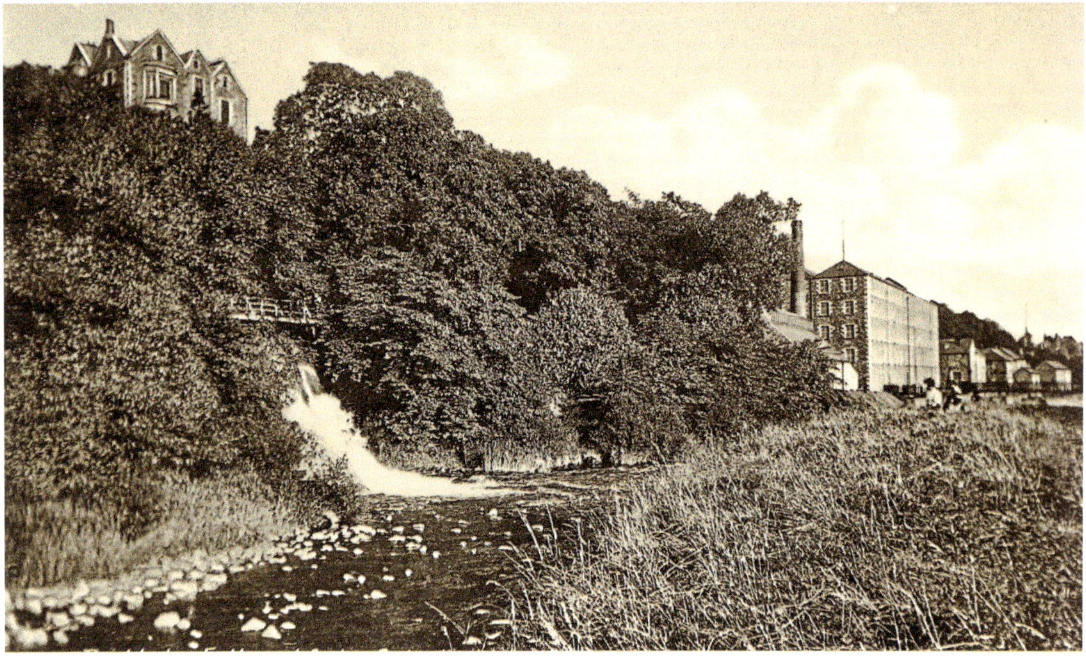

Buckholmburn Falls

Buckholmburn Falls just appearing below Buckholm Burn House, top left. Buckholm Mill, which closed in the early seventies, can be seen in the distance. All that remains of Buckholm Falls is an unusable walkway and the old workings of the sluice covered in tree branches and foliage.

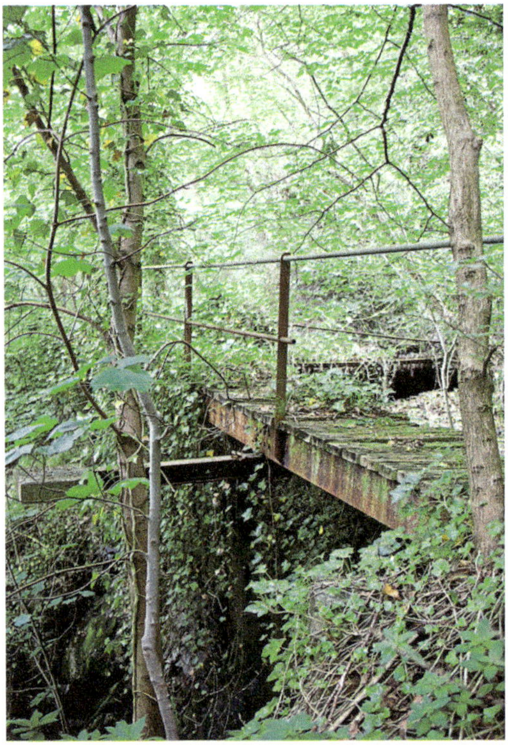

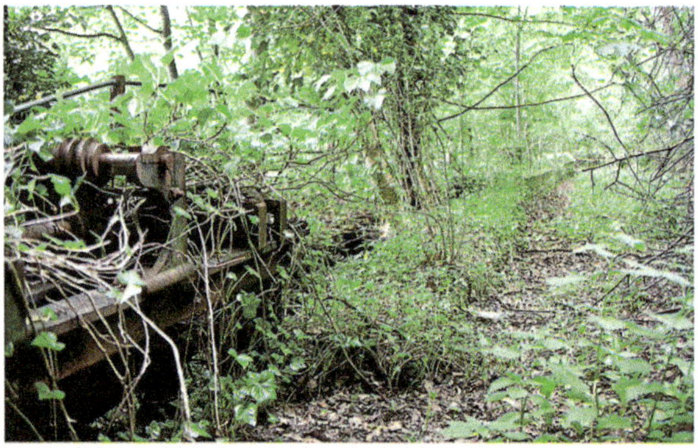

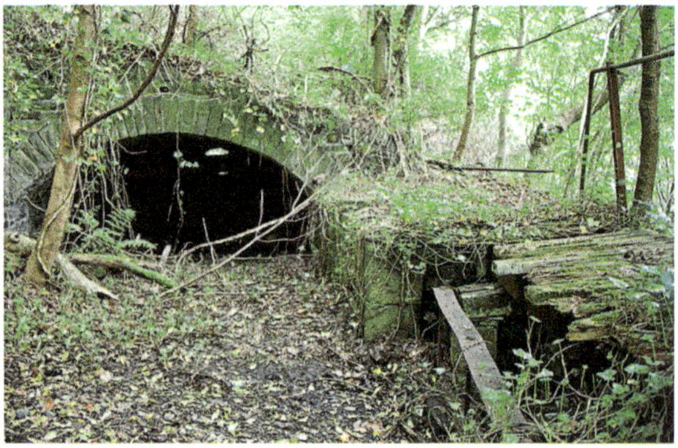

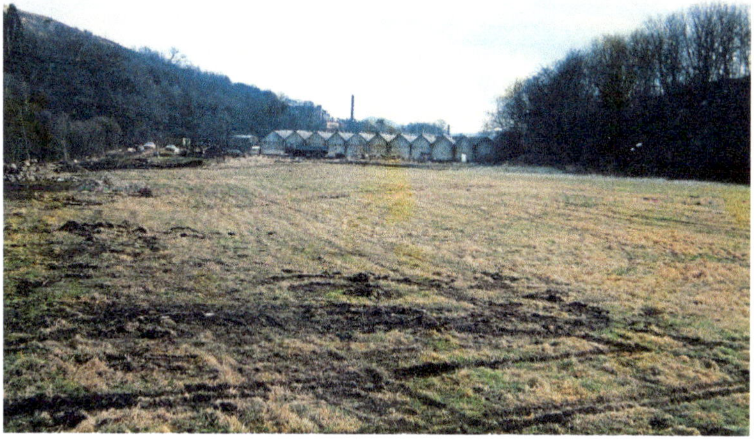

Buckholm Burn

This large expanse of land looking back to Buckholm Burn (seen top left among the trees) was acquired by S. & I. Thomson, an automotive salvage company, in the early 1980s. This land at one time was a sand quarry, then a market garden. The old buildings seen in the distance, now owned by the Wool Marketing Board, once stored essential supplies during the war years, such as gas masks etc. The drone image shows the extent of the salvage yard with many of the cars on frames stacked four high.

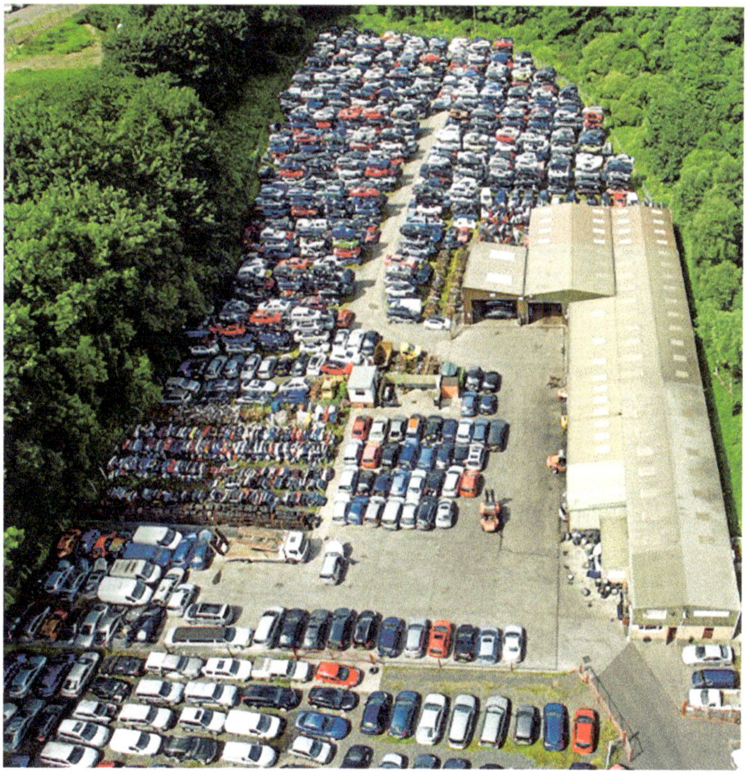

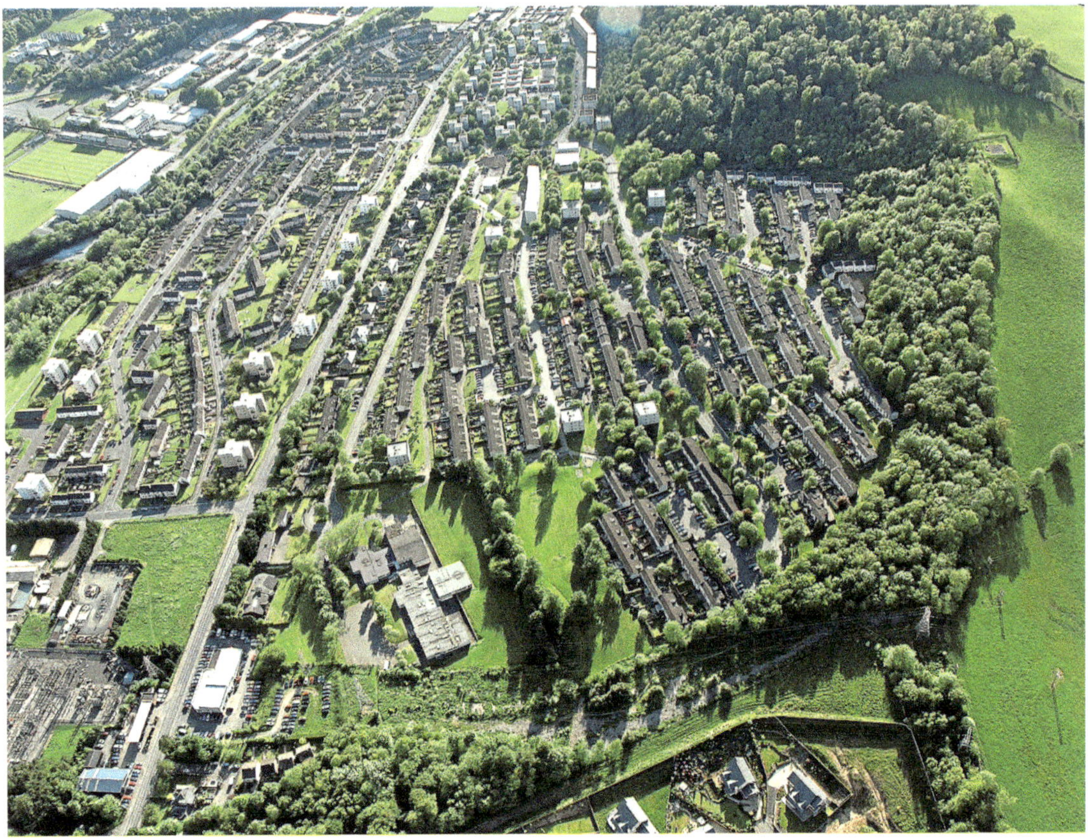

Langlee

Acknowledgements

My grateful thanks to my uncle James T. Walker, F.R.P.S, Justin Mihulka, Ron Ballantyne, Ewan Doyle, Effie Devlin, Neta Weatherly, Philip Macari, Sylvia Mitchell, Kirsty and Jamie Houghton, Phyllis Hancock, Craig Murray, Mary Young, Pat McMorran, Jim Lees, Neil Crooks, Don and Sandra Aitchison, Borders College, John Gray, the Codona family, Bill Lamb, Graeme Howlieson, Moira Whyte, Bill Brodie, Gary Adams, Cameron Architects, Lewis Roden, Carolyn and Isobel at Gala Day Services, Morag Dawson, Scott Bell, Scott Paterson, Tom and Charlotte Stanners, Joyce Maltman, Alwyn Johnston, and all who assisted me with this book. The drone images are courtesy of RC Innovations.

Also Available from Amberley Publishing

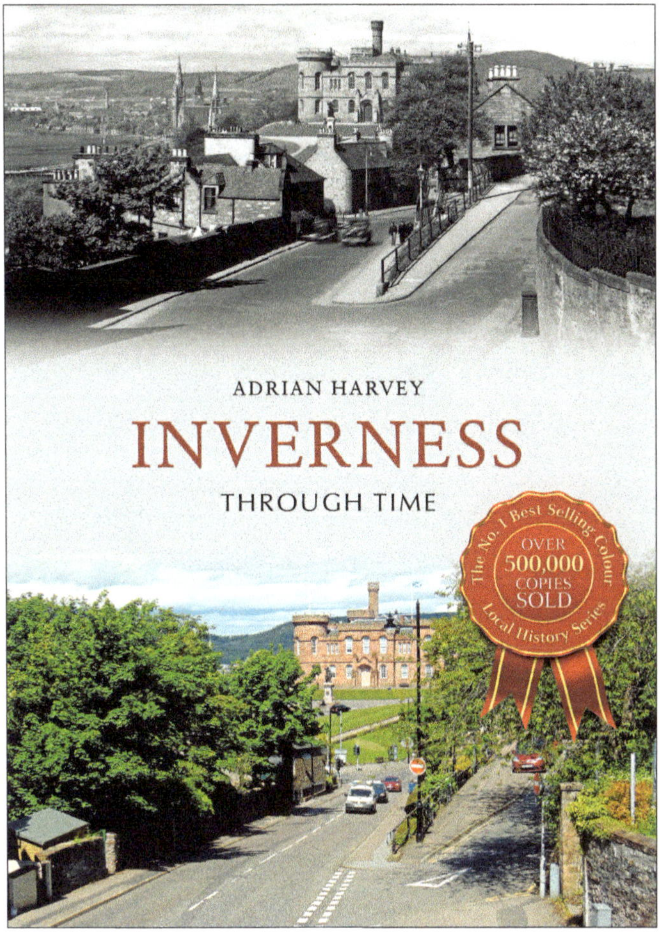

Paperback
180 illustrations
96 pages
978-1-4456-4199-7

Available now from all good bookshops or to order direct
please call 01453-847-800
www.amberley-books.com